Uli's Journey

ISBN 978-1-946886-45-3

Library of Congress Control Number: 2023905653

Copyright © 2023 by Uli Schackmann

All rights reserved. No part of this book may be used, reproduced, or transmitted in any manner whatsoever without permission of the publisher.

All photographs, unless indicated otherwise, are provided courtesy of Uli Schackmann.

Published by Middle River Press
Oakland Park, Florida
middleriverpress.com

First Printing — Printed in the USA

Uli's Journey

Angels Along the Way

Uli Schackmann

Acknowledgements

It takes many people working together to make a book come true. In my case, what started out as a dream turned into a daring adventure, and after sharing my story with many friends, their encouragement that I put my experience on paper inspired me to follow through. Thank you, friends!

I also want to thank Bruce and Judy Borich, founders of Middle River Press, an independent publishing company in Oakland Park, Florida. They have helped authors share their stories for almost two decades, publishing beautifully designed and thoroughly edited books. Judy and Bruce, your encouragement and guidance during the process of publishing this book meant more to me than I can express.

In addition, I extend my gratitude to Ryan Archer and Jennifer Archer of Archer Editing and Writing Services (archerediting.writing@gmail.com). In the early stages of writing my story, Ryan and Jennifer acted as developmental editor and line editor, respectively, offering insight and suggestions to strengthen the book.

I am grateful to artist-writer Christy Sheffield Sanford, who made editorial suggestions and encouraged me to finish my manuscript.

Also, my heartfelt thanks to Chantal Gagnon, who provided me with the most relaxing and beautiful writing space to put the first words on paper. Chantal, your nurturing, loving spirit and encouragement got me going.

Also a heartfelt thank you to Barbara Bridson and Vera Mallo for their very generous supoort in creating a beautiful space for me to work on this book.

Special thanks to Glen Weinzimer, former CEO and founder of the SmartRide, a two-day HIV/AIDS fundraising bicycle ride from Miami to Key West. The money it raises goes directly to agencies supporting individuals living with HIV/AIDS. Glen believed in me from the start, and his words rang in my ears throughout my six-thousand-mile journey: "If anyone can do it, it's you, Uli." I appreciate your encouragement, Glen, and your allowing me to be part of a fantastic organization for the past fifteen years.

Al Magdaleno, CEO and founder of Citizens of the World, a non-profit organization working on humanitarian issues, did pre-ride video production, interviewing friends who left encouraging words on video for me. The videos bolstered my spirits and helped motivate me to push on during my ride, especially on my most challenging days. Thank you, Al, for all you did for me, and thanks to my friends who left video messages.

Before my ride, the World AIDS Museum in Fort Lauderdale donated their space for a farewell party and fundraiser, for which I'm so very grateful. I'm also eternally thankful to Chuck Panozza from Styx for donating a band-autographed electric guitar to the fundraiser.

Thank you, Steven Barnes and Gary Mercado, former CEOs and owners of Bike America Bicycle stores, who graciously donated the bicycle I rode during my journey. Also, thanks to the staff at Bike America, especially Todd Wayne and Roque Medina, for helping me by providing the right supplies and training to fix my bike whenever necessary. Thanks, too, to Punnassa Nessa from Nessa's Shop for creating a special back carrier for Jackson in case I got stranded and had to walk.

Hailey Rank (Burke) took on the task of managing my social media communication during my journey. I so appreciate all you did, Hailey!

Special thanks to Will Spencer former VP of Kids in Distress and Leslie Franco (Cartaya) former Communications Director at Kids In Distress for putting my sponsor letter together

I also want to thank Gratitude Training and especially my Masterful Living (ML) 34 West Palm Beach team for all their unwavering and empowering support.

Finally, to all the angels I met along the way over the many miles of my journey, who graciously supported me with a ride, shelter, kindness, and encouraging words. Without you and your generosity, I could not have completed my ride, and this book would not exist.

Dedication

I dedicate this book to all the many people whose lives have been affected by HIV/AIDS and to all the dedicated scientists still working on a cure for HIV/AIDS.

And to my extraordinary companion, Jackson, who bravely endured six months of many challenging adventures on the road with the bravest heart and sweetest smile.

Proceeds from this book will benefit amfAR to continue their research for a cure for AIDS.

Prologue

[May 12, 2017] Fairbanks, AK

The repair shop called to say that my bicycle was finally ready. I picked it up and began the ride back to the hostel. Once I arrived, I had breakfast and talked to some other people staying there before I took off.

Because of the flat terrain, the riding was easier than before. Whenever I did come to an incline, I got off and walked the bike; with the trailer attached, it was too heavy for me to pedal uphill. Besides, my knees hurt, and I already felt burnt out.

Outside of Fairbanks, I rode past a town called North Pole and stopped to take pictures with Santa Claus and give him my Christmas wish list. Later, back on the road, I pedaled for a while, then got off again and pushed the bicycle up a steep incline that plateaued at the top.

Jackson and I stopped to catch our breath, and I thought about my journey so far. Climbing the steep inclines was entirely different from my training rides in Florida. Riding was beyond strenuous; I had never before experienced such a challenge or such a demand on my body and psyche. Still, the beauty, the immense splendor and sheer aloneness consumed me and filled me with such gratitude.

I was about to take off again when, suddenly, a giant grizzly appeared seventy to eighty feet up ahead, walking away from us. She had one heck of a big behind and a cub following at her right side.

Uncapping my bear spray, I looked at Jackson and put my finger over my lips. The bear terrified me, and I started trembling, but Jackson remained calm. The grizzly bear moved slowly forward, never turning to look back at us. She ambled slightly to the right and up a little embankment, disappearing momentarily behind a cluster of trees. When she emerged again, I saw that she had not one but two small cubs.

Fear paralyzed me. I thought about all the stinky items I carried in my saddle bags that the bears might smell. I stood frozen, yet in complete awe. I knew of nothing more dangerous than a grizzly bear emerging from hibernation with two cubs. Should I turn around? Should I try to pass the animals? I couldn't decide what to do, so I waited for quite some time until I was sure they had moved on.

By now, it was late, and I hadn't found a place to set up camp. I didn't relish the thought of camping in an area with a mama bear and her two cubs. I'd have to feed Jackson, but I would most likely go without dinner since cooking would fill the air with strong scents that might attract the bears.

I climbed on my bike and pedaled hard while looking for a safe place to pitch my tent. The side roads were all inaccessible due to snowpack; only the main road was clear. Panic fluttered in my chest. What if the bear found me during the night? I had the overwhelming feeling that humans didn't belong out here. Maybe my friends in Florida had been right; maybe it wasn't safe for me to be out in the middle of Alaska alone. What had I been thinking when I decided to make this journey? Had I become like my father—looking for adventures to stave off my restlessness?

Suddenly, lights appeared in my rearview mirrors. A truck approached me from behind. I raised my arms and waved frantically, hoping to get the driver's attention.

The truck pulled up next to me and stopped. "Do you need help?" the driver asked.

I told him I did, and he got out. We introduced ourselves. His name was Greg, and when I told him about the bear and her cubs, he helped me put all my gear in the back of his F-350 Ford truck.

Feeling blessed, divinely guided, and beyond lucky, I climbed in and looked out the passenger side window of Greg's truck into the wilds of Alaska. This was not my space. It belonged to the wildlife, to that bear and her cubs; I was only a visitor riding through their territory.

As the sky darkened, and we drove into the night, I told Greg my story.

FOR IMMEDIATE RELEASE

One-Woman HIV/AIDS

59 years old, Uli Schackmann attempting cross-country 6,000+ mile bicycle ride towing her dog Jackson and a 6 foot AIDS Red Ribbon Flag from Alaska to Florida to find an AIDS cure by 2020

Ft. Lauderdale, Florida, May 21, 2017—On May 8th, 2017, Uli Schackmann, the one-woman crusader started bicycling from Anchorage, Alaska to Key West, Schackmann is attempting this solo cycling trip to raise awareness and funds going to The Foundation for AIDS Research (amfAR) with the goal of finding a cure by 2020.

Her 6,000+ mile journey will be an unprecedented challenge, both physically and emotionally, spanning nearly seven months (from May to Nov 2017) and more than 6,000 miles. The arduous journey is symbolic of the struggle people living with HIV/AIDS face as they fight for normalcy. Schackmann began her journey from Anchorage, Alaska on May 8, 2017.

Uli is also looking for any kind hearts out there that may be able to house her and Jackson for a night on her historic journey for mankind.

"I am compelled to do this because I have witnessed the intimate nature of this disease and the human response to it," she said. "I don't need to explain that HIV knows no boundaries. It globally impacts men, women, and children.

It affects people of all racial, ethnic, and socioeconomic backgrounds. Education is essential to preventing the spread and ultimately eradicating HIV's path. My path across the North American continent will demonstrate that, with belief and commitment, anything is possible."

This is not the first time Schackmann has used two wheels to raise awareness for HIV/AIDS in various fundraising rides across the country for over twenty years. She has ridden or served crew for the SMART (Southern Most AIDS/HIV) Ride, a two-day 165-mile ride from Miami to Key West, Florida for 9 years.

In each event, she was the rider everyone knew due to her heavy steel bike affixed with a metal pole carrying the AIDS Flag for 17 years. Attached to the flag where tiny red ribbons, all given to her by friends who had lost a loved one to the disease or were too sick to ride themselves. For 17 years Schackmann has proudly ridden with this flag.

"One year we had unseasonably, record-breaking ICE-cold weather and crossing almost 43 bridges between Miami and Key West with torrential rain and frigid unforgiving environment," said Glen Weinzimer, SMART Ride founder. "Yet there was Uli, the last rider, working the hardest and riding with this enormous flag in extreme wind. Most would have given up under normal circumstances, but when you add the weight of her bicycle and the resistance of the flag as it whipped, it is a miracle what she accomplished. That is determination and a testament to her tenacity."

She has received support from the local Florida cycling community, shops and bikers alike. Bike America gifted Schackmann with a new bicycle and supplies needed for the journey including a trailer so her pup, Jackson, can join her on the adventure. Riders have joined her on training rides for company. Others have offered lodging along her route, words of encouragement, and even a celebratory meal.

Chuck Panozzo, co-founder and bass guitarist from the multi gold and platinum award winning rock band STYX was so moved, he donated an electric guitar to be raffled as a winning prize to those who donate $100 or more to amfAR and Uli's Journey.

amfAR, the Foundation for AIDS Research, is devoting its considerable resources to assist Ms. Schackmann in achieving her great goal.

"Breakthroughs come from being committed to something, even if the path to achieve it is unclear," Schackmann said. "Breakthroughs allow for sudden powerful insights that take us past our self-imposed limitations. Breakthroughs alter our sense of whom we are, alter the quality of our life."

For more information, please contact Al Magdaleno at 754-254-6215 or almagnow@yahoo.com

༄

I wanted to send you a note of support and a recommendation for Uli Schackman who is going to be making a cross-country bicycle tour for HIV and AIDS.

What I can say from the start, I wish there were more people in the world like Uli; she has pretty much dedicated her adult life to helping those infected, affected or at risk for HIV and AIDS. I met Uli almost two decades ago (boy that makes me feel even older than I look in the mirror) and she was a lady everyone knew because she rode a HEAVY steel bike with a metal pole carrying the AIDS Flag. Attached to the flag where tiny red ribbons, all given to her by friends who had lost someone or were too sick to ride themselves. For years Uli rode with this flag and that HEAVY bike across the country in different AIDS bicycle rides.

When we started, what is known as The SMART Ride,(www.thesmartride.org) Uli was there. One year we had unseasonably, record-breaking ICE-cold weather and crossing almost 43 bridges between Miami and Key West with torrential rain and frigid unforgiving environment, as people dropped out and got sagged, there was Uli, the last rider, working the hardest and riding with this Enormous Flag in extreme wind. That is determination and a testament to her tenacity, I am not sure I could do what she does with her bike and her fearless attitude to raise awareness on the road.

Most would have given up under normal circumstances, but when you add the weight of her bicycle, the resistance the flag caused as it whipped it is a miracle what she accomplished. I tell you this because Uli is determined and does follow through with her commitments; she has not wavered from this mission since the beginning of this pandemic. There was a time where emotionally I thought Uli would stop riding, I heard her say in an interview one time that the weight of symbolically carrying all those people on her journeys might be too much. She quickly embraced that fear and carries on.

I would ask that you endorse her on her journey and assist her with ways to raise money and raise awareness by being attached to AMFAR. I am hoping with your network across the country she will find safe heaven and organizations that embrace her vision to raise money for AmFar and ultimately a cure by 2020.

Sincerely,

Glen Weinzimer
Founder, The SMART Ride
100% back, 100% of the time.
Over $8.5 Million raised and returned since 2003

Chapter 1

Preparing for the Ride

[April 29, 2017] Florida

It was dusk—that magical time when day turns into evening and the sun begins its descent. A time when friends meet for drinks after work. A time for reflection. I sat at a table at the restaurant George's Alibi and wondered if I would be able to complete my planned six-thousand-mile solo bicycle journey from Alaska to Key West, Florida. I sipped my wine between bites of tuna nachos. *What in the world made me commit to such an endeavor?*

The prospect of such a trip had been growing in my mind since completing Gratitude Training in October 2016. The coaches had asked each trainee to declare their vision, and mine was to have a cure for AIDS by 2020. After planting that seed, the journey became a living thing.

A yearning to be in Alaska, to ride the lonely roads, filled me. The notion became unbearable during my last few months of employment, and I couldn't focus on anything else besides the ride. The longing became so large, it spread into my dreams, my heart, and my being.

What would it be like to be in Alaska?

What would it be like to ride my bicycle all alone on the Alaskan highway?

I had spent years cooped up in an office behind a computer, hungry for something different, something big, something that would let me know I was still alive. The election of Trump and his hateful efforts to deny people basic human rights only increased my yearning to do something different. I was ready for a new adventure, for Alaska, for the open road.

I imagined Alaska as vast, primal, wild, and large. However, I wouldn't truly know all it offered unless I experienced it for myself. I wanted to escape the pressures, boredom, and expectations of my daily routine. The idea of such a journey grew until it became impossible for me not to try it. Life wasn't fulfilling anymore, and something deep inside of me called for me to break out, to do something different.

I had been participating in local AIDS bicycle rides for twenty years. The rides raised money for local agencies to provide services such as free HIV testing, housing, support for medical bills, utility bills, and pet care. Funds raised also went to educate people on what to do next after receiving a positive test. The organization I was involved in had raised an enormous amount of money, yet it seemed the number of infected individuals never decreased. Broward County ranked high in the country for the number of new HIV infections each year.

I wanted to set a new goal for myself and for the world of HIV support. I wanted it to be something huge. I asked myself, *what is the end goal?*

A cure for AIDS by 2020.

Riding six thousand miles through two countries—eleven USA states and five Canadian provinces—to raise money for such a cure and to educate people about AIDS seemed a big enough goal.

After past rides, people often asked me, "Why, as a gay woman, do you ride for AIDS? Are you infected?"

It stunned me that AIDS was still stigmatized as a gay disease. I was not infected with HIV, although I was *affected* by the sheer number of Americans who had died of AIDS since its initial outbreak. From 1980 until 2021 over six hundred thousand Americans died of the disease. Worldwide, the numbers are much more staggering—in the millions.

For that reason and others, the call to undertake the biking adventure was so strong that I eventually quit my job, rented out my condo, and sold my new car. When a person gives up on their vision, they give up on themselves and their spirit dies. I refused to give up on my vision. I trained for the journey with paint cans and books in my saddle bags.

And, of course, Jackson, my loyal canine service companion, was always with me. I had decided that he would go on the bike trip as well.

I adopted Jackson when he was just nine months old. He already had experienced abuse and unkindness and was so timid when I met him. He didn't know how to play and was afraid of his own shadow. Now he has grown into a gentle, trusting, curious, loyal, and obedient canine.

He is an adorable, very expressive black Havanese. Jackson now loves playing with balls and stones and his favorite game is diving after rocks.

Three weeks before Jackson and I left, I shipped everything I would need to Alaska.

Preparing for the experience ahead of me reminded me of when I came to the USA from Germany on a six-month visiting visa; I had many of the same feelings of being called into action. When I left Germany at the age of twenty-six in 1986, I gave up my apartment, stored my few belongings in a friend's attic, and quit studying for my second degree six months before I was to graduate with high marks. I didn't speak English. I had only one suitcase, one duffle bag, and five thousand marks on me.

My decision concerned my friends, and they told me awful things about the United States. They spoke of gun violence, murderers, drug wars, killings, and rapes. I understood that they meant well. But I had been told I couldn't or shouldn't do this or that for most of my life, and I decided that I would no longer let fear and negativity paralyze me. I trusted my mind and spirit to carry me through.

Planning my bicycle trip was no different. The thought of me—a lone woman—riding across the USA and Canada concerned my friends. They worried about accidents, hit-and-runs, rapes, murders, and bears. All of these were legitimate concerns. I knew they worried out of love for me. However, I also knew that if I let them, their fears could stop me from achieving my dream. Letting go of fear makes a person unstoppable.

I was unstoppable. I had a vision much bigger than my fears. I trusted myself and my reasons for the adventure I was about to undertake.

As I sat in George's Alibi restaurant, sipping wine and eating nachos, I thought about the challenge of the journey ahead with both reservation and excitement. I watched the other diners around me—couples sharing an intimate conversation, a flirting look, a gentle touch. I became very aware that those intimate moments would be a rarity for me while on the trip. I understood that reality, yet I was ready. For the first time in ages, I felt alive. Once again, I had a purpose.

[May 2, 2017]

The World AIDS Museum in Wilton Manors is the first museum dedicated to the HIV/AIDS epidemic. The educational center there provides information on treatment & prevention of HIV. Whether infected or affected, almost all of us have been touched by this virus in some way.

The World AIDS Museum website (https://worldaidsmuseum.org) states:

> "The World AIDS Museum's signature exhibit is the informative and artfully designed Chronology of AIDS. The exhibit presents the progression of the pandemic juxtaposed against key global events. It skillfully summarizes the political winds that have buffeted the world's response to the pandemic, and respectfully honors those affected by the disease. Visitors gain insight into the emergence of the first symptoms, to subsequent worldwide political and social responses, and finally to today's pharmacological advances.
>
> The exhibit unveils the impact on marginalized groups in the United States and to affected populations worldwide.

> *A visit to the Museum is an accomplished multimedia experience rounded out with artwork, colorful graphics, audiovisual displays, and a trained docent who personalizes the tour."*

More than thirty friends came to the museum to wish me well, to contribute to amFAR's AIDS Cure by 2020 research, and to leave an inspirational video message for the many tough days ahead of me on the road. Al Magdaleno, a friend I met through our mutual participation in AIDS/HIV bicycle rides, organized the farewell party and created a video inviting friends to the event.

Seeing everyone and feeling their support inspired me. I gave a presentation in which I discussed my reasons for riding for a cure; then it was time to mingle and connect. I felt present in the moment and extremely blessed as old friends and new ones showered me with love and good wishes. I didn't want to let them down. Their expectations for my mission seemed equal to mine. I knew how fortunate I was to have so many wonderful people show up to support me and send me on my way.

But, despite their goodwill, I couldn't push aside thoughts of what was in store for me in the days ahead. I still had so much planning to do. When I reached Anchorage, I needed to buy supplies and make so many other preparations before I set out on my bike with Jackson.

Still, I loved who I had become—a woman creating her life, taking charge. I felt strong and empowered. I didn't take that feeling for granted.

[May 4, 2017]

My friend Barbara Bridson took Jackson and me to the airport. I had known Barbara and her partner, Vera, for many years. As she drove, Barbara radiated tension and unhappiness. After much silence, I looked at her and said, "I love you, and I am sorry I am worrying you and Vera so much, but this is something that is important to me. I need to do this."

Barbara cast a shy smile my way. "Do you have your bear spray?"

"No," I said. "That is one of the supplies I'll have to get when I am in Alaska."

"Is your sleeping bag warm enough?"

"I think so," I replied, although I didn't know for certain the truth of that statement.

"What will you do when you encounter a bear?"

"Honestly, Barbara, I don't know, and I can't worry about it, or I might not ever leave and go on this journey. I get that you really care about me and that what I'm doing scares you."

We spent the remainder of the drive in silence.

When we arrived at the airport, Barbara, Jackson, and I got out of the vehicle. I grabbed my bag filled with Jackson's food, Jackson's sweater, a blanket for the two of us, undies for me, my toiletries, my passport, and all of Jackson's travel papers, and swung it over my shoulder. I gave Barbara a big hug and promised to stay in touch.

Jackson and I walked into the airport and left Barbara and Florida behind. I would be a different person when I returned.

After checking in, Jackson and I boarded our flight to Seattle. We had a middle seat. The young lady to my left put a headset on right away, making it clear that she was not interested in a conversation. The lady to my right, however, was friendly and loved having Jackson lean on her. She made the flight comfortable for Jackson and me.

When the lady and I weren't conversing, my thoughts drifted to all the friends who had helped me prepare for this journey. Often, a man named Jody came to mind. He was the person who had suggested that I would need an iPhone and a Garmin, which was a device that tracked activity as well as acting as a GPS. I did purchase the iPhone, and Jody helped me set it up. Then, just the night before, he'd surprised me with a Garmin and promised to donate seven thousand dollars to my ride for a cure as soon as he sold his house. I was grateful to Jody and everyone else who had helped me make my dream a reality.

We arrived in Seattle more than five hours later, and I learned that our connecting flight to Anchorage had been canceled due to bad weather. After being booked on a later flight, I found a cushioned place, set up "camp," and Jackson and I slept for about three hours. When we woke up, we found a restaurant and ordered breakfast—meatballs without sauce for Jackson and a breakfast sandwich and a fresh cup of hot coffee for me. Jackson looked at me with big sleepy eyes, as if to say he wasn't sure what he'd rather do—eat the meatballs or lie back down and nap. I laughed, understanding completely; I felt the same. In the end, we both chose the food, and after we finished, we prepared to board our 6:00 a.m. flight to Alaska.

Chapter 2

Alaska—the Journey Begins

Flying into Anchorage was an adventure in itself. The approach for landing seemed incredibly long as we flew over the inlet, glaciers, and mountains that surround the city. I leaned forward as much as I could to take in the spectacular view—blue ice fields, glaciers, the water of the inlet covered with patches of floating ice, the enormous Chugach mountain range blanketed in white powder. Tears filled my eyes as I absorbed the sheer majestic beauty displayed below me. I had reached my destination. My journey could finally begin.

Suzy Walsh waited for us inside the airport. Suzy and I had become acquainted through Reverend Kevin Lee from the Metaphysical Church in Fort Lauderdale. Before my trip, the Reverend had held a Sunday sermon in which he blessed my bike, trailer, the flag, Jackson, and me. The service was beautiful, loving, and incredibly meaningful for me. During the blessing, I felt so much love and support from the congregation that I knew in my soul the trip would go well.

As Reverend Kevin blessed me with special oil from Israel, I openly wept, overwhelmed by the presence of love, spirit, and connection flowing through all things—in a word, the presence of God.

As a child, I grew up in an orphanage and regularly attended church. We had Sunday service, Catechism, Friday Rosary, all major church holidays, nun's jubilees, and our name days. The orphanage did not celebrate our birthdays. My name day is July 4th, the Holy Ulrich.

During that period of my life, I had mixed feelings about the Church and God. The Church taught us about a loving God who healed people through Christ, a God that wanted all his children to return to him in Heaven. But that was not my experience living with the nuns, priests, Erzieherinen, and my teachers. I learned through experience that humans are often hypocrites.

At the orphanage, those meant to protect us, beat us. Priests sexually abused children. If we ever asked the nuns about the abuse, they beat us more. I learned that the God they taught about was a mean white man, more human than divine and out for vengeance. As a child, I never felt I could trust God. I had a love/hate relationship with the Almighty that took many years to resolve.

By the time I made it to Reverend Kevin's service, my relationship with God had healed, although it was with a God the nuns and priests of my youth would not recognize.

Reverend Kevin had introduced me to Suzy via Facebook so that I would have a contact in Anchorage. Suzy and I corresponded and got to know each other, and she agreed to help me start the bicycle journey. A few weeks earlier, I had mailed all of my supplies to her house, where she graciously stored them for me.

Amazed and giddy to finally see Suzy in person, I hurried over to embrace her. What a loving and beautiful soul! She had opened her home and her heart to me. I felt welcomed and grateful.

Suzy was in the process of selling her house when I arrived and had already sold all the furniture in her guest bedroom. "I want you to have my bedroom," she insisted.

"No," I protested. "Where will you and your granddaughter sleep?"

"We can sleep in the guest room in sleeping bags."

"Absolutely not," I said. "I would feel awful for kicking you out of your room."

Suzy smiled and shook her head. "This is my home, and you are my guest. In a few days, you will be sleeping in a tent out in the elements. You need to get as much rest as you can, while you can."

I reluctantly agreed and moved my luggage into the master bedroom.

A free-spirited, spiritual woman, Suzy possessed a warm and generous heart. She offered to show me Anchorage and take me on a short trip to see the glaciers and wildlife.

In many ways, Anchorage looked to me like many big cities, with cars whizzing by and dust and fumes in the air. As we drove south of the city the next day, I was awed by the majestic, snow-covered mountains, the immense glaciers, the intensity and variety of the colors, and the vastness and wildness of the Alaskan countryside. With temperatures in the low forties, Jackson and I played in the snow, loving every minute of our time there. I felt the God-spirit inside of me. The experience moved me to tears.

While staying with Suzy, she also took me shopping. We went to Fred Meyer for groceries, and she told me about a moose that once came to the garden center and ate all the flowers and other greenery. We also shopped for the remainder of the gear that I would need for the wilderness leg of my journey—bear spray, a food drum, a large knife, a camp stove, a bell (to warn bears of our approach), a wind jacket, and food.

Later, back at Suzy's house, I "staged" all my gear and supplies in an empty room. I spread it all out and checked and double-checked that I had everything necessary for the first part of my journey. Once certain everything was in order, I packed the supplies into four saddlebags, placed my camping gear onto the carrier of Jackson's trailer, and checked my bike.

I was ready to go.

[May 8, 2017]

In the early morning, I loaded Jackson into his trailer and got on my bike. My nerves were high, but Jackson seemed content to sit and start the journey. Suzy offered to drive along with us in her car and guide us out of Anchorage. I accepted her offer, and as I pedaled away from her house, the gigantic AIDS Memorial Flag pulled taut in the wind. The trip had begun.

Suzy led us through town to the highway. Traffic was heavy, but the farther away from Anchorage I rode, the less intense it became. I moved slowly through the cool, windy hills surrounding the city, stopping numerous times to add layers of clothing, check on Jackson, and catch my breath. Even though I had trained in Florida for the ride, I wasn't prepared for steep hills and inclines. I often had to push the bike, trailer, Jackson, and myself up the hills—a combination of two-hundred and fifty pounds. I had just started the first leg of my trip and it was already more difficult than I could have imagined. Moving across highway exits and on-ramps was the worst. Vehicles came and went at such high speeds that my bike shook as if in an earthquake.

When I arrived at the final exit from Anchorage, I saw Suzy waiting at the roadside in her car. She jumped out and ran toward me. I stopped and tried to catch my breath.

"Be careful," she said, her voice worried. "Stay to the right. Watch out for bears."

"I'll do that," I promised.

"If you need anything at all, call me."

"I want to thank you for everything," I said.

We stood there looking at each other for a moment and then we embraced. Suzy returned to her car and pulled away.

As she disappeared in the distance, the immense country's silence enveloped me. Jackson and I were alone. I thought of bears and checked to make sure I had the bear repellent and my knife. Suddenly, I felt an overwhelming fear that paralyzed me, and it took every ounce of courage I could gather to get back on my bike and pedal away from Anchorage, my past, and all the people who had doubted me and told me I couldn't—or shouldn't—go through with my mission.

I reminded myself that I'd had ample time to prepare for this journey, and that those diagnosed with HIV/AIDS aren't so fortunate. Then a thought struck me: if struggling with life or a disease, whom could I trust? With whom could I share my diagnosis, the betrayal of my body?

I began to weep. During my ride, I would begin to understand what it meant to live with HIV/AIDS, depression, and any other disease.

I wanted to move faster, but my body wouldn't allow it. Could I even trust it anymore? Cars sped by. Could they see that I was struggling? Could they see the pain in my arms and hands, the ache in my knees, the strain on my lungs?

I was only hours into my ride. What had I gotten myself into?

Blue lights appeared in my mirrors as I pedaled up the highway. I moved to the far-right side of the road, and a police car slowed and then stopped behind me. I looked around, confused. I was the only person on the road. I stopped, and the officer walked up to me. "Good morning, Officer," I said, then jokingly added, "I hope I wasn't speeding."

He smiled. "No. You weren't speeding. I appreciate you keeping to the right side of the road. What are you doing all the way out here on this bike?"

"Today is my first day on a six-thousand-mile journey from Alaska to Key West," I said. I gestured toward the small trailer behind my bike. "That's my dog, Jackson. We're riding for a cure for AIDS."

"That's unbelievable," he replied, sounding shocked. "It's extremely dangerous riding on this road, though. I hate to say it, but I need you to take the bike path out of town. I can't have you on the highway."

"There's a bike path out of Anchorage?" I asked, surprised.

"Yes. It's on the other side of the highway. It goes for about thirty miles before it re-enters the highway again."

"That's great." I glanced across the highway. "How do I get over there?"

The officer looked behind us. "You have to go back to the bridge, take the exit, and cross over to the bike path."

I laughed, hoping he was joking.

He looked serious. "I don't want you to get hurt on the first day. I want you to make it all the way to Key West."

My heart sank. After all my effort to make it this far, I would have to turn around. "There isn't another way?" I asked.

The officer shook his head. He wished me a good journey, and we took a picture together.

After he left, I wasn't sure if I should laugh or cry. I turned around and retraced my route to the bridge, found the bike path, and continued on my way. The weather was relentlessly cold and windy but I carried on.

After riding for what felt like hours, I saw a large area full of trailers and RVs. "Thank God," I muttered to myself. "This must be a campground." I pulled in and discovered it was an apartment building where the owner allowed people to store their campers. I found the owner, and he said for twenty dollars I could pitch my tent in his yard for the night.

I was exhausted, and the yard had a spectacular view, so I agreed. I set up the tent and made my bed. Even though I was surrounded by campers and in the man's yard, I was still terrified of a bear encounter. I put my bear spray, flashlight, whistle, and knife inside the tent beside where I'd be sleeping. I felt armed to the teeth, as if I'd be able to fight off anything that dared to enter—man or beast.

I decided to feed Jackson, but I couldn't open the bear drum—the canister that carried our food. After a while, I gave up trying and hid the drum between some trees far away from our tent. I also left my bag containing toiletries and my smelly clothes under a nearby trailer.

I wasn't sure how many miles I'd covered that day. I couldn't figure out how to program the Garmin GPS device that my friend Jody had given me to document my speed and miles.

Although I had no idea how far I'd gone, it was far enough to work up an appetite. The apartment building owner had told me about a gas station and restaurant just down the road, so Jackson and I walked that way to get a meal. After such a long and emotional first day, I relished sitting in the warm restaurant with a glass of red wine and listening to the music. I ordered food for the two of us, and the waitress allowed me to charge my phone. All the waitresses working there fell in love with Jackson and spoiled him after hearing about the mishap with the bear drum. They fed him grilled chicken and petted him at every opportunity; I think he thought he'd gone to dog heaven.

As we unwound, I couldn't help overhearing a conversation going on between three ladies at a table beside us. One of the women, probably in her seventies, had ridden her bike in an annual fundraising event that day. "It was so windy and cold," I heard her say, sounding out of breath. "It was such a difficult day."

"I'm sorry," I butted in, "but I couldn't help overhearing you. I started the first day of my six-thousand-mile ride to Florida today, and you're right—it was so windy and cold. I'm glad it wasn't just me!"

"That's amazing," the woman said. She smiled. "Would you care to join us? My name is Barb."

"I am Uli, and this is Jackson," I said. "We'd love to."

Jackson and I moved over to their table, and the women and I shared riding stories. I told them about the scope of my ride and its mission. I learned that we had traveled roughly twenty-eight miles that day, though my body felt as if I'd ridden a hundred. Before the women left, Barb donated thirty dollars to amfAR, and we all hugged and wished each other well.

It was only my first day on the road, but kindred spirits had already found their way into my life.

That first night in the tent, I wasn't tired mentally. Physically, however, my body craved a hot bath and a comfortable bed. As I lay there, exhausted, the thought of bears moving around outside the tent weighed heavy on my mind. Terror gripped me as I thought about being trapped inside my sleeping bag as a giant grizzly, hungry from months of hibernation, attacked. I knew I'd have to adjust to sleeping exposed in the wilderness. It would be an unavoidable aspect of the trip.

Branches creaked nearby. Jackson lifted his head and growled. Squirrels chatted, and birds sang until late in the night. Uncomfortable and cold, I snuggled with Jackson for warmth. It doesn't ever get truly dark in Alaska at that time of year; I found it impossible to gauge the time. Overhead, tree leaves rustled, sounding as if they whispered some forgotten, ancient language. At some point, I shut my eyes and fell asleep.

Jackson and my second night camping alone and in the cold.

Chapter 3

Guardian Angels

The next morning, I packed up everything and put it back on the bike. Then I fed Jackson some dog food I had not stored in the bear drum, and we left the apartment complex. I was still wary of attracting bears if I cooked or ate outside, so when I stopped at the nearest gas station to brush my teeth and get a cup of coffee, I also bought some banana bread for breakfast.

The cold, the wind, and a steady incline made for slow riding. The combined weight of the bike, the trailer, and Jackson sometimes made it feel as if I wasn't moving at all. Frustration set in when it took hours to reach the north side of Wasilla—a distance of approximately twenty to twenty-five miles.

I had pulled to the side of the road to look at my map when a van pulled alongside me and stopped. A man yelled through the window, "Are you okay?"

"I'm fine. I'm looking for a nearby campsite," I replied. "They all seem to be closed this time of year.'"

He nodded. "My name's Dave. I used to ride bicycles around these parts all the time. Whenever I got into trouble, someone always helped me out."

"You don't ride anymore?" I asked.

"No. I race sled dogs now. I'm training for the Iditarod. I was in the Army for thirty years, but I'm retired now." Dave seemed to think for a moment, then added, "It's getting late. I'll tell you what…if you want to, you can stay at my house tonight."

I glanced down at the map again. I didn't see any campsites nearby. I had a twinge of hesitation about spending the night at a strange man's house, but Dave was right—it was getting late. I told myself that now might be a good time to lean into trust and surrender; if I was going to complete my journey, I would need to have faith in the generosity of strangers. Dave might be a guardian angel, and wasn't the trip itself a total leap of faith? Didn't people living with AIDS have to have faith to get through each day?

Lifting my gaze from the map, I looked at Dave and said, "Thank you. I'd love to stay at your house if you're sure it's okay."

He opened the back of his van and reorganized the many bags of dog food he'd purchased in town. Then he helped me load my bike, the trailer, my saddle bags, and the flag into the vehicle. Jackson and I climbed into the front passenger seat beside Dave and off we went.

Dave was a pleasant man. While he drove, he told me he was engaged; he and his fiancé were to be wed in two months. His eyes lit up when he spoke of starting his new life. He had recently purchased his house, a place far off the beaten path that would allow him to focus full-time on breeding, training, and racing his Alaskan malamute dogs. The fifty-four-acre property consisted of the main house, two run-down storage buildings, a mill, and two sheds.

As soon as we arrived, I heard dogs barking. Dave helped me unload my gear from the van, and I helped him unload the enormous bags of dog food. He wanted to introduce me to his dogs, so we made our way over to where all sixteen of them were tied to tree stumps. They greeted us with excited barks and growls, jumping energetically and pulling the chains tight against the stumps. The dogs were huge, and the entire situation intimidated and frightened me. My mind raced back to a day when a large dog attacked Jackson and me at a park, but I pushed the memory aside and mustered my courage as Dave fed the dogs.

When he finished, we climbed aboard his ATV and toured the rest of his property. When we drove past a large, rusted-out school bus in the middle of a wooded area, I wondered how it came to be there. It seemed like a forgotten ancient ruin reclaimed by nature. I thought of Christopher J. McCandless, aka "Alexander Supertramp," a man made famous by the novel turned movie, *Into the Wild*. He'd entered the Alaskan wilderness alone and died there in a deserted school bus that he'd used for shelter. A hunter found his body; at death, McCandless weighed only sixty-seven pounds. The thought of him reminded me again of the enormity and danger of my own journey. Would the Alaskan wilderness claim me as well?

Later that evening, back at Dave's house, I washed my biking clothes down in his cold cellar and then took a hot shower. Refreshed, I returned to the main floor, where I found a fire burning in the fireplace and Dave in the kitchen cooking dinner. I was glad to be clean, warm, and about to eat a hot meal.

After dinner, we sat by the fire and talked. Dave smoked pot as he told me about his life. "My fiancé is a teacher," he said. "She plans to retire in two months and move in here with me. After we get married, she'll start trapping full-time."

"What kind of trapping does she do?" I asked.

"She traps for furs," he replied, motioning at the walls. "She trapped those. Skinned them, too."

I looked around the room and noticed all the animal furs: fox, wolf, and wolverine. The difference in our lifestyles was not lost on me.

"I'm in the process of remodeling this house," he continued. "I need to finish the upstairs bathroom. I don't want her to have to shower in that cold cellar. Everything's up there—bathtub, sink, toilet, lights, mirrors."

Dave had an unusual way of smoking pot that he said he learned while serving in Vietnam. He placed the marijuana on a knife, lit it on fire, then inhaled the smoke through a small pipe. He exhaled large puffs that drifted toward me. I didn't use marijuana, but the second-hand smoke relaxed my aching body, so I didn't mind him doing it.

"Can you come give me some pointers on how to organize the bathroom?" he asked.

"Sure, I'll take a look," I said.

We got up and went to the partially remodeled bathroom, and I told him where I thought I would put the toilet, tub, and sink. While we discussed the possibilities, Dave's phone rang, and he excused himself to go answer it.

I left the bathroom and sat down again, listening as he talked to a person whom I assumed was his fiancé. He shared the details of his day with the caller, including picking me up and me helping him with the bathroom design. I suddenly heard a woman yelling on the other end of the line, and Dave quickly took the phone outside to continue the conversation. Feeling awkward, I sat in the living room for what seemed like an eternity, waiting for him to return. When he did, he looked shaken and embarrassed.

"Listen," he said. "I'm really sorry about this, but she isn't my wife yet, and I want her to be. If I don't get you out of here right now, she said she will get on a bush plane *tonight* and get you out herself."

Dumbfounded, I looked at the countless skinned animals that covered the walls—beasts that, earlier, Dave had told me his fiancé had caught, killed, and skinned. "No problem," I said. "I'm out of here."

I packed my wet clothes into my bag, and we climbed into the van again. Dave drove Jackson and me to a campsite. The forest service hadn't yet opened it, so nobody else was there.

"Make a campfire to keep the bears away," Dave advised.

"I will. Thank you for the shower and the meal."

We wished each other luck, and Dave drove away. Despite how our meeting had ended, I considered him to be a guardian angel.

I set up camp next to a river and collected damp wood and leaves to start a fire. Once lit, the fire billowed smoke throughout the site. The area was so peaceful and beautiful, though, that I forgot all about the previous hours. I even forgot about Trump spewing his hatred throughout the world, and all the other reasons I was out here in the first place. I was surrounded by sheer magnificence and beauty, and I tapped into the stillness and my connection to God.

Later, Jackson and I lay in the tent, cuddled up for warmth. I closed my eyes and listened to the sound of the wind in the trees outside the tent. Letting the night and nature's symphony drift over me, I sent my thanks and gratitude out to the Universe and fell into a deep sleep.

I woke in the early morning and left camp without breakfast. Dave had told me about a nearby restaurant, and I wanted to eat inside as often as possible. I pedaled as fast as I could, the promise of fresh coffee and bacon propelling me forward. Dave's idea of "nearby" and mine obviously differed. I traveled many miles without ever coming upon a restaurant. My heart pounded like a drum. My legs burned. My Garmin still didn't work. My phone was long dead. At that moment, the only positive in my life was the scenery. Magnificent, breathtaking, gorgeous; no word could accurately describe it, and it only became more beautiful the closer I came to Denali National Park.

I saw my first two moose and stopped the bike as quietly as I could. I crept toward the moose to get a better look. Their size and beauty awed me and filled me with delight. I took a few pictures before continuing on my way. The encounter reenergized me. I now rode with joy, present in the moment, feeling as if God's arms embraced me; however, I still moved at a snail's pace.

After many hours of riding, Jackson and I finally arrived at the gas station and restaurant in the town of Trapper Creek. We stopped for a late breakfast. I ordered coffee, milk, a bottle of Alaskan Amber beer, bacon, eggs, potatoes, and toast. Jackson had hamburger meat mixed with egg. We both ate greedily and to our fill.

I told the waitresses about our trip and experiences so far, and they seemed in awe of my mission. Of course, they fell in love with Jackson, and the women spoiled him to no end. The attention Jackson brought to the cause, not to mention the freebies, could not be discounted.

The waitresses told me the truck stop had hot showers and a laundry, and I jumped at the opportunity to dry the wet clothes in my bag from the night before at Dave's. I was on the road and now operated on a different timeline; I did what I could when I had the opportunity to do it. No one expected me at a destination at a certain time, so I moved at my own speed. I had no place to go but forward.

However, not moving forward fast enough for my liking frustrated me. The hills became steeper, the wind stronger, and the cold more intense as we approached Denali. I'd slowed to five to six miles per hour. I began pushing the bike up each incline as I didn't have low enough gears to pedal. The effort exhausted me.

When we finally reached the south side of Denali, the highest peak in North America, the view took my breath away. At a lookout point, I stopped to snap a few pictures. Other tourists had gathered at the vantage point to do the same, and I spoke with two young men on their way to Fairbanks. After expressing my concern about finding a campsite for the night, they agreed to text me if they saw anything promising within ten miles.

Alaskan Highway 1 North

Jackson and I took the opportunity to rest, take pictures, and bask beneath the greatness of Denali. Eventually, the guys I'd met did text me, saying I'd find a campsite a mile up the road. Giddy and relieved, I jumped back on the bike and kept climbing. Sure enough, I saw the turn-off for the campgrounds after riding about a mile. I made the turn and followed the markers, climbing ever higher. Eventually, I got off and pushed the bike and trailer up the never-ending incline until I couldn't take another step. Although I'd been so happy after receiving the text message only a short time before, now tears ran down my dirt-covered face as I made a deal with myself, with God, with the Universe, with anyone who might be able to hear. Until I reached the top, I would stop and rest at each new turn before making my way to the next one. With knees that burned like fire, a heart beating like a drum, and electrical charges in my elbows, I kept my end of the bargain.

At the top, the view revealed itself to me. I stood directly across from Denali, all 20,310 feet of her. Denali is an Athabaskan word roughly translated as "the tall one" in English. It is the third most prominent and third most isolated peak on Earth after Mount Everest and Aconcagua, and I had ridden my bike there. I dropped to my knees, awed and physically drained. My sobs pierced the silence. I cried from exhaustion, from years of being alone, abandoned, from the overwhelming connection to nature I felt in that moment, in gratitude for all I had already accomplished so far.

Filled with euphoria and pride, I searched the campgrounds for a ranger. When I found one, he was preparing to leave for the day. "Hello, sir," I said. "Is there a place that I could camp for the night?"

"The park is still closed for the season," he explained.

I began to quiver, and tears welled in my eyes again. "Please," I pleaded. "I have ridden my bike all the way here. I don't have the energy to go anywhere else."

The ranger studied me and sighed. "Okay. You can stay for the night."

Denali National Park, the highest mountain in North America

"Thank you! Thank you!" I replied, wanting to hug him. "Can I ask you one more favor?"

Looking at me quizzically, he nodded.

"Could you show me how to open my bear drum? I haven't been able to open it all trip."

A grin appeared on the ranger's face. "I can do that," he said. "Show me where it is."

We walked to my bike, and I removed the drum from the trailer. He opened the drum quickly, and I felt a sense of relief. "Thank you again," I said. "Jackson and I can have dinner tonight."

"You're welcome. I'm glad that you have it. You need to be very careful this time of year. The bears have just come out of hibernation and are hungry and aggressive."

"I will be," I said.

"Be safe," he said. "Pick any site you want."

With that, he packed up and left Jackson and me to fend for ourselves.

Denali glowed brilliantly in the late evening sun, and I walked the grounds looking for a spot facing the mountain. What the ranger had said about bears came back to me. All the sites facing Denali cliffed-out to the front. If a bear came in behind the tent, I would be trapped. With that in mind, I changed my strategy and chose to set up my tent under the roof at the main pavilion.

I pitched the tent, parked the bike beside it, and surrounded my setup with picnic tables, creating a sort of backwoods fortress. If a bear came into camp, Jackson or I would hear it in time to get out of the tent with the bear repellent. I stored our food and other supplies in a nearby outhouse, returned to camp, and cleaned myself with baby wipes.

Jackson and I crawled into the tent and slept like the dead.

My campsite for the night. The park was still closed, but the ranger allowed me to stay. I am right across Denali National Park. Amazing view!

Denali National Park

We awoke from another frigid night to a cold, damp morning. I was glad I had slept under the pavilion; it had kept my gear dry. Before we hit the road, I walked to the cliff edge to greet the day, Denali, the birds, and to give thanks to God. I'd never felt so connected to nature. During the previous night, the world had become a magical place by virtue of its emptiness. The empowerment I felt sleeping alone in nature for the third night in a row gave me confidence that I could improvise and survive on my own.

Leaving camp was far easier than getting there. I coasted the bike downhill and braced myself against the cold morning air. The cold affected my entire body. It penetrated my clothes, my skin, and settled into my bones. I felt it in my artificial hip. My lips cracked and my nose ran; I blew my nose into a handkerchief as I rode but stopped doing so after a while because it ran continually. I put on a sweatband and covered it with a wool cap to retain the heat that rapidly escaped from the top of my head. All my mornings had been cold, but this morning was the coldest by far.

As the sun rose higher into the sky, I felt warmth spread throughout my body. Even the vegetation seemed to unfurl and reach skyward to drink in the sun's rays. It seemed unreal to me that I'd only recently left Florida's ninety-degree weather, and now I was sleeping on the ground, waking up to temperatures in the low thirties, and skipping breakfast for fear of being eaten by bears.

As I rode, I recalled being in the car with Suzy. She'd pointed into the clouds and said that I would be able to see Mount Denali from Anchorage on a clear day. Now I was on the other side of that mountain. It glowed pink in the sunlight and looked majestic towering over all the other surrounding peaks. Millions of evergreens blanketed the landscape, not tall and full like American Christmas trees, but stunted and skinny from the high latitude. I prayed that humans would preserve natural, wild places like Denali State Park.

Few cars passed me, and the silence was immense. I felt as tiny as an atom, and I occasionally screamed to alert bears, moose, and other dangerous wildlife of my presence. Screaming also helped me overcome my fear. The thought of encountering a hungry, aggressive bear paralyzed me, and my mind ran through different scenarios of what I'd do if I had to fight one off. *Pull the bear spray. Release the security clip. Flip to 'Spray.' Spray the bear. Wait. Don't run. Don't scream. Wait.*

I thought of times in my past when I had become overwhelmed while in a crowd, how I made myself invisible. People had walked by me as if I were a ghost. I wondered if I could use that trick on bears as well.

I let Jackson out of his trailer every hour. While he ran and stretched, I hugged trees and talked to flowers, animals, and God. My overwhelming feeling of connection to this place stayed with me as I climbed back onto my bike. But I snapped out of my trance when an eighteen-wheeler drove by so close that my bike shook violently. Gripping the handlebars in shock, I felt the tiredness in my body and bones as the truck raced off into the distance, once again leaving me alone in the silence.

We pushed north toward Fairbanks. I still couldn't get my Garmin to work, and my cellphone was almost dead again. After many hours, it rang, startling me. Not expecting a call, I pulled to the side of the road and answered. "Hello," I said, not recognizing the number.

"Is this Miss Uli Schackmann?" a female voice responded.

"Yes."

"This is the Alaskan Highway Patrol."

Dumbfounded, I looked around. I was alone in the middle of nowhere. Maybe I'd missed another bike path, I mused. "Why are you calling me? Am I on the wrong road?" I said, half teasing.

"I'm calling to see if you're okay," the woman answered. "Some of your friends in Florida called. They've been trying to reach you. I suggest you call them and let them know you're okay."

Touched and a bit flabbergasted that my friends were so worried about me that they'd called the Highway Patrol, I said, "I've been camping and haven't been able to charge my phone, so I've turned it off at times to save power. I'll contact them as soon as I get wi-fi and my phone is charged."

"That will be great. Safe travels."

I broke the connection and continued north.

Somewhere outside of Cantwell and north of Hurricane, I heard a loud *CLING*. Concerned, I pulled over to check out my bike's chain and tires; I even checked the saddlebags and the flag holder. Everything seemed to be in place, so I jumped back on, thinking I must've hit a piece of metal.

I tried to take off again, but the bike wouldn't budge. Looking it over a second time, I noticed that my back wheel looked like an egg; I'd broken a spoke and bent the rim.

I took Jackson out of the trailer to lighten the load and began pushing the bike up a hill. As few vehicles drove past, I waved my arms, hoping someone would stop. Eventually, a Mercedes-Benz cargo van pulled over. The driver, a man named Paul, tall, funny, New Yorker, with an inviting sweet smile, offered to take Jackson and me into town. Having no other options, I agreed, and we loaded my gear into the back of his empty van. I had met another guardian angel.

Paul informed me he had just arrived in Alaska. He flew there every year to help his friend Simon open his lodge for the summer. Simon owned the Camp Denali North Face Lodge and had left the van for Paul at the Anchorage airport.

When we arrived at the lodge office, three young women named Kelly, Meghan, and Theresa welcomed me to base camp, which was really a beautiful home. They showed me the shower, laundry, and kitchen, and I met Simon, a handsome, quiet, kind and athletic man. I felt so welcomed, and I immediately connected with the girls.

Since the actual lodge was far into the park, and the road was only clear of snow for thirty miles, Simon and Paul immediately flew out in Simon's small plane. I watched my guardian angel take off and disappear into the distance and knew God was looking after my well-being.

My angels Paul and Simon taking off to the Camp Denali North Face Lodge to get ready for the opening season

The view from the base camp of the Denali North Face Lodge

I returned to the house and made myself a cup of coffee while the girls called around to inquire about lodging for Jackson and me. Everything was closed; it was too early in the season to secure a place. The girls said I could stay at the lodge office, and they left me there for the night. I made dinner, did laundry, and took a shower before going to bed. I slept well and warm for the first time in many nights.

Megan came back to the lodge office the next morning and asked if I wanted to ride with her to Fairbanks to buy supplies for the lodge. I gratefully accepted, and we loaded my gear into her vehicle. When we arrived in Fairbanks, Megan took me to a bike shop, and we said our goodbyes. I thanked her for everything and asked that she relay my thanks to the others. She said she would and wished me well.

After I dropped my bike at the shop for repairs, Jackson and I took a taxi to the 7 Gables Hostel. Lucy, the owner, was welcoming and *hervorkommened*—accommodating. Because I had Jackson, I paid fifty dollars for a single room with a bathroom, which was a treat since snow remained on the ground and nightly temperatures were frigid.

I reorganized my supplies and mailed thirteen-and-a-half pounds of unnecessary gear back home. I now carried two bike outfits, one pair of long biking pants, one pair of biking shoes, one bathing suit, one pair of hiking pants, two pair of underpants, four t-shirts, biking gloves, a neck wrap, a baseball cap, a winter hat, a fleece jacket, a long sleeve biking shirt, a down jacket, a wind jacket, rain gear, toiletries, Jackson's first aid kit, my first aid kit, camping gear, a small shovel, toilet paper, baby wipes, a robe, two emergency blankets, one emergency sleeping bag, and the bear drum containing all of our food.

We spent three days in Fairbanks waiting on the shop to fix the bicycle. During that time, I rested, explored the town, and chatted with different guests at the hostel. I needed the break much more than I had realized. Not that I minded the loneliness of the road—it's what I'd yearned for when planning the trip. I had also wanted to experience the vastness, stillness, beauty, and wildness of Alaska, and while I had done so, most of my time riding through the state had been spent on a highway.

I felt proud of the distance I'd traveled. I already hungered for more of Alaska; I felt smaller and more vulnerable there than I ever had before and at the same time I felt huge, filled with strength and pride. I had an enormous amount of respect for the Alaskan environment and its wildlife, and it was exciting never knowing what might happen next.

I was unaware, of course, that the next day, I would encounter a grizzly and her cubs.

My bike packed and loaded, leaving Fairbanks, Alaska

Chapter 4

Crossing into Canada

Potholes, washboard sections, and heaves—nature-made "speed bumps" caused by melting, shifting permafrost—covered the Alaskan Highway. Greg, the man who had picked me up after my bear sighting, maneuvered his truck as best he could, but it bounced and rocked so much it reminded me of being on a plane experiencing turbulence.

As we drove, I held Jackson in my lap while sharing my adventures with Greg, and he told me about his family. He had a wife, kids, and a successful business he had built over many years of hard work.

In the middle of our conversation, Greg looked in the rearview mirror and exclaimed, "Oops! I think I lost your trailer!"

I glanced behind us. The trailer was nowhere in sight.

Greg turned the truck around, and we retraced our route. The trailer contained almost everything I needed; it was Jackson's home and the carrier for my camping equipment.

After stopping an oncoming truck, Greg asked the driver if he had seen a trailer on the road. The driver had, but said it was probably another sixty to ninety minutes down the road.

Greg looked at me and said, "I can't believe you aren't more upset about this."

I thought about that a moment, then replied, "When I started this ride, anger was an emotion I had to let go of. I made a promise to myself that, whatever happens on this journey, I will trust the process. There's nothing I can do about losing the trailer, and bitching or freaking out won't help the situation."

"I'm impressed," he said, then fell silent for a while. Finally, he sighed and said, "You know, I made that same commitment to myself and to my family recently. Especially to my son. My car had broken down several times and then my rental cabins flooded, which meant no income for a while. I had been paying a guy to manage them, and when I got the call that they'd flooded, I got so angry with the manager that I screamed and swore at him and hit the wall with my fist."

Pausing, Greg glanced at me, shamefaced and obviously embarrassed. I could see that he was fighting back tears. I started to say something to comfort him but before I could, he looked away and started talking again.

"I didn't realize that my five-year-old son was in the cabin at the time and witnessed the whole thing," Greg said quietly. "It scared him, and he ran away from me." In a choked voice, he added, "*I* scared him. My son was afraid of me. He's just a little boy."

Tears filled my eyes as well. "I'm so sorry. I understand how others can be affected when we get angry," I said, trying to console him. "It can be hard to repair the damage."

Greg nodded in agreement. Swiping a tear from his face with a hand, he said, "I make it a point now to never react to situations like I did before. I apologized to my manager, my family, and especially to my son. I've been working non-stop to rebuild our relationship, to regain my son's trust and let him know he never has to fear me, that I would never hurt him."

I smiled. "I can tell you're a responsible person. You're compassionate and sensitive, and your commitment to your family is commendable."

Greg waved me off. "I'm not worthy of them."

I wanted to tell him that I doubted the truth of that statement, that I could tell just by his reaction to what he'd done that he made his family his priority, but before I could say anything, we both spotted the trailer on the road ahead.

Even though it was beaten up and ripped, I felt great relief and gratitude that we'd found it. We pulled over and got out, put the trailer in the bed of Greg's truck, and tied everything down.

Back on the road again, Greg drove a little faster than before. I sensed that he wanted to get home to his family as quickly as possible.

Soon, we saw a hitchhiker trudging through the wet snow up ahead. He looked wet and cold. Greg glanced at me, "Should we help him?"

I felt sorry for the man, and Greg did too. Before I knew it, the hitchhiker was in the front seat with us. He was young and very handsome, a Spaniard named Pauli. He was also soaked to the bone, tired, and ragged. Pauli told us he'd been traveling the world for the past five years and was on his way to Vancouver. Almost immediately, he fell asleep.

Greg and I continued our conversation while Pauli slept peacefully.

"A year or so ago," Greg said, "my wife and kids went on a hiking trip. I couldn't go because of my business. The morning after they left, I woke up alone and missed them so much. I felt so grateful and happy to have them in my life, and I realized that everything I'd gone through before I met my wife, good and bad, had led me to her and to us having a family together. So, I did something on a whim. Something kind of strange, I guess." He laughed.

Curious, I smiled at him. "What did you do?"

"I called all my previous girlfriends and told them what they had contributed to my life. I wished them all the best." He laughed again. "I even felt grateful to the ones who had dumped me. If they hadn't, I might never have gotten together with my wife."

"How did they take that?" I asked.

"One hung up on me. She was the only person I think I was ever really in love with other than my wife. Another one said she still was in love with me." He shook his head. "I don't feel anything other than gratitude for either one of them or the others anymore. It makes me wonder where love goes when a relationship ends."

That he had taken the time and effort to contact and acknowledge the women who had inspired and loved him amazed me. It seemed such a tribute to them and to himself for the choices he'd made.

It had grown later after searching so long for my trailer, and Greg knew he wouldn't make it home that night. He called a motel in Destruction Bay and made reservations for a room with two beds. After dropping Pauli off at a truck stop, we drove another half mile to the motel. Greg invited me to stay with him, and to my surprise, I accepted. I shared a room with an almost total stranger that night. I felt an amazing connection to Greg and trusted him completely after knowing him only a few hours.

The next morning, Pauli met us at the motel for breakfast. Greg offered to take Pauli closer to his destination, Haines Junction, and he rode with us in Greg's truck after we finished eating.

Much later, it was dark and quiet in the truck as we approached the Canadian border. Greg stopped the car a half mile from the crossing and requested that Pauli walk across. He explained to me later that because he didn't really know Pauli, he didn't want to take a chance that the young man might be carrying drugs or weapons.

Half asleep, Pauli pulled himself together, got out and grabbed his bag from the truck bed, said goodbye to us, and started walking.

A few minutes later, Greg and I pulled up at the crossing, greeted by bright lights and a few border officers. Greg, a Canadian, handed one of the officers his paperwork. The man checked it briefly, then asked for mine and Jackson's. Several questions followed: How long would I be staying in the country? Where in the country was I headed? I told them about my mission and my journey so far, and before I knew it, a small congregation of officers surrounded us, all listening raptly to my story. They all showed admiration for my effort and wished me a safe trip to Key West.

The officer checking my paperwork handed it to Greg since he was the driver, and we crossed over into Canada, pulling to the roadside and stopping to wait for Pauli to rejoin us. We waited a long time, watching from a distance as the officers spoke to him. We wondered if there was a problem with his paperwork when we saw him open his bag and take something out. Finally, though, they let him pass, and he made his way to us. As we took off into Canada, he explained that the delay had been caused by his possession of a small alarm gun that he kept in his bag for protection. He had had to leave it with the agents.

I regretted that it was too dark to see anything out the window as we drove further into a whole other country. I would've liked getting a feel for the place. Still, I gave silent thanks that I had made it safely this far.

When we reached Whitehorse, a city in Canada's Yukon territory, it was time for Greg and me to part ways. He dropped me at a motel, and we said goodbye, wishing each other well. I was happy to have met such an amazing, kind, loving, and generous giver. I thought he might be another angel in disguise.

June 18, 2017 ANCHORAGE (KTUU) -UPDATE, 4:45 p.m. WEDNESDAY: On Tuesday evening, the Alaska Department of Fish and Game shot and killed four bears. One of the dead black bears is believed to be responsible for Sunday's fatal Bird Ridge mauling.

UPDATE, 10:35 a.m. MONDAY: Alaska State Troopers have identified the victim of Sunday's bear mauling at Bird Ridge as 16-year-old Patrick Cooper of Anchorage.

ORIGINAL STORY: A parent's worst nightmare came to life this Father's Day when a teen running an annual trail race was fatally mauled by a bear near Bird Creek. Law enforcement officials and fellow competitors said a 16-year-old boy was participating in the Robert Spurr Memorial Hill Climb at Bird Ridge, which was being run for the 29th year straight. Dozens of runners, including the teen, toed the starting line that morning for the mountain race that begins at the start of Bird Ridge Trail, and meanders through heavily wooded terrain. As for the ascent, that's a 3,400-foot vertical climb that spans three miles for adult racers and half that for juniors, those who are 17 and younger taking on the mountain.

https://www.alaskasnewssource.com/content/news/Bear-mauling--429297643.html

Chapter 5

First Nations People & Trump Supporters

Jackson and I settled in at a motel outside of Whitehorse. The next day, I checked out the bike, trailer, and our supplies. The earlier crash had damaged the trailer. Three corners of the fabric had ripped; one rip was as big as my hand. The trailer frame was so bent and crooked, I wasn't sure I would be able to mend it, let alone ride with it. I asked the motel staff for some old rags and used them to patch the rips, covering it all with Gorilla Tape to keep Jackson dry. Satisfied with my improvisation and inventiveness, I took Jackson with me to catch the bus into town to explore Whitehorse.

As we walked along the river, I became increasingly saddened by the sight of many homeless First Nations People. I learned that First Nations People had made a powerful contribution to the area and had given up much. Early European immigrants had used the natives as slaves, relocated them, and introduced them to alcohol.

In the 19th century, the Canadian government thought it their responsibility to educate and care for aboriginal people in Canada, believing the natives' best chance for success in mainstream society was to learn English and adopt Christianity. Ideally, the newly converted would pass their adopted lifestyle on to their children and native traditions would diminish in a few generations. With that in mind and thinking children would be easier to mold than adults, they adopted a policy called "aggressive assimilation." Children were torn from their families and communities and put in government-funded residential schools run by the Catholic Church under the Department of Indian Affairs. Children in the schools lived in substandard conditions and were often physically and emotionally abused. They were forbidden to pray to their "Great Spirit." They weren't allowed to sing their native songs or speak their native language. When they wrote letters home to their families, they were forced to write them in English, which many parents and grandparents couldn't read.

Later, when students returned to their homes, they felt they no longer belonged, and most were not equipped to teach their parents anything they had learned. Many became ashamed of their heritage and lived in a sort of purgatory between the life taught by their culture and the modern ways taught at school. Assimilation had robbed them of the rich and nurturing community to which they'd been born.

I learned most of these facts when I visited The Yukon First Nations Culture & Tourism Association, where I found a very active and proud community teaching the young people the old songs, dances, stories, and rich craftworks. On the day I was there, an event took place that included a free health screening, free lunch, and the distribution of free second-hand clothing.

I sat with many of the people and was surprised to hear of the high HIV infection rate among First Nations people; they made up about eleven percent of new cases. The numbers could be attributed to a lack of access to testing, education, care, treatment, and the stigma still attached to HIV/AIDS. I interviewed a few people by video as they shared their experiences surrounding HIV/AIDS. The experience brought home the fact that, unlike humans, the HIV/AIDS virus does not discriminate.

The Association invited me to take part in the health screening, and they checked my blood pressure, blood sugar, and cholesterol. My blood pressure registered at 140/80—higher than it had ever been. Concerned, I later bought baby aspirin that I hoped would help control my blood pressure. But taking the aspirin worried me since it thins the blood; I feared having an accident and bleeding profusely.

Whitehorse, Yukon Territory, Canada, Healing Totem Project

After the health screening, I left and continued to walk through town, where I listened to the street musicians play. An older gentleman played the saxophone, and his virtuosity put me in a different world. I sat near him on a bench and let the warmth of the afternoon sun soak into my skin. I breathed in the beauty of the snow-capped mountains and the grand Yukon River that flows through Whitehorse. In that moment, I felt relaxed and worry-free.

A stunning, elegant woman strolled past. She didn't notice me, but I couldn't keep my eyes off her; her perfume intoxicated me. I watched her until she disappeared from my sight.

For my last night in Whitehorse, I treated myself to dinner at a local diner. I ordered an elk-bison-moose burger. After I ate, Jackson greedily lapped up my leftovers, no doubt excited to eat something other than dry dog food.

I hoped to make it to Greg's cabin the next day. He had invited me there for a free stay, and since it was en route, I had agreed to visit.

I felt reenergized and ready to get back on the road and test the repairs to my bike and trailer. I knew a long, interesting day stretched ahead of me.

Jackson and I left Whitehorse at dawn and were soon back on Highway 1. We headed south toward Marsh Lake—a ride of about forty miles. I felt like a vagabond with my crooked, shabby trailer, but was proud of my self-reliance and ingenuity. Thanks to the Gorilla Tape, Jackson was safe and dry, and my camping gear was securely tied down. I felt pleased with myself for making the repairs. If I knew anything, it was that I would have to rely on myself to survive.

Once again, I traveled a steep road. My knees burned with each turn of the crank, and I was ready to give up just outside of Marsh Lake. I had tried every ointment on the market for pain and swelling in my knees, lower back, neck, and elbows, and I took Aleve regularly. I had thought that the hills would become easier to climb the farther I got into the ride, but they didn't. More and more often, I had to stop and push the bike with Jackson either walking at my side or in front of me.

I began to cry, feeling as if I was getting nowhere fast. Jackson must've sensed my frustration; he began helping by walking ahead of me and pulling the bike and gear as I held his leash.

When I finally reached the turn-off to Greg's house, I saw that he lived forty kilometers off the Interstate (Highway 1). I couldn't imagine adding the additional distance to my trip. Discouraged, I chose to continue onward and not stop at Greg's. I felt guilty and in pain. With a heavy heart and tears in my eyes, I waved goodbye to the intersection and Greg and pedaled forward.

Black bear near road

Each time I rode downhill, I put Jackson back in his trailer. On this day, though, the head wind was so strong that I even had to peddle when going downhill—no breaks, just constant peddling. I tried to feel gratitude that at least it wasn't a side wind I battled; side winds are far worse than head winds, especially when on a highway with cars zipping by at seventy to eighty miles per hour, or if on a bridge. At such times, I held tight to my handlebars.

Somewhere after Marsh Lake, I stopped, in agony. A truck pulled up beside me, both the male driver and his female passenger looking quite concerned. "Do you need some help?" the driver asked.

Unable to speak, I just glanced at the older couple and nodded.

The driver, Nile, jumped out, and we reorganized the cargo bed of his truck so that we could put the bike, trailer, four saddle bags, flag, and trailer into it.

Linda, Nile's wife, gave me water. "You must be dehydrated," she said. "What are you doing all the way out here?"

I explained my story, and they shared theirs.

Nile and Linda were returning to their home in Wyoming from Alaska, where they had been visiting their daughter and son-in-law. While there, they had bought their son-in-law's truck.

I soon learned that Nile was once a coal miner, and both he and Linda were big Trump supporters. The longer we were together, the more I found them both lovable, adorable, and so helpful and kind.

Like me, Nile and Linda came from difficult backgrounds. As a child, Linda spent time in foster care before being adopted by her foster family. Both she and Nile exhibited respect, love, and appreciation for their experiences, their way of life, and their children. Nile explained his reasons for voting for Trump as well as his expectation that Trump would make America "great again." Since I so strongly disagreed with his politics, I mostly listened, believing it important to allow him to share his opinion. I reminded myself that's all it was—an opinion. It wasn't my truth, just as my opinions weren't Nile's and Linda's truth. We ended up having an amazing conversation.

Knowing I supported Hillary Clinton, Nile exhibited great patience with me. I sensed that he thought if he spoke softly and gave me some time, I would eventually understand his point of view and Trump. He and Linda shared a fascinating outlook on life, the environment, the economy, and politics. As Niles talked, Linda sometimes intervened to change the topic a bit or steer the conversation in a different direction. For example, when Nile and I got a bit heated with each other while discussing the environment, Linda interrupted. In the end, we all laughed, and they shared popcorn, candy, and water with me.

Linda told me that she and Nile met at a party when he came over and asked her to dance. I winked at Nile, and he smiled brightly at the memory and at my wink. I felt like I was on a trip with the parents I never had.

I thought back to my own childhood. My parents divorced when I was two years old, and my mom left me with my father. He spent time in and out of prison, mostly for petty theft, falsifying checks, and for not paying alimony, so my grandmother took care of me for three years before the State took custody, and I was put into an orphanage. Living with my grandmother was difficult. An alcoholic and impatient, she had no understanding, tolerance, or love for herself, let alone for a little child. Both sides of my family saw in me the parts of the other side they didn't like; my father's side of the family saw my mother in me, and my mother's side saw my dad in me. Often, my grandmother beat me with a wooden spoon until it broke, then we'd go to the store together to pick up a new wooden spoon.

Nile and Linda took me to Laird, where we spent the night. Since I couldn't find an available campsite or another motel room, I stayed with them at the Laird Lodge. We shared a wonderful dinner together just before the kitchen closed. Linda wanted to go to the hot springs, and I was excited to join in. After a long day driving, Nile couldn't wait to be alone with Jackson and watch TV, so Linda and I walked two miles over boardwalks and beautiful fields and forest to the hot springs. I couldn't have imagined a prettier location, and it felt so good to soak up all the heat of the springs, warming my chilled and aching bones.

At first, not many people were in the pool. However, soon a group of loud teenage kids joined us. They ignored the non-smoking signs and continued to smoke and be obnoxious until several people, including me, confronted them. They laughed at us, but the Forest Service eventually arrived and reprimanded the unruly teens. They left, and the springs became quiet and peaceful again, as intended.

Frozen lake along the way in Alberta

I sank into the water, letting my body and mind relax. Linda and I both went silent, drifting into our own worlds. I thought about how lucky I had been on my journey so far—lucky to have met Greg, Nile, and Linda. The political climate back home was intense, yet meeting Nile and Linda, two people with far different views than mine who, nevertheless, showed me such love and kindness, made me optimistic about our country's future. I had high hopes that, despite differing political views, my fellow citizens would one day stand together, understanding that we are all one family: AMERICANS.

The next morning, Nile and Linda said they would be happy to take me to their next stop, and I gladly accepted the offer since my entire body still hurt. We left very early and drove until about ten o'clock, when we stopped at a lodge and gas station to refuel and have breakfast. Jackson seemed quite happy with all the bacon and sausage Nile fed him.

After breakfast, the truck ride became quiet, with each of us preoccupied by our own thoughts. We shared an occasional story, food, and laughter, but the atmosphere was different than it had been the prior day—not uncomfortable, exactly, just as if we had nothing else to say. I think we had all shared everything we wanted to share.

We covered close to eight hundred miles that day. The road was paved or chip-sealed but still had some rough patches and steep inclines. From the Alaskan Highway, we made it over to Highway 40—the "Highway of Hell." The gravel road had no shoulder, was very steep, and hundreds of semi-trucks traveled it, groaning up the hills at fifteen to twenty miles per hour like slow-moving grizzlies. Nile was tense as he followed behind the trucks for long stretches. He would pass one, only to find himself stuck behind another. I napped on and off, but the road—one of the most dangerous I'd ever traveled—kept me on the edge of my seat. I was glad to be in a big pickup truck and not on my bicycle.

When we arrived in Grand Cache late that evening, I was relieved and so grateful that Nile drove all those hours and brought us safely into town.

With tears in my eyes, I said goodbye to Linda and Nile the next morning. They wanted me to come with them to Wyoming; I'm sure they would have driven me all the way home if I'd asked. But after two days of rest, I thought the time had come to get back in the saddle and start riding again.

Traveling with Linda and Nile had been a wonderful experience—one of love, connection, caring, and concern. I felt as if I'd known them forever. They clearly both loved Jackson and me, and they told me I had inspired them with my mission. We were all grateful to have met one another.

Chapter 6

Grand Cache & the Grandfather Ceremony

Grande Cache, Alberta, sits on a mountain plateau at an elevation of 4,200 feet. The city has views of twenty-one mountain peaks and two river valleys. A fur trader who "cached" a large supply of fur in the area during a winter between 1818 and 1821 gave the town its name. Adjacent to Willmore Wilderness Park—an unspoiled region featuring ancient glaciers, high mountain peaks, thick forests, and raging rivers—the area offers a true back-country experience with over 750 kilometers of trails.

After Jackson and I arrived, we walked around town and into the mountains. Some locals told me about the fourteen registered cougars that live in Grand Cache's surrounding area. I had no idea what a cougar looked like; until then, I had never heard the word.

Panic-stricken, I went back to the motel room I'd rented and Googled "Grande Cache cougars," then "What does one do when encountering a cougar?" I learned that a cougar is a wildcat, like our panthers in Florida. *Oh, shit... a cougar is a panther? There are fourteen registered cougars in Grand Cache?* Daily, I feared a run-in with bears, moose, wolverines, or eagles. Now I had to add cougars to the list of things that could kill me on this ride; that list was getting longer by the day.

Grande Cache was once a bustling coal mining town. After the mine closed, residents suffered greatly. Many lost jobs and homes, and a feeling of heaviness and loss engulfed the town. With the hope of rejuvenating the place where he grew up, a man named Dale Tuck began an ultra-marathon now known as the Canadian Death Race. Dale launched the first Death Race in August 2000, and 193 people participated. By 2010, the race attracted more than one thousand participants each year from around the world. The Death Race is a 125-kilometer foot race through the Canadian Rocky Mountains and includes three mountain summits, one major river crossing, and seventeen thousand feet of elevation change. Dave's event brought much needed diversity, money, and fun back to Grande Cache.

Twenty-one mountain peaks surround Grande Cache, and the city has a population of around thirty-five hundred. Visitors are encouraged to come and experience the Rocky Mountains, and hikers are offered a passport to stamp if they summit a mountain.

That night, I stopped at a pub and talked to some locals, all of whom were deeply engaged by the televised live ice hockey game between the Ottawa Oilers and the Pittsburgh Penguins. When the Canadian National Anthem played, an atmosphere of camaraderie and patriotism filled the place. The anthem was beautiful, and I became tearful. The game was fast, with plenty of action. Everyone in the pub was so intense that I really got into the game as well. I cheered with all the Canadians; I found their energy contagious.

After the game, I spoke with some guys about the cougar and bear situation in Alberta, especially around Grand Cache. The men told me that they heard stories all the time about missing house animals—mostly cats and dogs—and sometimes about attacks on children. That revelation struck me with fear, as I needed to ride through the area. The men gave me one piece of advice for a cougar encounter: "Make yourself look huge!"

At the pub, the owner's mother, Olga, worked as the chef. Olga had emigrated many years ago from Greece and was a wonderful cook. After eating an exquisite meal, I sent my compliments back to the kitchen. The next day, I went back, and Olga came out to meet me. We shared an enjoyable conversation, which Olga turned into a double serving of food. I finished everything, and my healthy appetite thrilled her.

In her mid-seventies, Olga was a small, strong woman from the

Grecian old country. She had the sweetest, warmest smile, despite her missing teeth. Like most emigrants, Olga was tough as nails, yet kind. She'd lost one of her sons years ago and had suffered deeply; I could tell that she still mourned the loss. She touched my heart, and I was glad to meet her. I felt that I touched her heart as well.

Bob, Olga's son, told me that my presence and adventurous spirit had opened something up in his mother that he hadn't seen in years. She was more caring, softer. She worried about me being alone on the road. When Olga and I said goodbye, we left each other with tears in our eyes.

Olga the chef of Vegas Bar and Grill, Grand Cache, Alberta

The next day, I stopped by the Grande Cache Recreation Center, home to a first-class aquatic center, hockey arena, curling rink, fitness center, climbing cave, meeting and party rooms, and a variety of sport, fitness, and community programs for all ages. I spoke to Lin, a woman who worked there, about my journey. She told me HIV/AIDS had affected her personally, and she agreed to do a video interview about her story. In the interview, Lin shared that her uncle became infected with AIDS in 1980. His doctors put him on medication, and he was doing well. She spoke of the stigma surrounding HIV/AIDS in the 80s and described the ways in which her uncle's diagnosis affected the entire family.

After completing the interview, Lin and I talked for quite a while and shared stories about life. Lin loved to hunt, collect mushrooms and berries, hike, and stay overnight in the mountains. She shared some very good tips for protecting myself from wildlife.

I never ceased to be surprised that people shared such deep and intimate parts of their life with me. As someone who had always been rather conservative when it came to talking about myself, their generosity of spirit and openness always left me in awe.

The next day, Jackson and I went back to the recreation center for me to swim in the pool, and I thought it to be the best pool I'd ever experienced. It had lap lines and whirlpool hot tubs. The center also had an open pool, a kiddie pool, and a water slide. It felt amazing to plunge around in the water and use some different muscle groups other than the ones I used when riding my bike.

After two days exploring Grand Cache, eating good food, resting my body, and making connections with the locals, the time had come to move on. I made plans to leave the next morning.

Dressed in layers suited to the frigid morning air, I started climbing again as soon as Jackson and I passed the Grande Cache city limits on Highway 40. After thirty miles, I heard a loud *BANG* from the back of my bicycle. Concerned, I jumped off, only to find that I had broken three spokes and damaged my rim. I was smack dab in the middle of nowhere on the "Highway from Hell."

I waved at several trucks as they passed by before I finally fetched a ride with a woman named Tammy who was driving from British Columbia to Hinton, Alberta, to pick up her mom. Her mother had traveled from a First Nations reservation in Ottawa. Tammy's family was First Nation Cree.

After learning of Tammy's heritage, I told her about my first Grandfather Ceremony experience—a peyote ritual associated with the Native American Navajo tribe. As we talked about it, the conversation transported me back into the circle with Grandfather.

A friend had invited me to attend the ceremony, and I agreed to do it without having the slightest knowledge of what would occur. A shaman sat our group in a circle and explained the ritual. We sang and passed around a rattle; then the shaman told us stories and prayed to Grandfather—the fire. After the prayer, the shaman gave us peyote to take. Making certain I took as much as the elders, I washed it down with some tea and made a commitment to stay awake and watch over the fire all night. The shaman said newbies, like me, could change positions during the ceremony. However, he insisted that all the natives remain kneeling throughout the entire night.

Soon, a Voice appeared in my head. At first, I thought it was only my thoughts, but I began to suspect the Voice was something else entirely.

"Uli," the Voice said. "Get ready; you are going to throw up. Let me know what you are going to expel."

Marveling over the fact that I could talk to myself in that way, I heard the Voice say, "*We* are talking to you now. Besides, you have no time for a discussion. You are getting ready to throw up."

"Please, don't let me throw up," I begged.

"It's going to happen, so what will you get rid of?" the Voice asked.

"Toxic people."

"Great!" the Voice said. "Who are they?"

I gave three names.

"Why are these people toxic?" the Voice asked.

I said why.

"Great job," the Voice replied. "Get ready; here it comes!"

I leaned forward and began to vomit. When finished, I sat back. I was uncomfortable, but I sang along with the rest of the group.

The Voice came again. "We are going to throw up again," it said.

"Please, no…not again. I don't want to vomit," I pleaded. "It makes me weak."

"This time, I need something bigger that you want to get rid of," the Voice demanded.

I shook my head.

The Voice would not retreat. "I want something larger than toxic people. Something you want to expel."

"I give up rage, anger, and resentment," I said.

"Why do you feel these emotions?"

"Because of my abandonment," I admitted, for the first time in my life.

The Voice sounded almost cheerful as it said, "Fantastic…good work! Okay, get ready, here it comes."

Sure enough, I vomited a second time.

Time passed slowly. I was sick, uncomfortable, and having a conversation with an unseen thing. I couldn't believe I'd paid to participate in this.

The group continued to sing and play drums. As they did, the Voice came again. "Get ready for another one," it said.

"Please, no more. I can't. I am exhausted and so tired. No more throwing up. *Please!*" I begged.

"I applaud you for your hard work and for not giving up," the Voice said. "Remember, you are not alone. We are with you. So, what is it that you want to expel? Let's dig a little deeper."

I shared my biggest fears in life: fear of failing, fear of not being good enough, fear of being alone, and fear of being homeless.

"Thank you for digging deep," the Voice replied, sounding pleased with my efforts. "When did those fears begin?"

"In my childhood," I said.

"Great job, Uli," the Voice said. "Now, get ready."

I leaned over and vomited a third time.

Dehydrated and exhausted, I fought to keep my eyes open. I tried to get comfortable. My butt and lower back hurt badly, and I couldn't find a comfortable position.

The Voice spoke again. "Uli, this is the last one, so make it enormous; dig as deep as you can."

I couldn't think. I shook my head for the Voice to stop.

"Go deep, Uli. You are doing great. Let it all out, especially now that you are going on your journey. Leave it behind."

I looked inside myself and dug as deep as I could until I found the last of it. "I try to live up to people's expectations of me. I have much insecurity. I judge others." I gave everything to the Voice.

The Voice responded with obvious delight and cheer as it praised me for working so hard. Then it asked, "Where and how in life do these show up?"

I answered; then I vomited for the last time.

My eyeballs felt as if they would pop out from all the retching. I'd traveled beyond myself. I was exhausted, but the experience was over.

Tammy kept driving, listening raptly as I told the story. I decided to share with her a dream that I had shortly after the Grandfather Ceremony. The elder, "Grandfather," appeared in my dream and showed me a room. Inside the room, a man blew glass. Grandfather pointed to some beautiful bottles the man had created, each one a different design and color. He pointed at the bottle stoppers, also made from glass and with beautiful designs on top of each one. The stoppers also were of different colors, designs, and sizes.

Grandfather explained that we must take care of them; they are fragile, especially the glass stoppers. He said we always come with the same stopper, but never with the same bottle; the bottle changes over time.

I understood he was telling me that we reincarnate—that the stoppers represent our souls, and the bottles represent our physical bodies.

He smiled, pleased that I understood.

I finished telling Tammy about the dream. She had listened patiently…attentively. She thought that the Voice I had heard was the voice of God.

I thought about that for a while. I found it comforting to think that God was working with me.

Glancing across at Tammy, I saw that she was crying. We sat in silence for a moment and wiped our eyes. She said my stories had affected her and reminded her of her mother, Mary, who had lived a difficult life. As I had learned while in Whitehorse, the Canadian government had seen to it that all First Nation children of Tammy's mother's generation went to Christian schools. What Tammy told me that I didn't know was that, at these schools, the children's heads were shaved, and they were told that their cultural beliefs were wrong and bad.

First Nations people take pride in their long hair; it ties them to Mother Earth and symbolizes the manifestation of spiritual growth. Braids are especially sacred. The three intertwined strands of the braid represent the strengthening of the body, mind, and spirit. Losing their braids cost the children much more than a loss of hair.

Tammy reiterated more of what I had learned at Whitehorse, stating that at the government-sanctioned Christian schools, the children weren't allowed to speak their language, sing their songs, or say their traditional prayers. In effect, the government and the schools stripped First Nations children of their culture and separated them from their families and communities for many years. The kids felt like strangers when they returned to their reservations.

Mary had lived in a Christian boarding school for many years. She forgot the First Peoples' ways and adopted those of the white people. Over time, Mary became a devout Catholic.

Tammy told me that her mother's high school sweetheart had been a young man named Ed. Ed, at twenty years old, got in trouble one night while partying with some people and getting very drunk. The next morning, the police woke him up and arrested him for the murder of the dead man lying beside him. Ed remembered that the man and a woman at the party had fought the night before, but he couldn't recall anything else. The authorities charged him with murder, and he went to prison for many years. Before he served his time, he promised Mary that, upon his release, he would find her and provide for her.

Many years later, Ed did return to find Mary. He attended Alcoholics Anonymous, cleaned up, and followed through on his promise. While in prison, he had also committed to changing the lives of inmates by taking them to AA meetings and by helping them integrate back into society. He followed through on that commitment as well.

Tammy said that Ed had died ten years prior, and that his death had been a devastating loss for Mary.

Tammy explained that Mary hadn't always been there for her and her two sisters. Her mom had married an abusive man, and one day Mary decided to take a rifle down from the rack and shoot him. Just in time, a neighbor came by and found Mary standing at the door, her eyes bruised and her face swollen, the rifle in her hand. The neighbor asked what she was doing, and Mary replied, "Today, I kill him!"

The neighbor took Mary home with her, and they talked and had tea. The woman saved Mary from shooting her husband. Afterward, Mary packed up Tammy and her sisters and left. But due to Mary's alcoholism, social services stepped in and took the children from Mary for a few years. Although a devout Catholic, Mary tried to drink away her pain, and even her close friend, Ed, couldn't stop her.

Tammy admitted to me that she felt conflicted about her mother. She loved her, but alcoholism caused Mary to behave in ways that embarrassed Tammy and made her feel ashamed.

Tammy told me that my dream about the colored bottles made her

Jackson camping

begin to understand that many good things existed between her and Mary that had been overshadowed by her mom's drinking. She was often afraid for her mom to visit because of her alcoholism. But now she thought that perhaps she could create a different sort of relationship with her mother by focusing on Mary's warmth, love, and beautiful, sweet smile rather than all the things wrong with her.

Tammy was the first of her family not to fall into addiction or get into trouble. She had raised two beautiful, strong, independent girls as well as her brother's children, and had taught them about their culture. It had been difficult for her to find information about the First Peoples' dances, prayers, songs, and traditions because so much of the knowledge about such things had been stolen by the government, but Tammy passed along whatever she found.

By the time we reached Hinton, I counted myself fortunate to have met Tammy. She was truly a beautiful, sensitive, powerful spirit. Through her, I learned that, by sharing my own stories, I can contribute positively to the listener, and by listening to the stories of others, I receive gifts as well. Tammy said to me, "The First Nations dances, stories, and culture helped my children and me understand who we are and where we come from. *In order to be sure of yourself, you need to know who you are.*"

I would remember that lesson often during my journey and after it ended.

Chapter 7

Jasper—New Friends, Old Friends, & Wildlife Encounters

Tammy dropped me off at the local bike shop in Hinton, a town located in Yellowhead County, Alberta, 81 kilometers (50 miles) northeast of Jasper and about 284 kilometers (176 miles) west of Alberta's capital city, Edmonton, in the Athabasca River valley.

A guy at the bike shop told me he couldn't completely repair the bike and suggested that after he did what he could, I take it to Jasper, the next closest town. He wouldn't guarantee that his repairs would hold up long, but he assured me that the shop in Jasper would have a larger selection of materials. I rode to the nearest campsite and slept there that night, waking several times to the sound of a train that came through the area almost every hour. The cold also kept me awake; it was only about forty degrees during the night. It was very quiet, and sometimes I heard the rustle of a rabbit or a squirrel outside the tent, or possibly a bird.

We spent the next day in town, having breakfast at A&W, then going to a visitor center where I uploaded and updated Facebook posts while my bike was being repaired. Due to my infrequent access to wi-fi, it was challenging to stay up to date on social media, my website, and other online sites, and it took forever to download pictures. It took so much out of me because I often wasn't sure of the names of the towns I had traveled through,

Jody requested that I send him a daily report of the names of the towns I had gone through, how many miles I rode and how much money I'd raised, and I inquired about his seven thousand dollar donation he promised.

He seemed frustrated with me for that, and he chastised me for my poor use of English in the few posts I did make, which he claimed made it impossible for anyone to relate to my riding experiences. I felt controlled by him, and after telling him so, he signed off on me; I never heard from him again. Honestly, I was relieved not to have to deal with him.

After finishing up at the visitor's center, Jackson and I went over to the Beaver Boardwalk for a nice little walk. As we navigated a trail through the woods, other hikers informed me of a recent cougar attack in the area. I stayed on high alert for the remainder of the walk.

That evening, we stopped at Smithy's Restaurant for an early dinner. A man named Steve, who was the owner's brother, greeted and seated us. We struck up a conversation about my trip when he asked about my bike and trailer, which he could see through the window. Steve claimed to be an outdoorsman and a guide. He knew the name of every mountain peak and told me about his experiences on each one either hang-gliding, skiing, or hiking. Other diners heard us talking, and they watched Jackson and me with curiosity etched on their faces as I ate the salmon, rice, and veggies I ordered and listened to Steve's stories. Tourists were not unusual to the area, but not many were traveling with a dog on a bicycle from Alaska to Key West.

At almost sixty years old, Steve was still quite attractive. Because he was also an adventurer, we hit it off. I enjoyed hearing about his adventures, especially his recounting of a near-death survival experience.

Once, Steve, his dog, and two of his friends went hiking in the mountains and got caught in an unexpected snowstorm that lasted almost four days. They dragged the little bit of hiking gear they'd brought under a fir tree where they all huddled and braved out the storm for almost five days, after which they were found by a rescue party. All of them survived, even Steve's dog. I heard old fears resurface in his voice as he told the tale, but I also heard a ring of certainty born of self-reliance. Those five days had made Steve into a more confident person, but he had not forgotten the sense of terror he and his friends had felt at the time, and he never would.

I finally had some reception on my phone, so I made some calls that evening. I felt lonely and desperately wanted to talk with friends. When I did, though, something seemed to be missing between us. The calls felt distant, disconnected, short. Their doubts about my journey were at the forefront of everything we discussed. After the last call, I felt more alone than I had before. I thought of Steve at the restaurant, and I realized that I felt more connected to the strangers I'd met on my journey than I did to old friends. The people I'd met so far accepted me and valued what I was doing. Their warm reception and encouragement made me feel as if the journey was worth the difficulty of climbing so many hills and the pain in my body. They focused on the contribution I was making rather than any potential dangers I faced. That realization was an uncomfortable eye-opener. I would ponder the reasons why it was true for a very long time.

The next day, I stopped at Smithy's and reconnected with Steve. He seemed happy to see me. I ate a hardy breakfast and rid myself of the cold in my bones. Steve offered to give me a ride to Jasper since he had to go there for business. I gladly accepted his offer. I didn't trust my bike to hold up all the way to Jasper. Besides, I wanted to hear more of Steve's adventure stories.

While we drove, we had another long conversation. He was an outdoorsman, which wasn't a rarity in Alberta, and he came from a well-known and respected family in Grand Cache. Still, Steve had many incorrect ideas about himself.

"I guess I'm just a loser," he told me. "The government shut down my outdoor business twice."

His business had included sky diving, hang gliding, mountain biking, kayaking, windsurfing, and camping. He claimed that the oil and coal industry shut him down.

Steve had hired an attorney to fight the closures, but after two years, he thought he'd run out of money and time on the statute of limitations.

"I really miss it," he said. "I loved working out in nature. I especially loved hiking and off-road biking."

His adventures interested me, and I liked his enthusiasm. Instead of sharing the mechanics of my trip, I shared how my journey had started because of a vision I had to find a cure for AIDS by 2020. I encouraged him to create a vision for himself.

"You're right," he said, clearly moved. "I gave up on my dream, and now I'm working for my brother at his restaurant."

He told me he still had an eight-room house in Grand Cache that he used to rent out to adventure travelers. Then the oil industry took over, and he started renting the house to roughnecks until the oil business went bust. Grande Cache didn't want to invest in tourism; instead, the town put all its resources into the oil and coal industries, so Steve lost his clients and his business. He had since moved to Hinton.

"I'm kind of excited about the idea of creating a new dream," he said.

"When you decide what it is," I replied, "tell others about your vision so they'll get inspired and encourage you and push you to succeed. That's what I did."

Steve got a bit teary-eyed. "Thanks for the pep talk. I needed it. I get the feeling we were meant to meet."

"You're very welcome."

"You want to get together Thursday evening?" he asked. "I'll be back in Jasper then, and I'd like to take you to dinner to thank you for inspiring me."

I smiled. "Sure. I'd like that."

Steve helped me find lodging in Jasper. All the motels and hotels were either booked or too expensive, so he suggested I rent a room in a home—something he said was common there. We found the perfect place; then he drove me to the bike shop to leave my bike and get the back wheel fixed. I was told it would take three days.

Snowing in Jasper, Alberta

When I got back to the house where I'd rented a room, Mr. and Ms. Robertson, the owners, said it would be fine for me to stay three nights. After settling in, taking a hot shower, and washing my old biking outfit, I felt like I was in heaven; I had a warm room and a comfortable bed.

That night, I thought about Steve, Tammy, and the many others that I had encountered on my journey so far, and I felt inspired and uplifted. Many thoughts ran through my head. Sometimes, I felt like a messenger for the people I met on the road. While they helped me move forward physically on my journey, I helped them realize their importance. It occurred to me that when we help others see their own greatness and power, their light shines and anything is possible.

The next day was cold and wet. Jackson and I cuddled and kept each other warm in our room.

That night, I took him with me to have dinner at the Downstream Restaurant. I had two glasses of red wine, a beautifully cooked elk steak covered with a peppercorn sauce, vegetables, and a potato. Perfectly seasoned and cooked, the food was delicious. Since I'd seen so much wildlife on my journey, I thought of Grandfather Spirit and blessed my food, giving thanks to the elk and Mother Earth for nurturing me. I honored the elk's life and wildness, grateful for the strength it would pass to me. Wanting the elk's spirit to live on in Jackson as well, I shared some of the meat with him.

The next morning, Jackson and I walked out of town toward the mountains while we waited for the bike. The fear of bears hung over me like a dark cloud or some bad dream. Jackson led me into the mountains and up to the top of a small summit. The intoxicating beauty and scents that surrounded me made me dizzy with delight. I was proud that we'd made it, but also afraid of bears and other wildlife. I constantly scanned left to right and above to the treetops, on the lookout for anything that might threaten our safety. Confirming my fears, we encountered a group of hikers, and they pointed at two giant black bears in the distance, meandering alongside some railroad tracks while eating grain that had fallen from the trains. From my perch in the woods, they seemed non-aggressive. Nevertheless, I reversed my direction and started slowly back toward town.

As I walked along the tracks, I spotted what I thought was a large dog, maybe a golden retriever, on my left across the way. A closer look stopped my heart; it was a cougar. Jackson and I were now sandwiched between two black bears and a cougar. Jackson obviously knew something was up; he stayed close to me, acting wary. The bears were a good distance away from us, but the cougar was way too close.

Scooping Jackson up, I threw him over my shoulder and grabbed my backpack in my free hand. Swinging the pack wildly and I made screaming noises. If a person had seen me at that moment, they would've thought me a lunatic. The cat must have thought so too; it quickly jumped into the high grass and bushes and disappeared.

Everything had happened so quickly that I felt in shock. The encounter had been too close for comfort, and I couldn't wait to get back to civilization. I felt I'd crossed some invisible line separating adventure from danger. Somehow, I'd managed to break out of my momentary paralysis and found the courage to make the bold move I'd made. I'd scared a cougar away. I was growing.

Early season tourists from around the world began arriving in Jasper. Even though I'd only been in town a few days, I had begun to think of myself as part of the local community. Whenever I walked down the street, I would greet or be greeted by familiar people, and we would make small talk. An amazing number of Germans were in Jasper. The Germans weren't as friendly as others I met; I connected better with those of other nationalities than with my own people. I crossed paths with Koreans, Europeans, Australians, Filipinos, Chinese, and people from many other far-off locations. On every corner it seemed, someone spoke German, and I was excited to hear my native tongue.

After staying three days with Sandy and Jean Robertson, I received notice that my bike was ready. The time had come to leave Jasper. I said goodbye to many new friends and headed out of town. It felt wonderful to be back in the saddle. I rode for about an hour before I heard the familiar sound of a broken spoke. I turned around and pushed the bike all the way back into town. I arrived back at the Robertson's house, and they greeted me with surprised expressions. I explained the situation, and they welcomed me back into their home, saying that I could stay as long as it took to fix the bike.

I settled back into the room, then returned to the bike shop. They thought that the rim could not support the weight I had on the bike. They ordered a new, stronger wheel and told me it would take four days for it to arrive.

Since I would be in Jasper a while longer, I contacted the local paper and asked if they'd be interested in interviewing me about my mission and journey. They scheduled a meeting the next morning with a man named Paul Clark, and he wrote the following article:

> Uli Schackmann is no stranger to long distance cycling but cycling from Alaska to Florida to raise money and awareness about AIDS is an entirely different challenge.
>
> With her dog in tow, the German-born American citizen left Anchorage in early May and recently stopped in Jasper as part of her 9,600-kilometer journey to Key West, Florida.
>
> "I'm riding because I want to bring awareness and educate others about HIV and AIDS," said Schackmann, who is raising money for amfAR, an international organization dedicated to AIDS research. "I aligned with them because they have the same ambition, which is a cure for AIDS by 2020."
>
> For the past eighteen years, the 58-year-old has been participating in long distance bike rides throughout the United States to raise awareness about AIDS. She said she hopes to complete her current journey in the next six or seven months. Her unplanned stop in Jasper in mid-May was only supposed to last for a few days before she headed to Banff, but almost two weeks later she said the kindness and generosity shown by locals has made it difficult to leave. When she first showed up, she couldn't find a place to stay so she decided to knock on a few random doors in town to see if someone had room for her and her six-year-old dog, named Jackson. It only took a few knocks before she came upon Sandy and Jean Robinson, who warmly welcomed her in with open arms.

"They couldn't have been any kinder," said Schackmann. "I paid for three nights, but we had snow so they said I couldn't leave because it was too cold and there would be too much snow if I headed down to Banff so I stayed."

A few days later she tried to depart, but only part-way down Highway 93 her bike broke down, so she had to return to Jasper. While waiting for her bike to be fixed, she stayed with the same couple for another four days, free of charge. "I told Jean I don't know what it is about this place, but it's pulling me always back in."

And the friendly hospitality didn't stop there. To help her get on her way, Freewheel Cycle fixed her bike, but only charged her for the parts, while the Jasper Veterinary Clinic offered to groom her dog free of charge.

She said the journey, of course, hasn't been without its challenges. While cycling through the Yukon she came face to face with a grizzly bear and her two young cubs. "That was scary," recalled Schackmann. "They were just heading up a hill when I came, and I tell you, my heart went up in my throat." Spooked by the encounter, she rode a bit further before flagging down a passing motorist. "There was nothing out there. I didn't see a sign for the next campsite, there were no human beings and hardly any cars. It was really, really lonely out there." Adding to the challenge, a lot of the campsites along the way were still closed and covered in snow. "It was just too intense. I couldn't relax or sleep." To get herself out of the situation she flagged down a passing car, which drove her the remaining 800 miles to Whitehorse. Despite being in the middle of nowhere, she said she learned a lot from the experience. "It made me very present to people who are living with HIV or AIDS and coming out and how lonely that would have been for them."

Reflecting on her journey so far, she couldn't say enough about Jasper's generosity. "I had the most amazing stay here. People couldn't have been any nicer, more welcoming, and kinder. It was just an amazing experience."

To donate to amfAR, visit her GoFundMe page: Uli's Journey. People can also support her personal costs by donating to her Crowdrise page under the same name.

"HIV AIDS is here, and we have to address it and hopefully we find a cure and not just make a difference in the United States and Canada, but across the world." Paul Clarke; editor@fitzhugh.ca

The interview went well. It amazed me to look at myself and see how much I had grown and was still growing. Once, I had been so shy I could hardly talk to others. Now, I had become powerful, inspirational, courageous, bold. What a journey I had taken to initiate that growth. I felt proud that I'd challenged myself by opening to change.

I stayed with Sandy and Jean Robertson for two weeks, and they only charged me for three days. They loved Jackson and took pity on me because their children had traveled in Europe and Asia in the past and had relied on the generosity of strangers to help them in a pinch. Both Robertsons were born and raised in Jasper. I found them to be proud, kind, generous, hard-working people, content and happy parents and grandparents.

Sandy, a tall, handsome gentleman and artist, had painted many beautiful scenes from around Jasper. He also told wonderful stories. In his youth, his parents owned the supermarket in Jasper. One day during that time, a Hollywood film production crew stopped at the store to buy supplies. They asked Sandy where they could rent an office. Sandy's parents ended up renting their office to the film crew, and Sandy helped to find twenty men to act as Canadian Mounties for a movie the film crew was making.

When Sandy showed up on set with his twenty Mounties, one being himself, he saw Marilyn Monroe there. During a break in filming, he went over to Marilyn, introduced himself, and started to crack jokes with her. She seemed enamored with Sandy and spent time with him from then on, allowing him to take pictures with her. He still had a glow in his eyes when he showed me some of those photos. He talked fondly about Marilyn, and he sang me some songs from the movie.

After the movie completed filming and the production left town, word got around in Hollywood to contact Sandy's family when filming in or around Jasper National Park. Due to that, Sandy had met many stars and had many stories to tell.

I continued my exploration of Jasper and the surrounding area, aware more than ever of the beauty, God spirit, and the amazing kindness of the people there. My self-confidence had grown since starting the ride, as had my self-reliance and strength. I felt gratified and proud.

I often walked outside of town and took the trails into the woods. On one of my hikes, I saw bear signs everywhere. On full alert, I walked farther into the forest, the dense canopy of trees blocking out the light and making it difficult to see. In my mind, I went over again what I would do if I encountered a bear face-to-face. Finally, I turned around; I wasn't sure how far into the forest the trail went.

I walked along a fast-moving river on my right. A grove of thin trees and brush surrounded me. I still had quite a way to go before reaching the road when I saw a bear squatting at the edge of the tree line. I thought of the bear spray in my hip pack, but I froze in place, unable to move a muscle, as did Jackson beside me. Staring straight at us, the bear froze too. I stared back, wondering if he would turn away or if he would run at us. I had replayed this scenario in my mind many times, but now it was real, and I didn't know what to do.

Free-running calving elk cows (They can be very aggressive as they are very protective of their young)

The bear and I continued our stare down. I mustered the nerve to move my hand just enough to adjust my glasses and squinted, trying to get a better look. The bear hadn't moved an inch for the entire time I'd been watching him, and that had been quite a while. Taking a deep breath, I inched forward a step, then another, moving closer to the bear, who just happened to be squatting in the spot that was my only way out of there. Slowly, I moved closer.

As I closed the distance between myself and the bear, I realized it wasn't a bear at all. I had been staring down a burned-out tree stump.

Relief swept over me, and I began laughing at my mistake. But my reaction at encountering what I'd thought was a bear also worried me. Had I responded in the proper way? I wasn't sure.

Two days later, I read an article in the local paper about a bear attack on a hiker on the same trail I'd been traveling. It was a sobering read, and I realized that a simple walk through the wilderness can become serious in a blink. I couldn't help thinking that I'd been divinely guided and protected on my journey so far. I felt grateful.

I had arrived in Jasper after two months on the road, and I'd found it refreshing to see a gay sticker on the Coco Coffee Shop's front window. I almost skipped my way into the establishment, where the friendly staff greeted me. Until then, I hadn't realized how much I had missed those rainbow colors, and it delighted me to know I was welcome there.

As I walked the streets of Jasper during those first days, I saw that many stores had a rainbow sticker on the door or in a window. A town of only forty-five hundred people, Jasper didn't have a large gay population, but residents seemed open to diversity and freedom of expression; almost anything goes in Jasper. Before the tourists started to show up, I did my part to support the economy. I loved that Jasper had a small town feel while still welcoming diversity. During my time there, I always felt welcomed and accepted. People chatted with me on the street and in cafes—a great feeling.

As temperatures rose, Jasper donned a spring dress. The air held the sweet scent of lilacs, intoxicating me. Filled with joy, I breathed deeply. I imagined I could feel the grass stretching out to touch the blanket of warmth I felt drifting over me. A kaleidoscope of colors appeared, all the plants and flowers eager to share their glory. They seemed to grow by the minute, their perfume becoming stronger by the day. It was intense and wild.

In Jasper, people love their gardens; Jean's garden boasted labrador tea, buttercups, and baneberry. Neighborhood lawns looked like beautiful fields, beckoning me to picnic in them, read, relax. I couldn't get enough of their simple beauty.

Most everyone I met suggested I visit Lake Maligne. When I decided to, a blizzard hit. The weather turned cold again overnight, and up to two feet of snow was dumped on Jasper. The snowstorm coincided with the return of my bike, repaired and ready to go. Jane and Sandy suggested that I stay until the roads cleared, and I agreed.

While we waited for the roads to be safe to travel by bike, I rented a motorcycle with a sidecar and a driver. Jackson rode in the sidecar, and I sat behind the driver on a beautiful ride to Lake Maligne that took my breath away. Surrounded by Rocky Mountain peaks and three visible glaciers, it seemed magical, a Garden of Eden. I felt surrounded by the gods and spirits that called the place home.

I found myself paying more attention to my thoughts than I ever had before. While on the road, alone on my bike, I always felt tense, on alert for wildlife crossing the road or ready to attack, for traffic passing by at high speeds. I never had time to drift into my thoughts, to let go of my tension and relax, to enjoy my surroundings from a different perspective, as I did now. Staying in Jasper had allowed me that reprieve.

The ride had taught me that I don't need much to live and to be happy. The passing miles had made me realize that everything is temporary, and the present moment is really all I have. Every experience I encountered was a learning opportunity that called me to trust and believe, to open and surrender, to be kind. I made every effort to relax into the lessons; the alternative would be to become hardened. I did my best to nurture myself with love and respect. When I did, it always came back to me. I imprinted myself on the people I met and allowed them to imprint themselves on me; we left footprints on one another's hearts.

Tomorrow, Jackson and I would head south to Banff. I had mixed feelings about leaving. I was ready to continue my journey, but I would miss Jasper.

That Friday night, Steve drove from Hinton to see me. I knew he liked me, but I wasn't sure if he was straight or gay. I wondered why I couldn't find a woman who would drive so far at 7:40 pm to spend two hours with me. Steve told me that he had missed me since our last dinner. It was a fantastic feeling to know that someone missed me, thought of me, and was willing to drive so far to see me. However, I soon realized that Steve didn't know I am gay.

"Are you dating anyone?" he asked.

"No," I replied. "I have been single for quite a while. Just out here flying solo."

He smiled, obviously pleased. But, almost as quickly, Steve steered the conversation back into a victimized "poor me" role, and I found myself internally impatient. Steve might have sensed my irritation; he immediately switched gears and said, "I guess I need to stay focused on my vision and stop complaining."

I smiled. "You got it."

With that, he began to share his dreams with me, and I was happy to hear that he had a plan other than sitting in self-pity.

Chapter 8

On to Calgary

It was time to say goodbye to Jasper. I knew that this beautiful town and its warm and welcoming people would always be in my heart. Jasper was one of the most lovely, easy-going Alpine towns I had visited. I felt so welcomed, and the residents treated me like a long-lost friend. Surrounded by the Rockies, immense forests, and lakes, it was breathtaking. Everywhere I went and every experience I had brought me closer to God and myself. I understood that, in Jasper, I reflected nature and all the people around me.

Steve showed up at the Robertson's unannounced and offered to drive me through the Rockies. He told me that snow still covered the roadsides, and he worried about me riding through the mountains alone. He also wanted to show me the beauty of the Rockies and visit some of his adventure sites.

I agreed to let him take me. With a heavy heart, I helped him load his van. As we drove away from the Robertson's house, I truly felt as if I'd left something behind.

Before we drove out of Jasper, we went to a field beside the library where my little companion Jackson could run loose and let out some energy before being cooped up for our trip. I brought his bone, and he was content. It brought me great joy to watch him play.

Soon we drove on the Icefields Parkway, also known as Highway 93, which is rated as one of the top drives in the world. The Icefield Parkway, a 232-kilometer highway, winds along the Continental Divide through soaring mountain peaks, icefields, and vast sweeping valleys of thick pine and large forests. The abundance of wildlife in the park had me peering around every turn in anticipation of another encounter. The pristine wilderness awed me and took my breath away. In fact, the Canadian Rockies are a UNESCO World Heritage Site.

We stopped to walk along a magnificent limestone gorge, then went on to the Athabasca Falls, which are approximately 30 kilometers south of Jasper. The falls cut through rocks and openings onto sweeping mountain vistas. Thousands of years of fast-flowing water have carved away smooth formations, leaving pretty little crevices and swirling whirlpools ranging from milky white to aqua blue. They were only one stunning part of Alberta's legendary Jasper National Park.

Later, we stopped again at the Athabasca Glacier, one of the six principal "toes" of the Columbia Icefield. The glacier currently recedes at a rate of about five meters per year, which is more than alarming. Scientists had posted signs where the icefield used to be, and the signs showed the speed at which the glaciers recede each year, which was at a record high.

Steve was a wonderful guide. He knew the names of every mountain peak and shared his experiences of each mountain either as a hang glider, skier, hiker, or survivor. I heard the most colorful and adventurous stories. As we walked close to the ice field, Steve also told me many stories about people disappearing in the glacier crevasses. I learned that the body of a young man who had gone missing almost twenty years in the past was found only a few years before my trip. Then Steve told me an incredible survival story about a man who fell more than thirty meters into a glacier crevasse. The man climbed out of the crevasse on his own, a feat of luck and endurance that stunned rescuers.

I suffered some misfortune in the park as well, though not life threatening. I broke my eyeglasses, and the soles of my cycling shoes peeled off. They were the only pair of shoes I had.

We made our way south toward Banff, and we stopped at Lake Louise. Lake Louise is both a town and a glacier-fed lake that is the most beautiful aqua color. The water looked inviting; it sparkled as if covered with diamonds. I wanted to jump into its gorgeous depths. It reminded me of Lake Edith and Lake Annette, near Jasper, that I visited while staying there. I swam in the frigid water at both places and felt invigorated afterward. I would have loved to swim in Lake Louise as well; however, we continued our journey on the trail. The beauty, the connection to nature, and the majestic wilderness stunned me.

While hiking outside of Banff, we met a man named John, a participant in the Tour Divide, a long-distance bicycle race from Banff to Mexico that was scheduled to start the next morning. The Tour Divide is the longest mountain bike race in the world, running nearly three thousand miles through the Rockies, from Canada to Mexico. However, the distance is not the only challenge—the total ascent of two hundred thousand feet is the equivalent of scaling Mount Everest nearly seven times. Bears, mountain lions, and wolves in the north, and rattlesnakes and tarantulas in the south, also present great risk.

The Tour Divide race clock runs twenty-four-hours a day. Other than access to public facilities such as stores, motels, and bike shops, participants aren't allowed any outside support. The record time to complete the Tour Divide is thirteen days, twenty-two hours, and fifty-one minutes. Unlike the Tour de France, winners do not receive a fabulous yellow jersey or prize money; for them, the journey is the reward. I felt an immediate connection to the racers.

A retired Marine, John lived in Seattle and was homeless. He rode his bicycle in Seattle to get around. One day, a couple of guys from a local bike club met him, and John began to ride with them. Members of the club noticed his natural talent, and someone donated a better bike to John.

Over coffee one morning, his buddies told him about the Tour Divide. Immediately, John knew the race was his calling. He trained every day, kept his bike buddies updated on his progress, and received their encouragement and support. John told me that since the ride was self-sufficient, he felt that he had an advantage over other racers because he was used to sleeping outside.

Two of his buddies drove him to Banff for the race. They spoke to me of what an inspiration John was to the other club members. They agreed that he had a large and generous heart and said that John had already won because the club had raised enough money to rent an apartment for him. When John returned to Seattle, he'd meet with a surprise—a furnished home would be waiting for him.

Before leaving, we all hugged and wished one another safe travels. In a world that can often be full of hate, John's story left me feeling inspired.

Steve and I drove farther down the road before stopping in Canmore, a town just west of Calgary. Craggy, tooth-like mountains surround the village, the most famous being the Three Sisters and Charity Peak.

It was late, and I was ready to go to sleep. Instead of putting my tent up, Steve invited me to sleep in his old van. I gladly accepted, as it was still cold and wet at night. We cooked dinner together, and he shared many more stories. As I listened to his calm, soothing voice, I drifted peacefully into sleep.

Early the next morning, we headed out on Route 1, the Trans-Canada Highway. As we continued through the Banff National Park, we stopped frequently to admire the beauty and return to nature by hiking again. It felt wonderful to walk around instead of pedaling. My knees still burned when I walked, but not as bad as when I rode the bike or pushed it uphill.

At the end of the day, we arrived in Cochrane, a town noted for its Western heritage, unique buildings, popular Main Street, and small-town hospitality. Steve's sister, Ann Marie, also happened to live in Cochrane. We pulled up to her house and knocked.

When Ann Marie opened the door, a startled look crossed her face. "Steve, what are you doing here?" she asked.

I could tell we had caught her by surprise. She wore dressy clothes and was obviously about to go out for the night.

"I was about to meet my boyfriend at the theater!" she said.

After welcoming us in, she made a call to her boyfriend, Ian, who was able to procure two more tickets to the show.

My heart sank. "I don't have any clothing besides my bike outfits," I confessed to her.

"Come with me," she said.

Ann Marie took me to her closet and dressed me in her clothes. I felt like I was intruding on her, but she didn't seem to mind. Her strength, grace, and composure impressed me.

A few minutes later, we were back in the car and off to Calgary to see *The Brides in the Bath Murders*, a play about the notorious British serial killer George Joseph Smith. I hadn't seen live theater in quite some time. After such a long stretch on the road and in smaller towns, it felt nice to be in a big city.

Steve and I spent the next three nights with Ann Marie and Ian. We went ballroom dancing in Calgary and had a fantastic time. Steve and his sister also set up an interview for me with the Cochrane newspaper.

Uli's Journey to Find a Cure for AIDS—CochraneNow: Cochrane, Alberta's latest news, sports, weather, community events. Written by Noel Edey, Friday, Jun 09 2017, 9:37 PM

Uli Schackmann is on a journey from Anchorage, AK to Key West, FL during which she hopes to raise awareness and funds to find a cure for AIDS by 2020. Between two donation sites, Crowdrise and GoFundMe, she has currently raised over $7,000 in support of amfAR.org, the Foundation for AIDS Research.

"I am compelled to do this because I have witnessed the intimate nature of this disease and the human response to it," says Schackmann. The Fort Lauderdale resident hopes to complete the 8,200 km trip by Nov. 18 and considers her ride symbolic of the struggle so many people living with HIV will face for the rest of their lives. "My path across the North American continent will demonstrate that with belief and commitment anything is possible."

While she has never been personally affected by the infection, she has been supporting the aims of amFAR for 18 years and has participated in many of their charity rides to help support local agencies provide services. But as time went on it seemed there was an endless stream of new cases coming forward and so she set her sights on a bigger target. Schackmann also finds it's not a topic of discussion for the younger generation, and she is concerned they lack knowledge of the serious nature of the infection.

"Just when you thought you have supported people, there's a younger generation of people coming up that are infected by HIV who need services and support. So I thought it was more important to focus on something bigger, which is a cure for AIDS."

Her companion on the trip is six-year-old Jackson, a 20lb. dog that she pulls behind in a bike carrier.

"He's an amazing companion, and he's traveling in a dog trailer behind, but when we get to the hills he has to get out and start pushing."

She also flies a 5'x3' HIV/AIDS red ribbon flag mounted on her bike that also includes a number of little red flags given to her by friends before her departure.

Schackmann has already faced many challenges in this daunting quest that's taking her through a large segment in

Canada for the first time in her life. Fortunately, along the way she has met people willing to lend a hand.

Steve Tocher, of Hinton, was one such person. When her bicycle broke down in Hinton, he took some time off work to get her back on track. His sister in Cochrane also provided accommodations for a few days to give her time to recharge before she departed on June 12.

According to the Public Health Agency of Canada, an estimated 75,500 were living with HIV in 2014. AIDS first surfaced in Canada in 1982. While the number of cases declined for over a decade, it began to rise again in the late 1990s and now increases at a rate of about 2,500 people annually. Sexual contact between men is the leading cause, but the infection is also spread by injection drug use and heterosexual contact. About a quarter of those with HIV are women.

Strides have been made to reduce the number of deaths from HIV/AIDS.

Neither Steve's brother nor his parents knew where he had gone and called Ann Marie, concerned about him; he had not contacted his family, and they were worried sick. Ann Marie explained to them that Steve had arrived a few days before with a woman, and he was okay. However, it was time for Steve to return home. It was time for me to move on as well.

Steve was short on money, so I paid for his gas and gave him some extra for food on his long drive back to Hinton. The farewell was bittersweet. I felt as if I was leaving my big brother, but at the same time, I was excited to get back on the road and continue my journey. We hugged each other and said our goodbyes. I knew I'd found an amazing, gentle, adventurous soul in Steve. What an amazing man.

The thirty-five-mile ride to Calgary proved uneventful, and my mind drifted pleasantly. I made my way to my friend Elizabeth's house, and she met me at the door wearing sweatpants and a sweater, her hair wild and free. She looked so down to earth, and I immediately found her more attractive than I had when we met in Florida for the first time. Our mutual friend, Bob, had tried to set us up, but we didn't connect back then. Now, I found her to be more authentic, natural, and strong as she welcomed me into her home.

"First things first," she said, handing me a cold drink.

While I relaxed with my beverage for a bit, then settled into my room and stored my bike and trailer, Elizabeth drew me a hot bubble bath, complete with candlelight and meditation music. The bathtub was so large and deep it could easily have fit two people. I was in heaven.

The next day, Elizabeth took me into Calgary and showed me the sights. That afternoon, we ate organic Albertan grass-fed steak at a fancy restaurant called Hy's Steakhouse & Cocktail Bar. As she ordered, our waiter smiled, obviously approving of her choice of steaks.

Elizabeth told the waiter about me, and he mentioned that the general manager, Barb, participated in triathlons. A few minutes later, he returned with Barb in tow, and we talked about my mission to help find a cure for AIDS by 2020. When the food arrived, I blessed the meal, as I'd been doing since Jasper, and dug into the most delicious and tender meat I'd had in a very long time. I instantly understood why Alberta beef is famous.

Sean, our dessert waiter, presented our dessert on a plate that had "Uli's Journey" written on the rim in chocolate letters. Confused, I asked, "How did you know?"

"The whole restaurant knows," he replied with a smile.

The restaurant's outstanding service and attention to detail blew me away. To top everything off, when Elizabeth asked for the bill, our waiter explained that Barb and the staff wanted to donate the meal to my cause. My eyes welled with tears as Elizabeth and I stared in shock at the two hundred dollar tab.

Elizabeth left a large tip for our servers, and we exited the restaurant, stunned. As I had so many times before on the trip, I marveled at the connection I felt to complete strangers.

The days on the road finally caught up with me, and I came down with a terrible cold. My nose and eyes ran. My body ached. While nursing me back to health, Elizabeth caught the same illness. For two days, we both stayed in bed and tried to help each other as best we could.

We eventually recovered, and I prepared to leave Calgary. Though Elizabeth had arranged for Jackson and me to be guests of honor in an annual kids' safety ride called Pedal to Metal Kids Bicycle Parade first. Along with about fifty children, parents, and political representatives from Ottawa, I decorated my bike and we rode a few miles through the city. I loved riding with the children, and at the end of the day, I raised another $190 for amfAR.

After the parade, Elizabeth and I returned to her house and I gathered my things. I would be riding on the plains now and wouldn't need my mountain gear any longer. I gave my bear drum, some specialized food, and specialized camping gear to Elizabeth's neighbor in exchange for an online donation to amfAR. The loss of gear would greatly lighten my load.

I was ready to get back on the road.

Chapter 9

A Shift in the Journey & in Me

Elizabeth drove me to the town of Strathmore, where we finally said our goodbyes. We had become good friends during my stay, and I was so grateful that I didn't have to ride with my trailer and Jackson through Calgary traffic.

Riding out of Strathmore through flat farm and ranch land was easy. Jackson and I rode all the way to Bassano, a fifty-eight-mile trek. I stopped every hour so that Jackson could run and play in the surrounding fields. The stops also provided an opportunity to hydrate, but each one added another five to ten minutes to the trip. Sometimes, large herds of cattle greeted us with loud "moos," and I often stretched my tired body out in the grass and stared up into the clouds, watching in tranquil fascination as they moved across the sky.

Although I had removed twelve to fifteen pounds of gear from my bike before leaving Calgary, I felt no difference in weight or speed. With all my remaining supplies, the bike still felt heavy, and my top speed was only ten to fourteen miles per hour.

Gravel, potholes, and washboards covered the shoulder of Canadian Highway 1, as well as glass and debris, adding difficulty to the ride. I had a hard choice: stay on the shoulder and risk getting stranded with a punctured tire, or ride on the road itself and risk getting hit. On the road, vehicles passed me at seventy miles an hour, and my bike and trailer shook violently. I grew increasingly tense and crossing highway entrances and exits didn't help. I decided stranded was better than dead, but when we finally arrived in Bassano late that evening, the extra time spent maneuvering the road's shoulder and starting and stopping had exhausted me.

The ride to Brooks exhausted me as well. The days never seemed to get any easier. I checked into the Travelodge Motel across from a Denny's restaurant. After a hot shower, I washed my clothes, then headed over to the restaurant to eat an early dinner.

A gentleman sitting parallel to me caught my attention, and we began to chat. "My name is Ed," he said.

"Uli," I replied.

"Are you visiting here?"

"Not really. Just passing through."

"You have to see the Dinosaur Provincial Park while you're here," he said. "It's about twenty miles away and worth seeing."

"There is nothing on Earth that would get me back on my bicycle today," I responded.

Ed chuckled. "You're riding a bike?"

I told him a bit about my story.

"I could drive you to the park after dinner," Ed said.

I agreed to go with him.

After finishing my dinner, I went back to the hotel and relaxed a bit; then Ed picked me up. During the drive, he told me that the Dinosaur Provincial Park is a UNESCO World Heritage Site. It is known as one of the locations with the most dinosaur fossils in the world. Fifty-eight dinosaur species have been discovered, and more than five hundred specimens have been removed from the park and can now be seen in many different museums worldwide.

The park had a prehistoric feel. I learned that paleontologists had recently found a standing T-Rex in a hillside at the park—a once-in-a-lifetime find. They cut it out, and the bones and tendons remained intact.

As we walked through the park and Ed rattled off fascinating stories about it, I heard a different type of rattle ahead of me. I spotted a rattlesnake about two feet away. Frightened, I sprung up and backward at once, pulling Jackson along with me. As the snake slithered away, I shrieked and trembled.

Ed remained calm and tried to ease my nerves. He told me that snakes are plentiful there because the park protects them. Hearing this, I suggested we finish the tour by car.

While driving, Ed not only told me about the park; he also talked about his life. He was a wonderful storyteller and had found an eager listener in me.

Ed grew up in Ottawa in a wealthy family. Before his birth, his parents lost their best friends in a car accident. The friends left behind four children, and Ed's parents adopted them despite having three children of their own.

After the adoptions, Ed's father, Ted, an engineer and inventor, invented the soft drink machines that are common today. Soon, the machines made the family quite wealthy, and Ted and his wife went on to have three more children, the youngest of which was Ed.

A thorough businessman whom Ed compared to Donald Trump, Ted insisted that all ten of his children call him by his first name. When they came of age, most of the children went to work for Ted in the family business in sales, accounting, management, or as board members of the company. Ed's oldest sibling, Ricky, was put in charge of protecting both their father and Ed. As the president of a feared motorcycle gang called the Satans, Ricky was well-suited for the job. He saw to it that his youngest brother had a bodyguard and a personal driver.

Ed worked for his father for many years in different roles. He represented the company at conventions, worked in overseas sales, and eventually became the company's ambassador and accountant.

Many politicians courted Ted for donations, and his connection to powerful people grew, as did his ruthlessness. Whenever a customer didn't pay or a politician didn't come through for him after he donated to their campaign, Ted sent Ricky to collect or punish them. As a result of these encounters, many dead bodies were found in trash cans, rivers, and fields. Everyone knew that Ricky was responsible for the deaths, but nobody could prove it, and having a father with influential friends didn't hurt. Consequently, Ricky was never arrested.

Once, Ed showed up immediately after Ricky killed a man. When the police arrived, Ed kept them preoccupied so that his brother could slip away to a safe place where he would never be found. Even if the cops had found him, their father had so many politicians, judges, and police officers in his pocket that Ricky and the rest of the family could literally get away with murder.

Often, Ted came to Ed and asked him to make money "disappear," and Ed would find a way to alter the books.

Stunned by his stories, I stated that Ed came from a *mafia* family, adding that he was the money launderer for their operation. Ed didn't see it that way. In fact, he laughed and said that my comments were the funniest thing anyone had ever said to him. But I believe he knew it was true because when that life became too much for him and he couldn't stand the pressure anymore, Ed took his wife and daughter, left Ottawa, and moved to Saskatchewan.

Ed bought a home in Saskatchewan, but he was a very sick man at the time—overweight, a heavy smoker, and a drinker. Soon after he and his family moved into the new house, his wife and grown daughter kicked him out, (saying that he was dying anyway) and Ed became depressed, angry, and furious with life. Fortunately, friends stepped in and told him that he needed help, so he went to see a doctor and a therapist and turned his health around. He stopped drinking and smoking and completely changed his diet.

At the time I met Ed, it had been four years since he had begun to heal, and I thought he looked amazing. His transformation even amazed his doctors; they couldn't believe he was still alive.

Ed had a wonderful attitude and a great sense of humor. He had bought another house in Saskatchewan across from the old one, where his wife and daughter still lived. He said they wanted him back, but he loved his freedom and the life he had created, and he had filed for a divorce from his wife.

Lying in bed that night, I thought of all the stories Ed had told me. I looked at the piece of paper he had given me before we parted company. On it he'd written his number and the words: "If you have any problems on the road and need anything, call me."

I stared into the darkness of the room and asked myself if I would ever call Ed after everything I'd experienced and heard that day. I felt flattered that he was so protective of me; yet, at the same time, I feared he might think I owed him something if he did me a favor. He had been wonderful and funny, but his connection to the mafia, if real, scared me a bit.

I left Brooks the next morning and headed toward Medicine Hat. After much consideration, I chose to head east on the Trans Canadian Highway instead of taking a southern route through beautiful cowboy country. The rattlesnake encounter on the previous day had spooked me, and the long stretches without any towns, people, or campsites also weighed in on my decision.

Cars zipped past me with unbelievable speed, shaking my rig every time, especially when an eighteen-wheeler rumbled by. The riding was strenuous, tense, and noisy. I missed Alaska's quiet, wide-open spaces.

I sensed a change in my journey. I'd felt it shifting the night before I left Calgary. The ride from Alaska to Calgary had been one of not knowing what to expect, one of discovery. In the great, wild northern forests, I'd had to trust the Universe and surrender to its magic. Calgary had been a bookend to something, the closing fireworks to an unbelievable expanse of unpopulated wilderness.

This new stretch of ride would be different; it already was. The scenery had totally changed. Rolling hills intertwined with flat farmland. Cows, sheep, llamas, and other domesticated livestock had replaced bears, moose, deer, and elk. Outside of Calgary, nothing much existed for as far as the eye could see. I would have to plan my days carefully, as distances between towns could be quite long and there were no places to camp.

As I pedaled down the four-lane highway, cars and trucks raced by at seventy to ninety miles an hour. I don't think they noticed me or the AIDS flag; I felt very lonely out there. In fact, I'd never felt as alone as I did on that highway.

After a while, I resigned myself to whatever was next and the loneliness of being alone. It was different, difficult, and tough. The feeling reminded me of the first outbreaks of AIDS, when everyone was put on drug cocktails and strict medications, and friends and family left the sick by themselves to go blind, suffer, and die alone. In my moment of resignation, I was sure some of those sick from days gone by had also resigned themselves to whatever was next. And to the loneliness.

I was incredibly thankful for Jackson, my companion and only constant. We stopped outside of Medicine Hat, and I watched him run and play in a nearby field. After a while, I called out to him, and he trotted over. He was so patient with me. I petted him, and he loved on me.

A sense of accomplishment ran through me; but, as I stared off into the distance, I felt the weight of what lay ahead. The miles to go. The tears. The new people. The unknown.

I saw the world changing all around me and understood that I was changing as well.

My journey continued east on the Trans Canadian Highway. As I rode myself into the landscape, beautiful weather embraced me. Vehicles zipped by, and I felt like an invisible Lone Ranger. My heart overflowed as a breeze swayed the trees. I thought they appeared to be dancing with the wind, and soon that wind started dancing with me, gently at first, then more exuberantly.

After hours of riding, I finally made it to Medicine Hat and checked into the cheapest motel I could find, booking the room for two nights to recuperate. My knees, elbows, and neck had flared up again; they burned like fire.

With a population of 63,230, Medicine Hat is located along the South Saskatchewan River. The name "Medicine Hat" refers to the eagle tail feather headdress once worn by Blackfoot medicine men. More than one legend exists to explain how the town got its name. One involves a battle between a Blackfoot tribe and a Cree tribe. According to the legend, the headdress belonging to a Cree medicine man fell off him as he fled across the Saskatchewan River to escape Blackfoot warriors.

Medicine Hat sits in the South Saskatchewan River valley. Within the city, Seven Persons Creek and Ross Creek flow into the river. The valley is striking, with the stream tributaries, the river, multiple cliffs, rolling hills, and flat grassy areas.

After settling in, I took a taxi ride to Kin Coulee Park to re-center myself. The park has over one hundred acres to explore. Jackson and I walked for hours, exploring and reconnecting with nature—regaining my strength, determination, and commitment to my mission. I also delighted in watching Jackson run and roll in the grass.

During our walk, we came upon a tunnel, and Jackson and I walked through it. At first, darkness surrounded me, with just a little light at the end. But the farther I stepped into the darkness, the brighter the light at the end of the tunnel became. It seemed a metaphor for my journey, for my entire life, and for people living with HIV/AIDS.

Early on the morning that Jackson and I left Medicine Hat, we set off east on the Trans-Canada Highway under a beautiful, sunny, blue sky dotted with fluffy white clouds. When I looked in my rearview mirror, however, I saw frightening, dark clouds building behind me. I thought I could outrun the storm; I pushed forward at what must've been seventeen to eighteen miles per hour, the fastest I had ridden on my journey. At first, the speed exhilarated me; I didn't realize that the storm was closing in on me rapidly from behind.

Suddenly, the clouds changed overhead and seemed much lower. Rain began to fall, and the temperature dropped. My legs turned red from the cold, and my fingers became numb. Soaking wet, I stopped to put on warmer clothes and rain gear; Jackson was drenched too.

As I changed my clothes on the highway, the cars passing by seemed to drive faster than before, trying to get out of the storm. I had no wi-fi and no way of knowing the severity of the approaching storm.

All at once, a gust of wind roared up and threw me to the ground on my back. The bike and trailer combo landed on top of me. I untangled from the wreckage, jumped up, and checked on Jackson. He was wet, but fine. Still terrified, I fixed the bike and pedaled as fast as I could toward the nearest town. Along the way, I looked for some type of shelter—a barn, a construction site, a garage, a big pipe cauldron—that we could get into or under to protect us from the storm. I didn't see anything, but I knew I had to find a safe place for us to wait out the weather.

Despite having numb hands and feet, I pushed myself as hard as I could, battling the wind and rain until, finally, I made it to the small town of Irvine, a tiny hamlet of 291 residents in Alberta that is located approximately thirty miles east of Medicine Hat. The town's only hotel was under renovation, so I pushed the bike through the small community screaming, "Hello!"

I spotted a man walking along the street; he looked as wet as Jackson and me. Seemingly surprised by my yelling, he approached and asked, "What do you need?"

"We're looking for shelter," I replied.

The man looked me up and down with empathetic eyes, then said, "Follow me."

He introduced himself as Dennis, and we walked to his house and put the bike and trailer in his backyard, covered everything with a tarp. Then Jackson and I followed him inside. Warmth enveloped me as we entered the cluttered living room, and I met Dennis's daughter, Gabriel. She got a towel and dried Jackson, while Dennis made hot cocoa.

The temperature outside had dropped to four degrees Celsius. I sipped my hot cocoa and became acquainted with Dennis and his daughter. He talked about the extremely unpredictable weather patterns in Saskatchewan and said that the weather could change in an instant.

As we talked, I became aware of the sparse furnishings around us. Nothing matched, and the few pieces of furniture were packed into the small living space. But as financially poor as he must've been, Dennis was equally as rich in generosity and kindness.

Gabriel showed me her dad's medallions that he had earned while serving in the military, both in the United States and in Canada. A citizen of both countries, Dennis had served eight years in the U.S. Reserve, many years in the Canadian military, and had completed tours of Iraq before being honorably discharged. At the time we met, he was studying to become a registered nurse, like his wife.

Although only thirteen years old, Gabriel told me she had delivered the local newspaper for three years to help support the family, beginning her route at six o'clock each morning. In the winter, winds could drop the temperature to -40 degrees Fahrenheit. On her route, she had encountered aggressive dogs, coyotes, and other wildlife.

Gabriel spoke proudly of her father. As she showed me his medals, she told the stories behind each one. She told me Dennis had been a medic before returning to civilian life. Then he worked in the oil industry in Alberta until a recession hit and he lost his job. He then moved the family back to Irvine and became a beekeeper, tending close to seventy hives, which he still did. Gabriel showed me hundreds of glass jars in the kitchen, some empty and some filled with golden honey.

Dennis's bees were located in Walsh, another tiny town about 20 km away from Irving. To make a living, Dennis sold honey, pollen, and cones at stores in both towns. I learned a lot from Gabriel and Dennis about starting a colony—what to do when the drones don't have a queen and how to manipulate the hive into thinking they *do* have a queen.

After the storm passed that afternoon, Dennis offered to take me to Maple Creek, the nearest town with accommodations. We unloaded bee supplies from his truck and loaded my bike, trailer, and other gear. Then he drove me the 75 km to Maple Creek and took me to a motel. He and his daughter had been incredibly kind, welcoming, and generous to me, even though I knew they didn't have much to share. I felt their family's struggle, but also their love, happiness, and admiration of one another.

I thanked Dennis for his support and for the wonderful stories he and Gabriel had told me. We hugged and went our separate ways. I knew I'd crossed paths with two more angels on my journey, two of many I'd met since leaving Alaska. I couldn't have made it so far without them.

After I checked into the motel, I emptied all my saddle bags, spread out the AIDS Memorial flag, then emptied the trailer and carrier to let everything dry overnight. My room looked like a gypsy camp. I laughed when I found a jar of honey in my helmet, knowing that either Dennis or Gabriel must've hidden it there.

I went to the motel's adjoining restaurant and bar and ordered dinner and a drink. The place was packed with interesting people, some playing pool or slot machines, others engaged in conversation over food and drink. I met several friendly folks, and the hot meal, drink, and interesting conversations hit the spot, but I was exhausted and ready for bed.

Late that night, the wind howled outside, and rain pummeled the motel roof. I was grateful to be in a safe place and not in my tent.

The next morning, I returned to the restaurant and had breakfast before getting back on the road. Everyone in the place seemed to know about my Alaska to Florida bicycle journey. One person, a gentleman named Jon, called me over and invited me to join him for breakfast. He was at least sixty-five, tall with an athletic build, and had gray hair and a beard. His inviting blue eyes seemed to smile at me. I sat across from him, and we shared stories over breakfast.

A cyclist like me, Jon was traveling from Seattle and going as far east as he could in one week's time, after which his wife would pick him up. We talked about our experiences on the road, our encounters, and all the people we had met so far. I told Jon about the pain in my neck, lower back, and elbows. He said he also experienced a lot of pain, but he smoked pot, which helped him tremendously. He offered me some, but I declined. I would be reentering the United States soon and didn't feel comfortable traveling from one country to another while carrying marijuana.

I was ready to leave and hit the road again, but most of my supplies remained damp, and I wasn't looking forward to wearing wet clothes and shoes. The weather report predicted a clear sky in the morning and severe thunder and lightning storms in the afternoon.

I headed toward the Trans-Canada Highway, eight miles away, and as soon as I hit the Canadian Transit, the strong west wind pushed me down the road at great speed. My bike and trailer felt ready to take flight as I sped down the highway, gripping the handlebars for dear life. When an eighteen-wheeler passed me by, I gripped them even harder. The prior day's weather experience stayed at the front of my mind; I didn't want to go through anything like that again.

At eleven o'clock that morning, I was between Gull Lake and Swift Current when the weather changed in the exact way it had the day before. The temperature dropped, and dark clouds moved in. Once again, I was alone on the road. And again, I looked for shelter but found nothing. I glanced in the rearview mirror and stopped riding, horrified by what I saw—a sky so dark I began to panic.

Just then, a white Mercedes-Benz SUV stopped, and the driver, a woman named Tanis, asked if I needed help. She was headed for Regina, where she lived, and said she could take me all the way there. I took the trailer, carrier, flag, and saddle bags off my bike and organized everything in her car. My packing skills amazed Tanis. Little did she know that I was now an old pro.

As I had with all my "angels" on the road, I shared my journey with Tanis, then listened to her life story. She spoke of her two marriages and her three grown children. She said that she had gone through the worst experience of her life four years ago when a drunk driver killed her oldest daughter in a hit and run incident. If the driver had stopped, he might have saved her daughter's life. Instead, she had died alone on the road, and Tanis felt her suffering. I was certain Tanis had picked me up because of the way her daughter had died.

The police eventually found the hit and run driver. After a two-year court case, he was sentenced to two years in prison. Tanis sounded angry when she told me about the sentence; she felt he had gotten away with murder.

Her family had all grieved so differently—none of them able to help one another, each in their own world, consumed by their grief. Tanis went into a deep depression from which she'd only recently emerged. Her depression had removed her from the rest of her family; her husband, Shawn, had stepped in to take over her responsibilities. Each time she had tried to pull herself together, she fell apart again, while Shawn fought to keep the family united. He worked, came home, and helped Tanis with the kids and household chores. At night, he cried over the loss of their daughter.

Their youngest child, a boy, became angry, depressed, and a rebel. He quit high school, isolated himself, and didn't want to see his friends. He felt alone, misunderstood, and empty. After a year, he started to work at his father's construction business and then started one of his own.

To deal with her grief, their middle child, a girl, moved out and got her own place, a boyfriend, and had a child. Tragically, her husband died of cancer, and the little girl, Anna, was left without a father. I could tell that her granddaughter was the light of Tanis's life.

It took the entire family four years to heal, but in the process, they rediscovered their love for one another, along with a deep connection and understanding that only death can create. I was moved by Tanis's willingness to share her anguish, anger, and newfound joy.

During our drive, Tanis called her husband and said, "Honey, I am bringing a guest tonight. Please take the steak from the freezer and make some potatoes."

That Tanis had picked up a stranger on the road and was bringing her to their home for dinner and a one-night stay surprised Shawn, but he agreed.

Tanis was half First Nations Cree and half Caucasian (German & Polish). Growing up, she and her siblings experienced rejection from the Caucasian side of the family because of their native blood. At the same time, the First Nation side of the family rejected them because they were part white. It was a very confusing time for them, but eventually, they realized that they possessed something very special—the knowledge and customs of two different cultures. She said that to have a foot in both worlds was something like being bilingual.

When we arrived at her home, Shawn was in the middle of setting the table for our steak dinner. After Tanis shared my story with him, he welcomed me warmly. I had the honey from Dennis and thought I'd offer it for our meal. Tanis used it, along with other spices, to cover the steak. The meal was delicious. Afterward, Shawn invited me to watch a Canadian football game on television.

When the game finished, it was time for bed. I helped Tanis prepare her granddaughter's room for me to sleep in and said goodnight.

I left Tanis and Shawn after breakfast the next morning and headed downtown to find an inexpensive place to stay. I got a second-floor motel room and had to carry my bike, trailer, AIDS Memorial Flag, and four saddle bags upstairs. Physically, the journey had challenged my body. My hands were always asleep in the morning, and it took a while to get them moving. My knees hurt, and so did my neck, shoulders, calves, and ankles. I moved my legs slowly at night for fear that I might get painful muscle cramps.

I settled in and contacted the local media to try to drum up some publicity. Afterward, I walked through Regina, exploring the city. Canada was turning 150 years old, and many celebrations were underway in Regina. The 150th birthday marked a significant moment in the History of Canada—when Quebec, Ontario, New Brunswick, and Nova Scotia united to create the Canadian Confederation, or the Dominion of Canada. I saw Native dancing, different performances, vendors, street festivals, and food vendors throughout the city.

I hadn't been in a city for quite some time. A part of me enjoyed it, with all the activities. Another part of me craved quiet and alone time. It felt strange to be present to both experiences, and my conflicting emotions confused me. It had taken some time to get used to, but I had become more comfortable with being alone as the ride progressed. Still, at times I felt I was in a place where I didn't belong, and I longed for something I couldn't define. My moods regularly shifted between excitement and frustration, loneliness and an almost mystical feeling of connection to the land and the people I met along the way.

The day before, I had spoken to Grandfather Spirit. I explained that I felt lost and unsettled, and I asked for guidance. I knew I needed to find the strength to trust and surrender again, to allow experiences to unfold and take shape without fear and worrying. From the outside, I was outgoing, sharing, and confident. However, internally, I struggled with melancholy.

The journey had been so incredibly challenging. I had let go of my fear of wildlife. I had learned to trust strangers, to allow others to contribute. I had created intimate connections through sharing. Yet, while in Regina, I felt agitated, sad, like I was in mourning. I didn't know why I felt as I did. Sometimes, I even sensed I was dying—whether my body or my ego, I wasn't sure.

However, when my body and mind felt in sync, I connected to nature and to the serene, to myself and to my spirit. The challenge of the ride and the kindness and support I had received from so many strangers had changed and impacted me. I was not the same person anymore. Something had shifted.

Chapter 10

Interviews & Storm Clouds

While eating lunch at a little outdoor restaurant, I saw a single young woman sitting alone. A voice in my head told me to invite her to my table. I dismissed the idea twice, but the voice persisted. Before I knew it, I had walked over to the young woman's table, and I invited her to join me. At first, she hesitated, but then she agreed, and we had lunch together.

Her name was Buff and she told me that she was a massage therapist; she worked mainly in sports medicine. I told her about myself as well. Buff admitted that she had been addicted to cocaine but was now sober. Her brother had paid for her to do CHOICE, and it was a life-changing experience for her.

Buff and the rest of her family had no relationship with her father. They were angry with him for taking their grandmother's land after her death. He sold it, took the money, and they never heard from him again.

Buff and her brother grew up on a farm and had very difficult childhoods. They were part First Nation and part Caucasian, and Buff felt she didn't belong to either group. Growing up, she couldn't see a future for herself outside of the small community in which she lived. At age thirty-six, she finally left and moved to Regina, where she went to massage therapy school.

It was obvious to me that Buff had done a lot of work on herself and that her spirit was calling her to discover the next step. We both believed coincidences didn't exist—that we were meant to meet.

Buff had a friend named Shawn who produced a local podcast. The one-hour program, called *The Story of U*, featured homeless people, First Nation people, politicians, workers, and more. She introduced me to Shawn via phone and told him she thought my story would be great for the show. Shawn thought so, too. We had a brief conversation, after which he scheduled me for an interview later that night at seven o'clock. If I had ignored that little voice in my head that told me to talk to Buff, I would not have had that opportunity.

That evening, I took a taxi ride over to Shawn's place. The house was messy, though the recording studio was well-organized and clean.

Guests of the podcast told stories from their own perspective. Stories could be about anything from abuse, mental illness, overcoming obstacles—the list was unlimited. Shawn and I sat and chatted to get to know each other better. He had a full build and was muscular and tall. Charming, smart, and funny, he asked great questions. Finally, we put on our headsets and started the one-hour interview.

Shawn made sharing easy. He asked questions about my childhood, my years in the orphanage, my coming to America, and my year in America while waiting for my green card. I talked about the years I lived in San Francisco, my move to New England, my move to Florida, my participation in the local AIDS bicycle rides, and my reasons for riding from Alaska to Key West for a Cure for AIDS by 2020. The interview went well and was aired soon after our meeting. It can be heard here: https://storyofupodcast.com/2017/07/03/chapter-41-uli/

After meeting with Shawn, I returned to my room to find a message from Global News TV. The station wanted to interview me as well. I agreed, and we made an appointment for the next morning at the Prince Wales Rd., a shopping mall. I had planned to leave town much earlier, but I thought doing as many interviews as possible was a smart decision.

The next morning, a young woman and a camera man arrived at the mall, and the woman asked me questions. I also rode in circles around the parking lot while they videoed me. Later, after we said our goodbyes, they took more footage of me as I rode out of Regina.

I made good time to Indian Head, a town in southeast Saskatchewan, Canada, forty-three miles east of Regina on the Trans-Canada Highway.

Indian Head had its beginnings in 1882 as the first settlers, mainly of Scottish origin, arrived to make their homes. It wasn't incorporated as a town, however, until 1902. The town is known for its federally operated experimental farm and tree nursery, which has produced and distributed seedlings since 1901.

With the Qu'Appelle River on one side and the Qu'Appelle Valley and Canadian Prairies on the other, Indian Head sits on hilly grasslands strewn with poplar-covered cliffs and exposed bogs. The town's estimated population is 1,910.

Jackson and I arrived in town during a blustery windstorm. Sand blew off the ground and twirled around like a mini tornado. Unsecured objects began to take flight. Local people I met assured me that such weather was normal for the area, so I tried not to worry.

I found a cheap motel with an attached Indian food restaurant. Indian food is a favorite of mine, so I couldn't believe my luck at finding a place that served it in the middle of the Canadian countryside. As I checked in, I smelled curry, cumin, and other Indian spices.

Upon opening the restaurant door, I saw an old Indian man in traditional clothing asleep right next to the entrance. The Hindi language flowed from a television. I took these as good signs the food would be authentic and delicious. I ordered and was pleased to find that I'd been right; I indulged in all the flavors and spice I could stomach, enjoying it all.

After dinner, I walked around town and stopped at the visitor's center, where I found some retired female volunteers who were eager to chat with a new visitor. Besides getting information on the town, I also heard stories about other visitors. The ladies spoke fondly of a handsome, young Italian cyclist. They praised him so enthusiastically, they almost sounded smitten. They said that, once, when a female cyclist came to town, they had attempted to set her up with the handsome Italian. I found their stories highly amusing. It seems elderly women the world over are matchmakers.

I left Indian Head around seven o'clock the next morning and headed toward the town of Grenfell. The day was beautiful and sunny but very gusty, and it took great effort to peddle into the wind. Prairie and farmland still surrounded me, and I went long stretches of time without any human contact. I had begun to get used to the eighteen wheelers and the noise of cars passing me by.

After riding for some time, I thought I heard someone calling my name. Assuming the sound of the wind was playing tricks on me, I started laughing when, again, I heard, "Uli!" The voice was distinct this time; someone had called my name.

I stopped the bike, and in my rearview mirror, I saw another cyclist behind me. The woman rode up beside me, and with the warmest smile said, "Hi, Uli. My name is Anna. I was hoping I would catch up with you."

Confused, I asked, "Have we met?"

"No," she said. "I heard about you from the ladies at the visitor's center in Indian Head."

Since we were in the middle of a highway, we took off riding together until we found a safer place to rest—an old cemetery. Jackson ran and played while Anna and I shared a quick lunch, my first meal of the day.

The night before, Anna had arrived at the visitor's center shortly after I'd left. Since she was a cyclist, the ladies shared my story with her. In fact, not only did they share my story, the matchmakers also tried to hook Anna up with the handsome Italian man they'd told me about. We both laughed over that.

Anna said she told the women she wasn't interested as she was riding from Vancouver to Newfoundland to meet a different young man. I heard excitement in her voice when she talked about him.

After our conversation, we walked around the cemetery and read some of the gravestones. I remembered when I did Gratitude Training, and one of our exercises was to walk alone, silently, through a cemetery and be present to the people who had died. During the exercise, I stopped and read a dedication to a young man who had died during a war at the age of nineteen. Even though I'd never known him, I stood and cried at his grave. I felt the pain of loss that his family and friends must've experienced. I also became acutely aware of my good fortune; I was alive and experiencing adventures.

Anna and I walked in silence as well, and I saw more graves belonging to military sons, fathers, and husbands who had fought wars and been killed. Other graves with military honors attached belonged to people who had served but had lived on afterward and grown old. Some of the deceased were middle aged, in the prime of their lives, when a tragic accident or illness took them, no doubt leaving loved ones in grief. And then there were the graves belonging to children of all ages, some of them only a few months old. Anna and I wondered what happened to those babies. We thought about their mothers, their fathers, and others who must have been devastated by their loss. Did the parents' marriage survive after the child's death? Could it? Or is that sort of grief so massive no couple could withstand it?

It was time to move on. Anna and I hugged each other and wished one another a safe ride. As we rode onto the highway, I couldn't keep up with Anna. In no time at all, she appeared as a speck in the distance.

When I reached Grenfell, I stopped and decided to call it a day. Exhausted and hurting, I found a motel. I was grateful to be there; the afternoon had brought another thunder and lightning storm. After settling in, Jackson and I walked over to a Subway sandwich place—the closest restaurant to our motel.

We met a woman there who said her twenty-two-year-old dog had died last week; he had looked just like Jackson. She cried while petting Jackson, and he licked away her tears. The woman said her daughter had given birth just before the dog died; it was as if the dog had waited for the baby to arrive before he passed away. I gave the woman a big hug, then Jackson and I left to return to our room and eat.

After I finished eating my sandwich, I called the local paper. They were interested in my story and requested I stop by that very afternoon. I did, and they asked me questions about my trip and took my picture. Later, the photo and a caption appeared in the local paper, but the interview was never printed.

Our next destination was Moosomin, a small town located fifty-eight miles from Grenfell. I had come to expect late afternoon thunderstorms; however, on that day, Jackson and I were not so lucky; the storms started sooner. Although clear skies had greeted us as we took off from Grenfell, the morning soon grew dark. Gale force winds, thunder, and lightning quickly followed. I was lucky to wave down a pickup truck. The two men inside the cab, Barry and Randy, took me the rest of the way to Moosomin—a short ride by car. I was so grateful for the ride and relieved to be safely out of the lightning storm.

The town of Moosomin had a population of about three thousand residents. Most worked either in farming or the oil, gas, or potash mining industries.

Barry and Randy both worked as commercial window installers in Saskatoon, a town about eight hours away from their home in Winnipeg. They worked primarily on commercial high-rise buildings—a very dangerous job. In fact, many co-workers had fallen to their deaths. Barry had been in the business for thirty years, and Randy for six. They typically worked away from home for two weeks and then went home for a long weekend. Barry missed his family while he was away and preferred to work closer to home. However, Randy enjoyed the schedule—it gave him more freedom. Both had worked before in the USA and loved the States, especially California and the Pacific Ocean area.

The men dropped me off at the Prairie Motel. Motels were cheap and mostly shabby in that area of Canada, and the Prairie was no exception. It had little to no hot water, a grimy bathtub and sink, a filthy shower curtain, and a very soft mattress. I still felt blessed to be out of the storm—sheltered, safe, warm, and comfortable.

After the storm passed, I went for a walk and explored the town before visiting the local newspaper. I got an interview and a photo shoot right then and there. The paper said it would publish my story the following Monday.

Later that day, Barry and Randy returned to the motel. I had left my bicycle helmet and gloves in their truck, and they brought them to me. I couldn't believe they'd turned around and come back to do that; for many people, it would've been too much of an inconvenience. Not Barry and Randy. They went out of their way to make sure I had my stuff, and I was so appreciative.

It was steak night at the restaurant adjoining the motel. People arrived in hordes for the $7.99 steak dinner. I was tired of steak, so I ordered a stir-fry; a Chinese family owned the hotel and restaurant, so I thought it would be a good choice.

Most of the time when I went to a restaurant for breakfast or dinner, I saw men sitting together drinking coffee and chatting. The same was true on this night. It surprised me to learn that men gossip as much or more than women do.

At one point during dinner, an elderly couple, probably in their eighties, arrived. They held hands as they entered the restaurant, and the man walked with a cane. The woman wore a babushka; the man wore an old hat. She had a sweet, round face that reminded me of my grandmother—my father's mother. In fact, the woman's entire appearance reminded me of her. The heavy coat, the scarf around her neck, her heavy shoes. I didn't have loving thoughts of my grandmother.

She was inpatient with me. I was the daughter of her daughter-in-law, whom she hated, and she never let me forget it.

Watching the old woman brought back memories of when, between the ages of two and five, I lived with my grandmother after my parents divorced and before I went to the orphanage. I recalled the frequent beatings she gave me with a wooden spoon, and how when it broke, we would go to the store to buy a new one. I always knew that the new spoon wasn't for cooking; it was to be used to beat me again.

The elderly woman at the restaurant, however, only reminded me of my grandmother in appearance. She and the elderly man exhibited so much tenderness, affection, and love toward each other. She helped him walk, and he helped her cut up her steak. They ate in silence, looking at each other and nodding now and then.

I started to feel weird as I watched them, as if I intruded on their personal, intimate, and loving space. Still, I couldn't pull my gaze away. That two elderly people shared such respect for each other amazed me. I tried to be discreet and often looked out of the corner of my eye, my affection for them growing stronger with each second that passed.

When the bill for my meal arrived, I requested to pay for the elderly couple's food as well. Witnessing the kindness and loving care they shared had felt like a gift, and I wanted to repay them. I took their gentleness and humble demeanor back with me to my empty motel room and it filled the space.

Early the next morning, I returned to the restaurant for breakfast. I sat in the same spot as the night before and looked at the table the old couple had occupied. I closed my eyes. I could see the man cutting his wife's steak, their silent communication.

When my waiter arrived, I chatted with him about the weather, mentioning that it was not yet summer there. A guest four tables away overheard me and said, "Nope, it sure isn't!"

We began a conversation, and I invited him to join me. His name was Jason. Tough-looking, tattooed, and with a demeanor that said, "Don't mess with me," Jason seemed like a "man's man." He told me he was going through a divorce, and he missed his six-year-old daughter, whom he hadn't seen since the beginning of May. He also had suffered a back injury, which kept him out of work. He had become depressed over both situations and had been resorting to alcohol to drown out his pain and unhappiness. We talked about many things: my ride, relationships, his upcoming surgery, new possibilities. We shared laughter and listened to each other. Time passed too quickly, and after a while, I told Jason I had to hit the road.

"Which way are you going?" he asked.

"East," I said.

"I can give you a ride to Virdron," he replied.

I accepted, happy to have a lift and the company.

After loading my bike and trailer into Jason's truck and settling Jackson on my lap, we drove off together. He had so many insights about his relationship and the emotional support he'd expected from his ex-wife while they were married. He said that his back injury didn't cause the divorce, but rather it was his inability to share his feelings with his wife that ended his marriage. He had always feared that he would get hurt if he told her what he felt, and that whatever he shared would be used against him.

After a while, Jason looked at me and said, "I have never shared myself like this with anyone. You inspire me." He was saddened when we reached our destination. "If I could," he said, "I would drive you all the way to Florida just to continue our conversation."

I put my rig back together and headed toward the town of Alexander. After riding for a few hours, I saw dark clouds gathering overhead. I didn't want to get caught in another storm, so I pedaled hard until I reached a gas station. The employees there assured me that I would find motel accommodations a few miles ahead in Alexander. Ecstatic, I rode hard, using all my energy to outrun the storm that brewed above me.

When I pulled into Alexander, I sang with delight. However, my enthusiasm quickly dimmed when several residents I talked to claimed the town didn't have lodging. Hoping they were wrong, I checked for a motel, a bed and breakfast, a room for rent in a home—any kind of shelter for the night. I would have settled for a spot in a barn or a garage. But I found nothing.

I left town and headed back out to the Trans-Canada Highway. I had to stop several times to take care of Jackson, and I wondered if he sensed my frustration and stress. He panted non-stop, and the sound of his breathing began to irritate me. Nothing I did worked to calm him down.

Before we made it to the town of Brandon, I faced two huge inclines and had to push the bike and trailer, destroying my back and knees. I counted fifty or one hundred steps as I pushed, then stopped for a drink of water and to catch my breath before continuing another fifty to one hundred steps. I repeated the process until I reached the top.

I finally arrived at a Super 8 Motel in Brandon. To my surprise, it had a hot tub and a pool. I was so tired that I decided to have food delivered from a nearby Smitty's; I had no energy to walk to a nearby restaurant. As I looked over the Smitty's menu, memories of another Smitty's in Hinton came up, which made me think of Steve. I missed his conversations, his stories, and his kind spirit.

After the eighty-seven-mile day I'd endured, soaking my sore bones in the hot tub felt great. Afterward, I returned to my room and enjoyed a salad with salmon for dinner. I needed to fix the trailer again; it was falling apart due to all the washboard roads and potholes I had bumped over in recent days. I took the old rug they'd given me at the hotel in Whitehorse and stitched up some ripped areas. Then I placed it over the trailer and secured everything with Gorilla Tape to waterproof it so Jackson would stay dry if we encountered another storm.

With the trailer tended, I gave Jackson a bath. He looked and smelled fantastic afterward, and I was sure he felt much better.

My knees burned like crazy; I took some medication and rubbed ointment all over my body. Drained, both physically and emotionally, I fell asleep as soon as my head hit the pillow.

Like other towns I had visited in Canada, Brandon had many activities planned for the country's 150th anniversary. I decided to stay an extra day to rest my exhausted body and participate in the fun.

Midday, I walked over to the riverbank—Brandon's "Central Park." Serene and beautiful, it provided an amazing location for the community's celebration. The events taking place commemorated one hundred and fifty years of the Canadian Confederation as well as one hundred and thirty-five years since the city of Brandon incorporated. First Nation Peoples and local entertainers performed for the crowd that had gathered at the riverbank. Children and families played games, took helicopter rides, and bought food from vendors. The Canadian flag flew everywhere.

Later that night, I watched fireworks from my motel room while I reflected on the beautiful, carefree day I'd spent in Brandon. I fell asleep and slept well, although my burning knees woke me up twice.

I left early the next morning and rode for hours, trying to beat the heat. By noon, the sun became brutally hot and unforgiving, and I moved slowly, stopping regularly to check on Jackson and give him some play time. We both needed lots of water, and we drank frequently, trying to cool down. It seemed that no matter how long I rested, I could never recover enough to reenergize. Still, I pushed forward, and just when I thought I couldn't go on, two young guys named Alex and Kyle stopped to see if I needed help. Indeed, I did.

After loading my bike and trailer in the bed of their truck, I climbed into the backseat of the cab. The cool air changed my mood in an instant, and I told them about my ride. Inspired, they offered to drive me all the way to the United States border. I thanked them but said that the nearest motel would be fine.

Alex and Kyle were on their way to Winnipeg to buy an engagement ring for Kyle's girlfriend. Kyle and the young woman had been together two years; his entire family embraced her and loved her as their own. She had no idea of Kyle's intentions, and I sensed his excitement.

We arrived at a Best Western in the town of Headingly and said our goodbyes. After I checked in, I began the difficult process of carting my gear up to the second floor; breaking everything down and getting it onto the elevator was no small feat.

After I showered and washed my dirty outfit, my stomach fell out from under me when I realized that I had left my phone in the vehicle with Alex and Kyle. I didn't even know their last names. I only knew that they were on their way to Winnipeg to buy an engagement ring, and I knew what they did for a living.

Panicked, I started calling every jeweler in Winnipeg, a city of seven hundred and fifty thousand people. Feeling lost and frustrated, I described Alex and Kyle to whoever would listen and left the motel's number with them. My trip diary and all the photographs I had taken on my journey were on my phone. Without it, I couldn't regularly update my friends to let them know where I was and that I was okay. I wouldn't be able to plan my routes, check for campgrounds, or find the nearest motel. I would have to buy a map.

I walked over to Denny's to calm down and have dinner. The waitress greeted me with a big smile and asked how I was doing. With tears in my eyes, I ordered a glass of wine and told her about my plight. Within no time, she came back with a glass of pinot grigio and the restaurant manager, Mario. He wanted to hear about my ride, and I invited him to sit with me. He listened intently to my story and became emotional as he told me that he had lost many friends to AIDS.

After a while, Mario left to assist a server, and when he returned, he sat an iPhone on my table. "I want you to have this," he said. "I have two, and I don't need this second one."

Stunned by his generosity, I thanked him profusely.

Soon, a young staff member showed me how to delete all of Mario's information from the phone, and when I left Denny's a short time later, I had a new iPhone, new friends, and a full stomach. My spirits soared so high I thought I could fly. Of course, I couldn't, instead, I skipped all the way back to the motel.

That night, I posted on my social media, asking my friends to send a 'Thank You' to Mario, the manager at the Denny's in Headingly.

The next day, I returned to the restaurant to thank Mario and his staff again and to say my goodbyes. Mario told me about the emails he had received from my friends. He also told me he had just found out that one of his best friends had died from complications of diabetes and HIV.

My mission felt more important than ever.

Chapter 11

Back in the USA

Jackson and I had been on the road for months, and we had experienced more than our fair share of ups and downs. While in Headingly, we saw a veterinarian to get Jackson's paperwork renewed for reentry into the United States. Jackson also got a good grooming, and I got a haircut. We both felt much better, and with all our chores accomplished, we left Headingly.

Back on Highway 12, we rode through the town of Steinbach. It was rush hour, and traffic became an issue. I had to ride in the car lane since the highway didn't have a shoulder. Outside of town, the road changed to a one-lane highway. At times, a long line of cars stretched behind me, following at about ten miles per hour. Fortunately, nobody got impatient enough to honk. I realized I must look like I was leading an AIDS Memorial parade, or even a funeral procession for an AIDS victim.

I finally reached a place where cars could pass me, and I rode for hours until my left knee became too painful. I knew I might hurt myself if I put much more pressure on it, so I began to ponder what to do next. Just then, a pick-up truck pulled alongside me. The driver, a man named Ian, had taken one look at me and knew I needed help. A very masculine, husky man with a kind and giving heart, he invited me to his house so I could rest and take care of my knee.

Ian told me he had just left the hospital, where he'd had his final treatment for prostate cancer. He lived on the Canadian/American border and had been a Canadian resident for more than thirty years after moving there from Jamaica. Ian worked for the railroad, and his job required that he fly all over Canada to deliver supplies and do repairs. He seemed to love his work, but his kids obviously took priority; he loved them more than anything else. Ian and his ex-wife had four adult children together, but he had recently adopted six Jamaican children on his own and was in the process of completing the paperwork necessary to bring them to Canada the following year.

When we made it to Ian's house, I met his sons, Ian Jr. and Patrick. Later that night, Patrick and his girlfriend made jerk chicken and rice for dinner. Ian offered me a place to spend the night, and I silently marveled at how my trust in the kindness and generosity of strangers usually turned out well; meeting an angel in disguise was always such an amazing gift.

The next morning, Ian asked me to stay one extra day to rest my knee. I decided that was a good idea, but I found it impossible to sit still and watch his family work. One son cut the grass on their large property, and I helped Ian organize and clean out his huge garage. He was thankful, and we shared a lot about our lives with each other while we worked.

While staying with Ian, Jackson also made a new acquaintance—Ian's cat. Jackson was excited to play with his four-legged friend. When the cat greeted us, he smelled terrible as he rubbed up against Jackson and me. I found out that he had encountered a skunk, and I had to give Jackson a bath and wash his vest as well as some of my clothes because the cat had transferred the smell to us.

On the morning we left Ian's house, I assured him and the rest of his family that we should be fine on the road. The weather was supposed to be good until late afternoon when a storm was expected. However, it started raining as soon as I made it to the highway. I had heard the storm would stay to the north, so I thought I could outrun it. As clouds formed all around us, I pedaled hard. The sky got so dark that the only light came from lightning flashes. The flag may as well have been a lightning rod, as it was the tallest structure in the area.

Frantic, I finally stopped, secured the flag on the trailer, and tried to wave down a truck. Only small cars stopped to help me, but they couldn't accommodate all my gear. After a while, a city employee in a pickup truck pulling a trailer stopped and gave me a lift to the nearest town. I didn't know where I was, only that I was safe and near the highway. I had broken my trailer in the storm and needed to make repairs. Everything inside of it was wet, and so were the saddle bags, Jackson, and I. The weather in the plains of Canada was unpredictable, and I could only hope we'd have better luck going forward.

The next morning, our gear was dry, and I had fixed the trailer. We headed south on Route 310 to re-enter the USA. I had mixed feelings about being back in my country—I was happy, but worried about the intolerance bubbling up in America. Our divisive president openly displayed hatred for almost every minority group; he both frightened and embarrassed me.

I made the final stretch to the border via a quiet two-lane road with no access to the shoulder. The silence gave me time to reflect about the past four months. Ahead, I saw the American flag and wanted to dance for joy; half of my journey was behind me.

Wearing a huge smile, I approached the border officer and answered all his questions. Soon, he returned my passport and Jackson's paperwork and welcomed me to the United States. I could hardly believe that I was back home.

I desperately wanted to call my friends and check in; however, because I'd lost my phone and the one Mario gave me was a Canadian device, I couldn't do so right away.

Jackson and I made the short ride to the town of Roseau and played tourist for the day. Then, early the next morning, we continued on Route 89 toward Grygla, about a forty-five-mile ride south. Pulling Jackson in the partially fixed trailer slowed me down. The trip took longer than I had planned. Still, after many hours and frequent stops for rest, we arrived safely.

We stayed in Grygla one night, continuing our journey south on Route 89 the next morning. After a couple of hours riding on the very quiet highway, I started to experience knee pain so sharp that I could no longer pedal. I pulled off the road and tried to wave down a vehicle for assistance.

I noted an immediate difference between Canada and the U.S. when it came to helping someone in need. Four vehicles stopped, and each driver explained to me in detail why they couldn't help me. Finally, a small pickup packed with three passengers, a cat, and supplies in the truck bed stopped. The driver, Darron, his wife, Leeann, and their teenage son, Dylan, assisted me in loading their already full little truck with my trailer, bike, AIDS flag, four saddle bags, Jackson, and me. It was no small task.

I felt a little uncomfortable taking time out of their schedule to rearrange everything, and the interior space was so tight that Dylan volunteered to sit in the truck bed, which was also loaded to the brim. Fearing for his safety, I told the family that Jackson and I would be more than happy sitting in the truck bed. Dylan, however, persisted. Being a teenage boy, I'm sure he thought it would be an adventure to sit in the back. After his parents gave him approval, I gladly gave in and took his spot inside.

The family dropped Jackson and me off at a small motel outside of Bemidji. After completing my usual settling-in routine, I limped down the street to the nearest restaurant, where I met two women who said they would be participating in an upcoming Red Ribbon Ride, a three-hundred-mile AIDS/HIV ride out of Minnesota. We immediately connected as we talked about all the rides they had accomplished in the past, and memories of my own rides flooded back to me:

Orlando to Miami.

Miami to Orlando.

Fort Lauderdale to Melbourne and back again.

The Twin Cities to Minneapolis.

Montreal to Portland.

Miami to Key West.

It felt great to talk to those with a similar cause. Content, I returned to the motel and immediately went to sleep.

The next morning, we headed toward the town of Hackensack. The road and the trip had become a slide show—one day after the next. I was somewhat weary of the routine. At the same time, the familiarity of going through the motions challenged me to pay attention, and because I could only rely on myself, I had to call on my strengths and awareness to make it through. Now that I was in the States, I felt like I was headed downhill.

As I rode through the beautiful countryside between Bemidji and Hackensack, Minnesota, I saw sporadic flashes of lakes, forests, and farm fields. I was in rural country. The route was mostly flat, and I had to keep pedaling to make progress. I stopped in Hackensack and checked into a cheap motel.

The next day, I awoke to a beautiful morning. After icing my knees, I took some Aleve. Feeling better, I rode into a beautiful landscape surrounded by lakes and open country.

Upon arriving in Baxter during the afternoon, I settled into a room at the AmericInn. I made a call to a local newspaper, and they seemed interested in my story. We made an appointment to meet later that afternoon.

One of the first things I'd done after arriving back in the United States was contact my phone carrier. My lost phone was insured, so I was able to get a new one. My friend Linda was going to meet me while I was in Baxter, and she had suggested that I have the new phone mailed to her mother's house. She would get it when visiting her mom up north and bring it to me.

The only thing I could do on Mario's phone was take pictures, make notes, and get on Facebook when connected to wi-fi in a restaurant or motel. I could also check the upcoming weather and plan my routes, but I had to write them down.

Later that evening, I connected with Linda and her mom, Betty, who happened to be in the same motel, on the same floor as me. Linda, who is a physical therapist in Ft. Lauderdale, brought me a powerful ointment for my pain as well as my replacement iPhone. I liked seeing a familiar face.

The next morning, Betty and Linda drove me to my friend Sara's house to drop off my bike, then we went to a Metro PC store in Minneapolis to activate my new phone, without much success. We were told I'd have to find an Apple store to set it up and restore all my data. After a relaxing lunch, we said our goodbyes, and I took care of my phone situation before taking a taxi ride back to Sara's.

Baxter Newspaper Article, July 17, 2017

> Uli Schackmann is riding her bicycle 5,800 miles from Anchorage, Alaska, to Key West, Fla., in order to raise money to find a cure for HIV/AIDS by 2020. But along her journey, in addition to collecting funds, she's also collecting a wealth of stories and experiences, which have touched her deeply.
>
> "It's not so much about the actual riding and the scenery," Schackmann said. "But it's really the people that I get in touch with, surrendering and trusting. And knowing everything will be okay."
>
> A man donated an iPhone 6 to Schackmann at a restaurant in Headingley, Manitoba, just outside of Winnipeg. She talked to the manager about her journey and told him about

her day, complete with bad weather and a lost cellphone. He told her he had two cellphones and could give one to her. She went back the next day to the thank the manager again, who told her why he donated the cellphone.

"He came over and said, 'I gave it to you because my friend died, and he died of AIDS,'" Schackmann said.

Schackmann stayed at the AmericInn in Baxter for a couple days this week, while she waited for a friend to meet her with a replacement cellphone and some supplies.

She got a ride Wednesday morning with a friend to Minneapolis, where she'll meet and stay with another friend. From there, she'll ride on through Wisconsin, Illinois, Pennsylvania and Virginia, before heading south along the coast to Key West.

Schackmann participated in the first AIDS bike ride in Florida 20 years ago, which she approached as more of a physical challenge. But after participating in a three-day ride to raise funds for a disease that was heavily stigmatized, she got the chance to meet riders who were affected by the disease.

Since then, she has completed numerous rides for HIV/AIDS throughout the U.S. and Canada, but this is the longest ride she's ever undertaken. These past rides raised money for services for people living with AIDS, which is important, she said. But for this longer ride, she wanted to undertake a more ambitious goal of finding a cure for HIV/AIDS by 2020.

"It seems that we just supply more people to the agencies that we just raised the money for," Schackmann said. "It's not getting less people coming to the agencies getting services."

Schackmann isn't totally alone on her ride, as her black-haired Havanese service/therapy dog Jackson rides with her in a trailer she tows. Other than some training rides before they left, it's Jackson's first time riding along with Schackmann.

"This little guy is amazing," Schackmann said. "He's curious, he's well-behaved, he's just taking it all in."

In addition to her trailer for Jackson and four saddle bags, Schackmann flies a white flag featuring a red ribbon, a common symbol for AIDS awareness. Along the way, people Schackmann met attached small red ribbons to the red ribbon on the flag, in honor of people affected by HIV/AIDS.

Finding friends

So far, people Schackmann met along her ride have been helpful, kind, generous and supportive, she said. Some of her favorite memories so far include total strangers taking her home and giving her food and shelter. A Jamaican man in tiny South Junction, Manitoba, near the U.S.-Canada border, let Schackmann into his home. She slept on his family's couch and ate Jamaican jerk chicken with them. "Absolutely wonderful," she said.

Schackmann got caught in a severe storm in Saskatchewan that blew her off her bike, she said. It was raining and freezing cold, she said, but she made it to the next town, where she started screaming for help. A man picked her up, made her some cocoa and drove her to the next town with a hotel or a motel.

Schackmann ran into communication issues along her journey because she had no cellphone service in Canada. Later on, she lost her cellphone altogether. She did have her camera, though, and was still able to take pictures. Whenever she found internet service, she was able to check Facebook and update her followers on her progress.

"They all find it very inspiring and think it's amazing to meet all these amazing people on the road," she said.

Ride logistics

Schackmann left Anchorage in the beginning of May and wants to reach Key West by Nov. 18, in order to ride in the Southern Most AIDS/HIV Ride. She has participated in the two-day, 165-mile ride from Miami to Key West for 20 years.

Schackmann plans her route by looking at her maps each night and determining her route for the following day. She knew she wanted to go from the most northern point of the U.S., Alaska, to the most southern point, in Key West. She left Anchorage and headed north to Fairbanks, at which point she started heading back south. She wanted to cross the border into Minnesota, in order to experience Midwest hospitality.

Schackmann is trying to ride 50 miles each day, she said, but that's not always the case. Some days she's been hampered by the weather. She tries to catch a ride with someone when the weather gets too severe, or when she can't physically ride anymore that day.

Schackmann carries a sleeping bag and tent for sleeping outdoors, but has been sleeping in hotels or motels since reaching Calgary, Alberta. The weather would hover just above freezing overnight, she said, so she decided to start sleeping indoors.

The Yukon Territory was breathtaking because of all the wildlife, Schackmann said. She saw a grizzly bear with two cubs, which got her heart racing, she said. Saskatchewan was flat but beautiful in its own way, she said, as was Manitoba. She was excited to cross over the U.S.-Canada border in Minnesota and see the U.S. flag. "It's like, 'Hey, I'm coming home again; let me come in,'" Schackmann said.

The physical toll of the ride has been tough, Schackmann said. She can pedal, walk and run, but sitting down and getting up is difficult. In the mornings, her pinky fingers are stuck in a curled position, from gripping the handlebars so much.

Visit *www.ulisjourney.com for more information on Schackmann's ride. People can support her cause by donating at GoFundMe or Crowdrise, by searching for "Uli's Journey." Money donated there goes to amfAR, the Foundation for AIDS Research, a nonprofit organization dedicated to the support of AIDS research, HIV prevention, treatment education and the advocacy of sound AIDS-related public policy, according to its website.*

SPENSER BICKETT may be reached at 218-855-5859 or spenser.bickett@brainerddispatch.com.
Follow on Twitter at www.twitter.com/spenserbickett.

Chapter 12

Taking Stock in Minneapolis

Jackson and I sat in a shady spot in Sara's backyard and waited for her to come home. It was still hot out, and my water supply had dwindled to almost nothing, but I managed to enjoy the peace and quiet. As minutes turned into hours, I meditated and inspected the area for a place to set up my tent. In case Sara didn't come home, I began mentally organizing a possible camp layout for the night.

I was wandering about the yard when Sara's neighbor showed up. Nancy had been watching me through a window and wondering who I was and what I was up to. I introduced myself and explained the situation, adding that my phone was dead and my water supply empty. Nancy left to refill my water bottle and brought it back a few minutes later along with some crackers and an extension cord so that I could charge my phone. We talked for a bit, and she said to just come over the fence if I needed anything else. Nancy's husband came by later, and he also said I should come over the garden fence if I needed anything.

Meeting the neighbors and receiving their offer of help put me more at ease as I returned to my task of finding a place to set up camp for the night. Sara's large yard had many apple trees, shrubs, and plenty of good, level places to pitch my tent. Since I'd informed the neighbor I might be camping there overnight, and I had dog food for Jackson and an energy bar for my dinner, my only worry was the bathroom situation. Obviously, no facilities existed in Sara's yard, and I wasn't comfortable imposing on the neighbors late at night should the need arise, despite their generous offers of assistance.

Late afternoon turned to evening. While dozing in a chair, a noise inside the house startled me awake. Relieved that Sara must finally be home, I jumped to my feet and walked to the back door. Sara answered my knock and greeted me with an expression of surprise that quickly transformed into a warm, welcoming smile. We embraced one another with joy.

"You're early!" Sara exclaimed. "I wasn't expecting you today."

"Did I miscommunicate?" I asked.

"It doesn't matter. I'm just glad you're here." She motioned me inside. "Sit down. Let's have a glass of wine."

Sara and I had met at Gratitude Training, a powerful leadership training course. She had been my "buddy" at the event, and we had challenged each other and supported one another's growth and development. Now, as we shared memories and new visions about our commitments and ways we could support one another in our next stage of life, it seemed nothing had changed between us. I appreciated Sara's willingness to engage in such a powerful conversation with me.

Too soon, it was time for bed. Sara made me feel comfortable and at home. Still, I wasn't tired. In Sara's guestroom bed, I remained awake for a long time, thinking about my day, about my Gratitude Training team, about how fortunate I had been on my amazing journey and all the wonderful friends who'd supported me.

The next morning, I woke up refreshed, and after a little breakfast, Sara and I went to Target to buy food and household supplies. While on my trip, I had quickly grown unaccustomed to the hustle and bustle of city shopping, and I felt wired up. Everything and everyone seemed to move too fast. Traffic…the people in the streets and in the store…the noise…it all overwhelmed me. I felt I couldn't handle the people and the situations taking place around me. I was happy when we finished and returned to Sara's house.

When she left for work later, Jackson and I explored the neighborhood. While we walked, I wondered about the travels ahead of me. I couldn't wait to find out what was next. Who else would I meet? What new adventures awaited me?

At 5:30 am the next day, Sara and I drove to the Mall of the Americas for the "Twin City to Chicago Red Ribbon Ride." I was excited to witness the event with my friend. I felt at home amongst the riders and excited to see them prepare for their three-day journey. Watching them brought thoughts of friends who had lost their lives to AIDS. I carried the AIDS Memorial Flag with me in memory of them, to encourage hope for a cure, and to inspire others to make a difference.

While there, I reconnected with two people, Tammy and Terry, I'd met recently at a restaurant and bar near Bemidji. Seeing them was like seeing old friends.

When the last rider had left, Sara and I made our way home. After she rested, then went to work, I took care of my phone issue, paid bills, did laundry, called NPR and a few newspapers, and picked up my bike from the shop where I'd left it for a tune up and repairs. I spent the rest of the day searching maps for the best route to Madison.

Later, I went to downtown St. Paul where I was to meet Sara for a wonderful gallery event. I was early, so I explored the gardens where the artwork was displayed.

When Sara showed up, we went inside, drank beer, and listened to the live music provided by an adorable hip-hop singer who everyone there seemed to know along with the lyrics to his songs. Later, he left, and the music changed to country and folk. Sara bumped into a couple of friends, two men who I initially thought were gay. I decided that wasn't the case when a woman named Rachel joined us, and I realized she was with the two men. Rachel announced she needed "a big beef injection." The others didn't seem to understand what she meant, but when I saw her smirk, I realized she wanted to have sex with a man.

Seemingly out of nowhere, an extremely handsome Jamaican dude showed up and started talking to us. I thought he was with the hip-hop band and that Sara and her friends knew him. He and I hit it off right away. I told him about my ride and about Germany, and we took some photos. Later, when the friends who'd accompanied him to the gallery event came over and announced they were ready to leave, he gave me a big hug before departing.

As I watched him walk away, Sara and the others stared at me with quizzical expressions. "What was that all about?" one of the guys asked.

I shrugged. "We were just talking. Why?"

He motioned to his friend. "We told him earlier that Rachel wanted to meet him. He didn't want to look too forward to her, so he started talking to you first."

I realized that because I'd monopolized the Jamaican guy's time, the handsome hunk had not had a chance to gravitate to Rachel. She'd lost her opportunity to have the great sex she "needed." I turned to her and shrugged again. "I had no idea. Sorry, Rachel." I guess she realized my innocent expression was genuine because she forgave me.

The next morning, I slept in and then went to Target to buy flip flops. They felt like heaven on my feet after wearing bike shoes for the past four months. After Sara got off work, she went to her dad's birthday party. She had invited me to join her, but I preferred to stay home.

I went to the library, put my route to Madison together, then went with Jackson to a beautiful outdoor Italian restaurant where I ate three different salads with grilled chicken and drank wine. Refills were free, and I lost track of how many times the waiter filled my glass.

The food was excellent, the atmosphere relaxing, and the staff super friendly. I enjoyed every bite, every sip of wine, every smile I received, and every kind conversation in which I took part. I felt like a new woman and stayed for hours.

While staying with Sara, we went to a tattoo artist, and at the age of fifty-nine, I got my first tattoo—three flying seagulls. Sara played my song from Gratitude Training, and I began to cry. I imagined myself as Jonathan the seagull, and all the love and powerful connections I'd experienced on my journey flooded back to me. My tears concerned the tattoo artist; he thought I was in pain. Sara explained my reasons for crying and put him more at ease.

Later, back at Sara's house, I cleaned out my saddle bags; then she drove me to the post office so I could ship three pounds of items home. Carrying so much weight on the bike was exhausting. Even without those three extra pounds, the bike was still extremely heavy. Not for the first time, I wished for a support vehicle.

So far, the ride had been both emotionally and physically challenging. Hours of planning went into it. My routes—which way to go, which areas to avoid. Did I want to take a longer, more scenic route, or go the faster way? Loneliness also challenged me, despite often finding myself in very good company. Sometimes, too, doubts crept in and tripped me up. I'd ask myself, *"What am I doing? Do I really believe this will make a difference in someone's life? Can I make myself push through? What is this doing to my body?"* I shared my struggles on Facebook, hoping to inspire others to fight any self-imposed resistance and follow their dreams.

Everywhere I went, I met people and told them about my journey and my mission to find a cure for AIDS by 2020. That sort of sharing could be emotionally taxing. Talking with friends at home about AIDS is one thing, but talking about the virus with complete strangers while on the road is quite another. I always worried about the reactions I might get, especially considering the political climate. Many people responded openly and in a quite friendly manner. However, some were not comfortable talking about AIDS because they saw it as a "gay disease." Fortunately, those encounters had been few and brief.

I also felt frustrated with some of the media outlets I'd contacted while on the road. Many had shown an interest in my effort, but their decision of whether to cover my story hinged on if they had a reporter available. If they did, I had to make myself available based on their schedule. If they didn't want to meet at a motel where I was staying, I had to ride to an agreed-upon meeting place, but not before making my gear, flag, and bike photo-friendly. Not every interview made it to print, and the ones that did weren't always shared with me. I often had to follow-up by calling from the road to find out their plans.

Jackson's care was also a huge responsibility. He needed daily exercise and TLC. In addition to my own supplies, I had to carry food and water for him.

The day after tomorrow we would be back on the road. I had my route from Minneapolis to Madison all mapped out. I was grateful for the time I'd had with Sara. We had reconnected and staying with her had allowed me to rest my knee and have extra play time with Jackson.

That night at Sara's, I had a weird dream about a former co-worker. We sat on a corner seat of a subway train and were on our way to her death, which I would observe. At some point, another person joined us—a friend of my co-worker's. I stood up to let the friend slide in next to her.

Suddenly, I realized we were headed for *my* death, not hers. I looked around, and the two women were gone. I was alone. Panic set in; I felt too young to die. I had too much juice left in me. I thought about escaping and looked for someone to help me.

The scene shifted. I now stood on the platform outside the train. I tried to step off, when a voice spoke to me, saying, "This is the best time for you to die. You have no home, no car, and no job. You wouldn't want to wait to die when you're old and shitting your pants, when you're a burden."

I started to relax and sat down, ready to die. Then I became aware the subway train was a gas chamber containing odorless, colorless gas.

I woke up in a sweat, my heart racing. Telling myself it was only a dream, I tried to ignore the fear in my bones and go back to sleep. My sense of foreboding had me at the edge of panic, and I couldn't shake it. I feared closing my eyes. I could only think about dying. Did I have everything in place in case of my death? Who would take care of Jackson if I died on the road? I reminded myself that Aiden had my will.

Reaching for my iPhone, I searched for articles about dreams of dying and what they mean. I read:

"Although such a dream may bring about feelings of fear and anxiety, it is no cause for alarm as it is often considered a positive symbol. Dreams of experiencing your own death usually mean that big changes are ahead. You may be moving on to new beginnings, leaving the past behind or opening up to spirituality."—Dreammoods.com

I felt relief.

Sara and I went to the Farmers Market and had breakfast. People, live music, and wonderful smells of freshly baked goods, fresh brewed coffee, and other goodies filled the market. I saw many brightly colored crafts on display. The chattering people seemed so happy to be a part of the colorful picture. I took it all in as I sat sipping my coffee. As people walked by, I overheard some of their conversations, their plans, and common concerns. I couldn't help wondering if those same concerns were still mine as well.

After we ate, I bought two huge flower bouquets, one for Sara, and one for her backyard neighbor. Then we headed back home; Sara had an engagement to attend.

After she left the house, I walked to a local bar for a beer. I met a man named Omar and talked to him about some of my experiences. I asked about his life and discovered that he came from Ethiopia but had fled that country when war erupted. To get refugee status and help, he knew he had to make it to Somalia. Traveling by foot with dozens of other refugees and only the clothes on his back, he had walked hundreds of miles to Somalia, to be greeted by war in that country as well.

Omar and the others with him traveled on in search of an escape from war, sleeping outside without shelter wherever they stopped and exposed to hungry lions and people carrying guns and machetes. He heard the lions at night, and he also heard screams when the lions captured their human prey. Terrified, Omar wasn't sure he would survive the ordeal.

Driven to continue walking, despite his fears, Omar focused on the possibility of finding a better life with new opportunities. He eventually made it to a safe zone and was processed then shipped off to Minnesota in the USA. He has lived there ever since. He became a teacher, met a woman and married, and they had five children. When we met, Omar's youngest child was two months old, and his oldest was fourteen years old. Omar spoke of wanting the best for his kids and of his fears for them due to the American political situation; he hated seeing the hatred and divisiveness taking place in his new country.

Omar said he taught his children to be respectful of others, even those with different values. But he knew they might not be extended the same courtesy. His children were American citizens, but they had dark skin and Ethiopian names. Tears filled his eyes as he mentioned his worry that something could happen to his children because they were "different." I understood his fears, but I could only tell him to have faith. I praised his courage and told him that his story, his commitment to a better life for himself, his family, and others, inspired me and gave me strength to continue my journey.

We hugged before we said goodbye. Only an hour earlier, we had met in the bar as total strangers. We left as friends.

Chapter 13

Minneapolis to Le Crosse

On Monday, July 17, I got a lift into Hastings just outside of Minneapolis, leaving me grateful I didn't have to deal with morning rush hour traffic through the city while riding my bike.

I started my ride on Route 10E. Traffic wasn't overly busy, consisting mostly of agricultural trucks and tractors pulling heavy equipment. Wind blew from the southeast, making pedaling a bit difficult. I navigated onto the shoulder of the road whenever I could, but cars still lined up behind me. Soon, the shoulder became narrower, filled with gravel, and impossible to ride on.

At one point, my bike started wobbling and picked up speed as the road began a gradual decline. I became more and more unsteady and knew I was in trouble. I couldn't escape the gravel as the bike veered left and I tried to gain traction. Cars that had lined up behind me, now passed alongside. Trying to avoid a collision, I hit the brake gently, causing the bike to swerve off the gravel shoulder toward the ditch, where I flew into the air and landed. The bike followed suit, and the trailer flipped with poor Jackson inside it. Without pausing, I jumped up and ran to check on him, and when I opened the wrecked trailer, he looked at me with big eyes as if to say, "What the hell just happened?"

Two young men who'd been working in a field across from the accident came running to check on us. Jackson and I were more than a little shook up. My knees bled, and I had scrapes on my legs, arms, and face. The guys wanted to call for help, but after calming down, I assured them that we were okay. They assisted me in getting the bike, trailer, flag, and four saddle bags put back together. Before I took off again, the guys urged me to "be safe and watch out for the gravel," then watched as I climbed back on the bike.

I tried to hide the fact that I was still a bit shaky and afraid as I maneuvered onto the road. I moved slowly, my confidence building with each push of a pedal. But I couldn't deny the fact that it hurt each time I extended a leg.

The wind hit full force against me as I traveled south on Route 35. A couple of times, I had to stop and get off to push the bike over rolling hills with steep inclines. The crash had caused me to lose a few trailer screws, and one side now scraped against a tire, slowing me down and causing the trailer to wobble. Twice, the chain came off the bike, and I fixed it. Whenever Jackson's squeak reached me, I climbed off to check on him, too.

Deciding that he and I both needed a break, I pushed on until I reached an ice cream store. I stopped to treat us both after our mishap. I ordered, and when the guy behind the counter handed me my cone the ice cream on top fell off, covering my bike gloves and legs! Wondering what else could possibly go wrong, I cleaned myself up and purchased another ice cream. After eating it, Jackson and I rode on.

Not long after leaving the ice cream store, I saw a sign for Bay City Campground. Relieved, I decided to end the day's ride early. When I reached the campground, I checked in and set up camp, then walked to the nearest gas station to get something to eat and a treat for Jackson; he had been so brave that day, and I wanted to reward him. Back at camp, we ate, then swam and played in the lake. Jackson enjoyed himself. I was relieved that he had forgotten about our accident.

Later, as I tended to my scraped knees and scratches, the neighbor camped beside me came over and invited me to dinner. I gladly accepted. While the campground owner used his tools to try to repair my trailer, I walked next door. Soon, a small group of cyclists arrived—four dads and their teenaged children, who were riding from Seattle to Maine. Each carried their own tent. The youngsters appeared to be tired, but when they finished putting up their tents, we chatted. I enjoyed their obvious excitement about their adventure. I understood their enthusiasm.

The Wisconsin Great River Road National Scenic Byway connects with thirty-three historic river towns—some of the oldest communities in Wisconsin. Throughout my journey, I had felt as if I was either back in Germany or back in time, since the architecture of the buildings in each town resembled that of late 18th or early 19th century buildings in Germany. Each of the thirty-three communities had a different story to tell. The unique river towns made the Wisconsin Great River Road journey an unforgettable experience.

Bay City, the location of the campground, sits at the head of vast Lake Pepin, and the community takes its name from its location on a large bay. A historical center sits beside the Conlin Log Home, a cabin built in 1856. Several historic houses that date back to the 19th century also call Bay City home, as well as an old jail and an historic grain elevator. Bay City's earliest residents made their living from the waters of Lake Pepin.

Jackson and I left Bay City Campground at 5:30 am on Tuesday, July 18, after no coffee, no shower, and no breakfast. I stopped at the playground to let Jackson run and play for a bit before we took off.

As soon as we hit Route 35, we began a two-mile-steep incline that sucked my energy dry. I got off and pushed the bike while Jackson stayed in the trailer; we were too near the road for him to walk next to me. The two-lane road was extremely narrow, and I passed by many trees and agricultural fields. At one of several historical marker lookouts along the Mississippi, I met two other female cyclists, one from Germany and the other from Idaho. They were on their way from Washington State to Maine. We took photos together, and they offered me sunscreen. After sharing a few stories, we took off together, but the girls soon left me in the dust.

The inclines seemed never-ending. I got off and pushed the bike over every hill, counting my steps. Sometimes I took fifty steps, sometimes one hundred, before stopping for a deep breath and a drink of water.

After reaching Maiden Rock, no more shoulder existed to ride on. I either rode or pushed the bike along with the traffic. The view of the Mississippi was breathtaking…stunning. On the other side of Stockholm, I once again had a two-foot shoulder on which to ride, and it was in great condition. Very smooth. No washboard. No gravel. No potholes. I felt like a town hopper, as the small towns I passed through were only eight to ten miles apart.

The heat bore down on Jackson and me. The girls I'd met earlier had told me that there was a 100% chance of a major storm that day, and the weather report backed that up, as did the ominous-looking clouds darkening above me. When I wasn't pushing the bike, I rode hard to try to distance myself from the oncoming storm. My eyes burned from the sweat streaming down my face—sweat and lotion that made my sunglasses slip down my nose. My skin felt sunburned.

At one stop along the way, I found Jackson squirming and panting inside the trailer. I poured our drinking water over him to cool him off. After that, I couldn't stop anymore because I was either mid-hill and pushing or down-hill and catching up—and always trying to outrun the storm.

Midday, Jackson and I checked into a motel in Pepin. "Enough for today," I said, consoling my bewildered canine pal. I was as exhausted as he was.

Once in our room, I washed my bike outfit and socks by hand, then took a shower. Afterward, Jackson and I walked through town.

Pepin is Laura Ingalls Wilder country. The renowned author of the immensely popular "Little House" series of books was born on a farm near Pepin in 1867. The Little House Wayside, located seven miles northwest of Pepin on County Road CC, marks the author's birthplace. Open year-round, it has a replica of the log cabin Wilder describes in

"Little House in the Big Woods." The three-acre site includes Pepin Village Park, which features a Laura Ingalls Wilder Memorial, the Pepin Depot Museum, and the Pepin Historical Museum. The latter focuses on local history and the Wilder legacy. Pepin also has a marina, a municipal swimming beach, and a courtesy dock. The waterfront is a wonderful spot to watch the boats navigating the Mississippi River.

Jackson and I found an open restaurant, and I ate my first meal of the day with a glass of pinot grigio while sitting at a table outside in the shade and enjoying the sights of the town. At one point, I felt as if I was being watched and turned to see a table of seven or eight patrons staring at me. Confused gazes lowered to my unimpressive breasts, and it occurred to me they were probably trying to decide if the solo person with the dog was a girl, a guy, or transgender. I wasn't bothered; I was just happy to be sitting in the shade drinking a glass of wine that numbed the pain in my body. I was happy, too, to be away from the storm I'd left behind.

Waving at the group, I called out a friendly "Hello!" although I wasn't in the mood to talk or to explain myself. I turned away and smiled.

Back at the hotel, I checked the news of the day and watched the Weather Channel while researching my route for the next day. Soon, I turned out the light and went to sleep, but awoke in the middle of the night to flashes of lightning and rumbles of thunder outside the window; I could've sworn the walls shook with each successive boom. I snuggled into the bed, glad to be sleeping in a warm, safe place instead of a tent.

We left Pepin around six-thirty on Wednesday morning, July 19. The terrain was beautiful, and I rode with tears in my eyes, grateful to experience it. Quiet and stillness surrounded me; I was consumed with awe, aware of being lucky and blessed. The mighty Mississippi kept me company on my right side, while agricultural fields and tree-covered hills kept me company on the left. From time to time, deer peeked from behind bushes and trees to greet us. Birds sang and butterflies fluttered around us. I had never felt so present with God.

As I had the day before, I climbed off my bike to push it over rolling hills and inclines, jumping back on whenever I reached the top and riding down. My knees and lower back ached from all the pushing, but I still enjoyed the journey.

After crossing forty miles, I was finished for the day and checked into a tastefully decorated room at a motel that was more upscale than the inexpensive places in which I typically stayed. It was a real treat—comfortable, sparkling clean, and so cozy. The owners were very accommodating and super nice to Jackson and me.

Another thunder and lightning storm woke me during the night, and I again counted my blessings that I had such a cozy room in which to sleep.

We got another early start the next morning. Since the motel didn't offer breakfast, I rode on an empty stomach. The small towns we passed through along the way were cute, and Jackson and I made a few pit stops. We played together alongside the Mississippi River, and Jackson even swam.

Later, when we stopped at a gas station, we met a group of teenage girls dressed as Dairy Princesses. They told me they were on their way to school and a storytelling event. The girls explained that they were Green County Dairy Queens, representing their communities as official hostesses for the Green County Ag Chest.

After the girls left, I made my way into Fountain City, a long, narrow town that stretches along the base of Eagle Bluff, which rises five hundred and fifty feet above the town and river below. Fountain City was named for an actual spring-fed fountain once located in the area and now boasts several unique restaurants, shops, and other attractions. It's a great place to watch barge traffic, but if Jackson and I

Jackson and me with the Dairy Princesses

were to stay at the campground four miles outside of town we wouldn't get a chance to enjoy that view. I decided to stay the night at a motel in town by the river.

After settling in, we had an early dinner at an Italian restaurant, where the waitress offered me a choice of two wines and let me sample both. One wine was a bit too sweet. The other was a dry white. I chose the white, but she brought the sweet wine by mistake. When I told her, she apologized, left that glass with me on the table, then brought another. It was the sweet wine again. As before, I told her, and she brought yet another glass…and made the same mistake!

Laughing, I said, "Don't worry. Apparently, the Great Spirit wants me to drink sweet, red wine tonight instead of dry white." A thought occurred to me. "Why don't you join me? Can you? I ordered a lot of food for one person, and I have more glasses of wine here than I can drink. Do you think your boss would let you?"

Francesca smiled. "I am the boss. I'm the owner of this place." She seemed to consider my offer for a moment, then said. "I'd love to join you. Thanks."

Sitting across from me, she sipped one of the glasses of wine and listened to the story about my journey. When I finished, she said she had a friend who died of AIDS.

"I appreciate what you're doing," she said. "Finding a cure for AIDS—bringing attention to the need—it's important."

"I appreciate your encouragement," I told her.

She insisted that dinner was her treat. What a beautiful gift.

On the walk back to the motel, I felt uplifted and strengthened, not only by the meal, but by the restaurant owner's spirit.

In bed a short time later, I struggled to find a comfortable position. Every part of me hurt from the neck down. I couldn't find the ointment Linda had given me, and I was too tired and sore to get up and look through my saddle bags. I promised myself I would find it the next day, and despite my discomfort, somehow managed to go to sleep.

Again, I was awakened during the night when my storm alert system went off. Several storms were moving across a seven-hundred-mile stretch of the Midwest, and that night at 12:02 am, the worst storm of my trip hit Fountain City. I had *never* experienced such a powerful lightning storm. Brilliant flashes of lightning continued, one after the other, and the thunder created a continuous roaring rumble. Rain beat relentlessly on the motel roof. Emergency vehicle sirens wailed outside, and my storm alert system went off several times during the night.

Despite the chaos, I was so tired I didn't leave the bed. I couldn't stop thinking about the four dads traveling by bike with their teenage kids that I had met at the last campsite, and I prayed for their safety. I was thankful for the roof over my head and that Jackson and I were safe and dry.

When morning came and I got underway again, I met three cyclists who had slept in a tent during the storm. Two of them—big, brawny guys—spoke about their experience during the night with fear still trembling in their voices. The third cyclist, a woman, remained very quiet as the men told of leaving everything and running for shelter when an emergency crew arrived at the campground to evacuate campers. Tents flooded and blew away. Many roads closed.

I felt blessed as they relayed their experience, divinely protected. I had originally intended to camp the night before and had decided only at the last minute to stay at a motel in town. I realized the importance of always trusting my inner voice.

The owner of the motel I had stayed at the night before had told me about a bike trail I should take, and I was excited to find it. After riding on for a while, I located the road that would lead me to the bike path. Pedaling hard and riding downhill, I covered the miles to the path quickly. When I arrived, I was disappointed to see a ranger putting up a sign that said the park and bike path were closed due to flooding. Turning my bike around, I started backtracking. I knew I would have to climb uphill now, adding extra miles to my already long day.

Jackson and I pushed on and eventually made it to the small town of Trempealeau. Main Street ran directly down to the Mississippi River. The Trempealeau Hotel is the most famous of all of Trempealeau's historic buildings and is listed in the National Register of Historic Places as a popular restaurant and lodging establishment.

Trempealeau, like many of the towns along the Mississippi River, reminded me of Europe. I thought it would be a good pit stop for Jackson and me. After a short break that included ice cream for Jackson and an iced coffee and Danish for me, we started off again.

While I was walking and pushing the bike up a hill, a van stopped me, and the driver, a woman named Shirley, poked her head out of the window and introduced herself. She eyed the big AIDS flag. "I noticed that you're limping. I thought I'd check on you."

I told her about my mission.

"That's amazing," she said, sounding truly awed. "Are you okay? What can I do?"

"My knees hurt, but I'm fine. There's nothing you can do, but thanks for asking."

"Let me help," she insisted. "Really, I'd like to. You're in pain. At least let me take you to the next town."

I shook my head. "Thank you again, but I'll be okay. I can make it."

She was persistent. "Why don't I check on you again in an hour?"

"Sure," I said.

An hour later, Shirley showed up again with a small trailer for my gear and drove me to the town of Le Crosse. She dropped me off at a Motel 6. I went in to make my reservation, and to my surprise, my credit card was rejected. Since I'd used the card to pay for my motel stay the previous night, I didn't understand what could be wrong.

I called my bank and was told the card had been canceled due to a merchant computer breach. The banker on the phone apologized for any inconvenience and said that a new card had already been mailed to my home address. I explained that I was on a six-thousand-mile bicycle trip and wouldn't be home for months. I had notified the bank of my journey in advance. But there wasn't anything he could do except connect me with a supervisor who suggested I stay for a week at the

Motel 6 in Le Crosse so they could mail a new card to me there. I asked if the bank would share the cost of my stay if I agreed to do that, and the supervisor laughed and transferred me to someone with more authority.

While I talked to the bank on my cell phone, Shirley drove me to the nearest Le Crosse branch. The branch manager there, who I later learned was named Sarah, overheard my phone conversation, which was going nowhere. Sarah asked for me to pass her the phone, and she set the guy straight, insisting that she would take over. And she did. Sarah passed the phone back to me, instructed me to take a deep breath, and asked me to trust her to take care of the situation.

She reminded me so much of my longtime friend Jeannine. The way she moved her hands. The way she spoke. She was patient, in control. I felt comforted by the familiarity of her resemblance to my friend, and tears of relief filled my eyes as I surrendered my problem to her, reminding myself that everything happens for a reason, even if I couldn't understand why at that moment. Deciding to just let go and trust the process rather than resisting, I strove for patience and humility, knowing that mindset would help me navigate the situation faster and more easily.

I left the bank with a temporary card that would work for the next ten days, and Sarah's assurance that my new permanent card would be waiting for me at the bank branch in Madison.

While I had been in the bank trying to resolve my issue, Shirley had been patiently waiting outside in her vehicle. She drove me all the way back to the motel and helped me cart all my things into my room. I was overwhelmed by her kindness—the kindness of a stranger. What we'd both intended to be a quick lift into town had turned into several hours. Shirley had not complained even once about the inconvenience.

To show my gratitude, I invited her to a late lunch. She declined, saying she needed to get home. I felt terrible for taking up so much of her time, but also thankful that she had appeared out of nowhere to help me. I knew I couldn't have resolved the situation with my credit card so quickly without her driving me around town.

The credit card situation showed me who I am in a crisis. At times, I had been close to surrendering to impatience and fear, but both Shirley and Sarah had empowered me to come at the problem from a place of trusting that everything would work out.

More storms blew in on Friday, and the weather report predicted continued severe activity throughout the day, so I decided to stay put. Happy to be dry and safe, I watched television, played with Jackson, and did laundry. I also read up on the town of La Crosse.

I learned that some of the tallest bluffs along the Wisconsin Great River Road are located around La Crosse, and with a population of over fifty thousand, it was the largest city I would pass through on my Wisconsin Great River Road journey. The community has a variety of restaurants, stores, museums, and historic attractions. It was once a major center for milling lumber. La Crosse's many historic buildings and large downtown districts date back to the 19th century, when the city was one of Wisconsin's most important centers for trade and commerce. I also found quite a bit of logging and steamboat history surrounding La Crosse.

The World's Largest Six Pack at the City Brewery and a giant statue of the patron saint of beer, King Gambrinus, are two of La Crosse's most famous man-made landmarks. The brewery has a long history that reflects the community's strong German heritage.

Chapter 14

Challenges, Lessons, & Dreams

After my day of research and relaxation, Jackson and I left La Crosse early on Saturday morning and began a rough ride of thirty miles. The bike's chain came off three times, and the road I traveled was in the worst condition I'd seen so far, with potholes and rough spots everywhere along the way. I tried to miss as many of them as I could, but my bike shook constantly, and poor Jackson was jarred and jolted inside the small trailer.

I rode slowly, zigzagging around as many bad spots as possible, and eventually arrived in a small town with a country store owned by Mennonites. I stopped for water and food, purchased three delicious fresh tomatoes, which I devoured, and inquired about camping facilities and motels in the area. After the last hill I'd climbed, I was ready to settle for the day.

Small cabins sat next to the country store, and I decided to rent one, even though the area around them was flooded from the storms. However, a music festival had been planned for that night, and even though it had canceled due to the weather, the cabins were all spoken for; nobody had canceled their reservation. I was informed that I'd find no rooms available in the tiny town as it didn't have any motels or hotels. My best bet for finding lodging was in the next town. I left the country store feeling frustrated and deflated.

As soon as I started off again on my bike, the buzzing of mosquitoes and flies surrounded me. I pressed on, crossing not only one giant hill, but two. The first one rose at a forty-five-percent incline and took me fifty-two minutes to climb. I pushed the bike while walking alongside of it most of the way.

Major roadwork was underway on the second hill, and flagmen

directed traffic. I spoke with one of them while waiting a half hour for my signal to go. He said he'd been stationed in Germany for three years while in the service, and he loved the country so much that he would've been happy to stay there longer. I enjoyed being taken down memory lane by his stories, and he seemed to feel the same about my stories. He shared the places he had visited while there and the food he'd loved, and by the time we parted ways, I was homesick.

Getting a little encouragement, directions, and warning, from a road construction worker about what lay ahead

The next hill was a real killer; I had to get off and push again. After thirty-eight minutes, I reached the top, exhausted. Only minutes later in Westby, I spotted a motel and checked in. I went through the usual end-of-day routine of washing my bike clothing, walking, playing with Jackson, then showering before going to dinner at the motel restaurant. I was quite happy to be inside, away from mosquitoes, flies, heat, and hills.

That night, relaxing in bed, I drifted off to sleep and dreamed about my life so far—my upbringing, my schooling, my relationships. In one of my dreams, it was dusk and the leaves on the trees all around me had changed to fall colors. People passed by, all of them wearing warm coats. A man in a large car that I thought might be a Mercedes-Benz quickly swerved into a parking space parallel to mine, even though another car had been ahead of him, waiting to pull in. The man got out of the Mercedes. Suddenly, as happens in dreams, the other car that had been waiting was no longer a car but three people who carried a heavy man by his arms and legs.

Furious at the Mercedes driver, I followed him from his car to a newsstand, calling out, "You could have found another parking space. Those men carrying that gentleman are struggling. You should have helped them!"

"I'm sorry," he said. "But I'm keeping the parking space."

I couldn't keep my voice from rising as I said, "You are very selfish and self-centered. You are a heartless man!"

When I woke up, I thought about what the dream might've meant and realized that, in the dream, I had felt the same way I did in Westby the previous day when I couldn't find a room, a cabin, or even a camping facility for the night. My frustration had intensified when I'd been forced to ride over the second hill, even though I was exhausted and hurting.

Jackson and I traveled Route 14 again on Sunday and experienced another rough day of riding. For a long period of time, no shoulder lined the side of the road, and I spent a lot of energy trying to dodge potholes. When I stopped to give Jackson a break, I discovered that one of the trailer tires had gone flat. I changed the tire but couldn't fill it with my little air pump. Leaving my bike and trailer behind, Jackson and I took both tires and walked to the nearest gas station to fill them with air.

I traveled rough roads all morning. In the afternoon, the shoulder changed, becoming wider and paved. Still, I encountered several frustrating, steep hills and had to stop several times to rest. Because I rode in the lowest gear, I seemed to hardly move forward; it felt as if someone held onto the back of the bike while I tried to break away.

It seemed a perfect analogy of my life. Sometimes I held myself back, thinking I'm not good enough, strong enough, smart enough. Other times, I allowed the opinions of others to hold me back by believing that I don't matter to them. As I pushed forward up another challenging hill, I told myself that I must be present for the ups and downs in my life. Would I let a mountain stop me? I was tired and weary, and a part of me thought that everyone should recognize my exhaustion and offer support, even if it wasn't easy to come by. All I wanted, most times, was something as simple as a place to pitch a tent, perhaps in a barn or a yard if there was no lodging available. So often, guardian angels appeared to provide assistance. However, sometimes, people didn't offer their help. Instead, they sent me on my way to figure it out by myself—like the person that told me there was no cabin for me to rent, no lodging in town, no campground.

Being left to my own devices taught me many lessons, though. I was learning to relax into my day, that my journey was not a race but a ride. Life, too, I had come to realize, is a journey, not a destination. I had experienced breakdowns, but that didn't mean that the day wasn't a good one. A day, even if it didn't play out as I'd envisioned it, was whatever I made of it. I was learning to look at the meaning I attached to such days. Feeling sorry for myself was the easy way out. I had a choice; I could go out and climb the hills that appeared in my life, or I could stay home, hide, and mope.

The two previous days had been challenging, but I had tackled the challenges and succeeded. In those two days, I had covered eighty rough miles of steep rolling hills. Ahead of me, I faced four more of those sneaky hills as well as more rain and incredible heat. I climbed off the bike and pushed again.

By 2:30 pm, the sun blazed so intensely I feared I'd collapse from a heat stroke. I must've looked pathetic because, right at that moment, an old pickup truck appeared out of nowhere and stopped alongside me. A middle-aged man and a boy sat inside. The man introduced himself, telling me his name was Randy, and the boy was his grandson. He asked, "Do you need help?"

I didn't answer; I just nodded my head.

Randy was covered in tattoos from the neck down and looked like a tough guy. I didn't care; he also looked like an angel to me. Together, we unhooked the trailer from the bike, took off the flag, and the four saddle bags, and loaded everything into the bed of his truck. Then Randy gave me some water. I drank it greedily, then gave some to Jackson. My supply was almost empty, and what little remained had grown hot in the sun.

After catching my breath and explaining to Randy and his grandson what I was doing out on the road, he told me that the nearest motel was only about seven miles away. I was relieved to hear it, and even more relieved that he would drive me there.

We made a short pit stop at a military memorial with hundreds of American flags. I took a quick picture before we started off on our way again. Randy talked while he drove. He had lived a hard life. His son—the boy's father—was disabled, and Randy was the primary caregiver for both his grandson and his son, providing for them financially and emotionally.

I listened to the difficulties and challenges he faced, noting that he displayed no resentment, anger, or self-pity. What a gift he was to me. Randy reminded me of the importance of being generous, tolerant, and kind.

Once at the motel and checked in, I settled my things in my room, then joined Randy and his grandson outside to express my thanks and say goodbye. They didn't leave right away. While I'd been inside, he had met a man passing by the motel with a story like his own, and they had immediately connected. The men and the boy sat outside for a while, the men smoking cigarettes and talking.

Sometime later, Randy knocked on my door. He wanted to thank *me*. I couldn't imagine what for and told him so. He said that if not for driving me to the motel, he wouldn't have met his new friend, who now sat out in his truck; Randy was going to give him a lift home. The two men had discovered that they were kindred spirits with much in common.

After he left, I soaked my aching body in the hot tub for a while and swam in the motel pool. Later, at dinner at a place called Cinco de Mayo, I treated myself to a delicious blueberry jalapeno margarita and the biggest burrito I'd ever seen. I saved some meat from the burrito for Jackson. Heidi, the waitress, was also covered in tattoos—it seemed to be a "thing" in this town. I showed her my one tiny tattoo, and we laughed together and talked a bit. She took great care of Jackson and me, which I appreciated.

On my walk back to the motel, I spied a small deer trapped belly deep in a stream. Having been in trouble and in need of help myself, I decided I should rescue the little guy. I climbed over the railing alongside the road and made my way down to the murky water. The deer saw me, startled, and jumped, freeing itself. I was glad he was out of the water and that I didn't have to get wet after all.

I felt so much better when I finally returned to the motel, both physically and emotionally. I reminded myself that I was privileged to undertake such a journey and to experience so much kindness, again and again, from total strangers. The miraculous beauty of human connection was sometimes so overwhelming that it made me cry, and this was one of those times.

On Monday morning, I met Louisiana, an employee at the motel who was about my age. Louisiana was a loud talker, and in her booming

My Angel Randy and his grandson

voice, she told me all about her two kids and getting "free government money." I wasn't sure if she was being cynical or serious.

Before I could break away to prepare for the day, she asked, "Do you know Jesus, Uli?"

I usually avoid religious and political conversations, so I just mumbled, "Uh huh."

She nodded. "That's good," she replied, her expression serious. "Do you also know that He died for you?"

"Uh huh," I mumbled again.

She paused for a long moment, then added, "He died for me, too."

"I'm glad He didn't just die for me," I said, suppressing a smile.

"If you didn't already know Him, I would've introduced you to Him. My relationship with Him is special. It's immediate and free—no cellphones needed," she said.

My smile broke through. "I promise, I'm okay. I have a special connection to God, too."

Louisiana nodded. "That's good. Will you pray with me?"

"Sure."

She took my hands in hers and asked for my safe journey to Key West and that I might find the true Jesus in my heart. When she finished, I asked God for an open heart, health, success, and kindness in her life. Then we hugged and said our goodbyes.

I thought her prayer in her booming voice must've surely woken up a couple of the travelers who walked into the motel during our session, looking a bit confused about what was going on.

I left the motel early enough to give me time to climb any unexpected hills. Jackson and I started off on a bike trail, and after covering four or five miles, came upon two fallen trees, remnants from the storm, that blocked the way. We turned around and made it back to the road.

I had planned to ride thirty-one miles to Arenas with a few stops in some of the towns along the way. My first stop was at a fresh butcher shop in a market that was clean and beautiful, with an abundance of different kinds of meats and cheeses. I bought a smoked dog bone for Jackson.

A gas station in the next town was our second stop, and we met three local gentlemen there who fell in love with Jackson. We talked while they took turns holding my dog and feeding him treats. I spent more time there than I'd intended, which made that day's journey take longer than expected. I just couldn't make myself hurry off after seeing how the men adored Jackson. Plus, they were so supportive of my mission that my heart filled with joy.

I had a much-needed good day of riding through amazing scenery. I spent the time enjoying myself…and dreaming.

Chapter 15

More Angels & Birthday Celebrations

I town-hopped on Tuesday, stopping in each place to allow Jackson to run and play. That strategy mentally cut down the mileage to Madison; instead of thinking I had to go sixty miles in total, I shot for ten miles to a pit stop in the next little town, then twelve to the next one, and fifteen to the next. It worked, and I had another good day.

In one town, I met a nice couple from Los Angeles at a cute little coffee shop. They said they came to Wisconsin every year and recommended that I go to the university by the lake in Madison, where someone at the student center might assist in finding accommodations for me or helping with any other needs I had. Thankful for the information, I said goodbye and left, making my way nearer to Madison.

At one point during my ride, I spotted a guy ahead standing next to a parked car. He seemed to be cheering me on. My first thought was "How amazing. Does this guy know what I am riding for?" But as I drew closer, I realized that the guy cheering was a man named Dan who I'd met at the Spring Valley Inn, where I'd stayed the night before. I recalled that he was on his way to the airport today to pick up his boyfriend, a producer at PBS. The boyfriend was flying in from Bali to celebrate his birthday.

The night before, Dan had introduced me to the motel owner, and the three of us had a glass of wine together as well as a good conversation. When we parted, he had promised to contribute to my ride. When I pulled up next to Dan on Route 24, we took some pictures together and wished each other well, then I was off again.

Soon, I saw a sign: "Fourteen miles to Madison." I was so excited!

The wind had been constant since 9:30 am and always coming at me. I was thrilled to be so close to my destination for the day.

I took Route 14, which brought me to Route 12, where I was detoured directly to a highway that I followed to the first exit, my knees shaking as vehicles whizzed by me at seventy-five to eighty miles per hour. It was frightening, and my bike shook, too.

After exiting the highway, I asked several pedestrians for directions to Madison and was told by all of them about a bike pass that leads to the university and Madison. More excited than ever, I rode with vigor. My enthusiasm soon waned as the trek dragged on, and I found myself climbing hills in the countryside. I was exhausted and disappointed that my exit from the highway had taken me the long way to my destination.

Feeling dehydrated, I stopped at a gas station to get something to drink and ask for directions. Two employees and some customers took one look at Jackson and me and hurried over. They gave us water and had us lie down on the store's tile floor to cool off. After gaining my strength and my voice again, I shared our story and told them about my dilemma with our detour; it had already added an extra ten miles to my planned thirty-seven-mile ride.

After more cool water and armed with new and more accurate directions, I was ready to take off again when a customer named Sue approached me and offered to drive us the remaining eighteen miles to Madison. Her car, though, was loaded with supplies, and I didn't see any place for my things. Sue suggested we leave the bike, trailer, flag, and saddle bags at the store; she could pick it all up later. I couldn't think of being separated from my bike, so I declined her wonderful offer, but before I left, she gave me her phone number in case I needed any help while on the road. I gave her my number as well, then Jackson and I took off.

The route took me over many rolling hills, and the brutal sun beat down on us. I had traveled about nine miles from the store when I saw Sue waiting on the side of the road. She waved and called me over. I admit to being somewhat irritated at being forced to stop; I would soon face another incline, and I had generated some good speed after coming down a hill. Sue must've noticed my mood. She apologized, explaining that she had given me an old phone number earlier in error. She gave me her new phone number and, again, offered me a ride.

As it turned out, we were right in front of Sue's workplace, but I still wasn't willing to leave my things. However, I didn't think I could ride my bike another mile and there didn't seem to be any motels nearby. I asked Sue to call an SUV or van taxi to take me into Madison, which she did.

It took a good twenty minutes for the taxi to arrive. In the meantime, Sue waited with me outside of her workplace, a government treatment center for people with developmental disabilities; she'd been employed there since the mid-nineties. She said she also taught a class at the university.

When my taxi came, Sue paid the forty-dollar cost for the ride, and as I helped the driver load my things, she offered to host a dinner while I was in Madison, saying I could tell the group about my ride for an AIDS cure.

I took off in the taxi, thinking that my journey had been one of miracles.

My temporary credit card worked fine when I checked in at Motel 6. Jackson and I settled into our room and cleaned up, and I felt like a human again, though my body still hurt all over.

I walked to the nearest restaurant and enjoyed a hot, high-carb meal. The noisy atmosphere made me anxious, so I quickly returned to the motel after finishing. The red light on my room phone was flashing, indicating I had a message. I listened and was surprised to learn that Sue was in the lobby; she wanted to take me out to eat Indian food. I hurried to the lobby and apologized, explaining that I'd just had dinner. I went with her to the restaurant anyway, where we met up with two of her friends and had a wonderful time.

That night, I dreamed that I hid behind an anonymous woman who sat in a chair and watched Karen Ansell try on different clothes—nice, expensive outfits, including a pair of awesome green pants. She wore an unusual bra; it was white, elastic, and oddly angelic, stretching all the way up her neck. The bra alone cost over a hundred dollars. I came out from behind the chair and told her to get it. "Life is short," I said. "You love it, so you should buy it."

The dream changed. I sat at a table with two friends. Two men were also present, and one of them insulted me. My normal reaction would be to become defensive and aggressive, but in the dream, I told the rude man how his words made me feel. I told him, too, that I was lonely. The dream continued with me moving to a different table to distance myself from the two men, but they soon followed me. Again, I expressed my emotions to the men and walked away rather than lashing out in defense.

I awoke the next morning certain that the ride, my experiences while on the road, and Trump's hatred were showing up in my dreams. I felt pleased by the way my dream self had responded to conflict.

That morning, I went to the bank to pick up my new credit card. From there, I dropped my bike and trailer at a bike shop and was told the estimated cost of the necessary maintenance and repairs was four hundred and fifty dollars. There was no getting around it; I left the bike and trailer to be fixed.

Wanting to stay busy, I contacted a local newspaper and scheduled an interview for nine o'clock the next morning. They asked for an exclusive, so I promised I would not contact any other Madison papers about my story.

Later in the day, I checked the Twin Cities Red Ribbon Ride website. Since Sarah and I had attended the opening ceremony, I was curious to find out if my ride for an AIDS cure was mentioned and if they'd posted photographs of us with my bike and the AIDS flag. I didn't find a single picture or mention of my mission. The Smart Ride was the same—no photos or mentions posted. Had I been naïve to think we all ride for a cure?

I watched the news and the Weather Channel from my room. President Trump's "them versus us" rhetoric discouraged me; it made the country's political climate worse. When had Russia become an ally of the United States while I, apparently, became an enemy simply because I'm a liberal Democrat?

I took a deep breath, turned off the television, then texted Sue, inviting her to join me for dinner.

I met with Sean from the local paper on Thursday. We spent two and a half hours talking about my cure for AIDS mission, and he took lots of notes. The interview went well, but despite his newspaper's request that I give them an exclusive, I later found out that they never published an article about my story.

Following the interview, I ran errands, taking Jackson along with me. We went to the pet store to buy his food, to Home Depot for waterproof tape, to AAA for maps, and to a thrift store where I purchased a t-shirt and a pair of shorts.

Sue texted me during the day about going to dinner again. I said I would, and she picked me up early that evening. Several of her friends met us. One woman, Kathy, was there with her partner, also named Kathy. Another couple, also women, told me they had met three years before on Match.com. The second couple arrived on electric bikes and invited me to ride one. Holy Moses! What a difference from my traditional bike. The pull was incredible. I was almost convinced to ask if they would trade one of their bikes for mine.

We ate dinner at a downtown restaurant by the water, and I enjoyed the company. I never imagined when I met Sue at the gas station that she would end up helping me get to Madison and then introduce me to a great group of gay women! All of them were so curious about my journey and so supportive. Sue wouldn't allow me to pay for her dinner, and she paid for mine. It was a lovely evening filled with delicious food, fun women, and great conversations. Sue had turned out to be an angel.

I took an Uber to the Capitol on Friday, July 28, and played tourist. I had a wonderful, relaxing day visiting the Supreme Court and the lake side of town. While I explored, Sue called and invited me to spend time in town with her on the following day, Saturday. I was still waiting on my bike, so I accepted.

We went to the Farmer's Market near the Capitol the next morning and to the university. Jackson swam in the lake, and we played his favorite water game, which consisted of me throwing a stone into the water and him diving in to retrieve it. We ate breakfast and lunch while out, then went to pick up my bike. Later that evening, Sue and I had dinner at a unique little Japanese restaurant.

When back in my room for the night, the odor of well-used carpet in the cheap motel assaulted my senses, and I started to cry. I couldn't pinpoint the exact reason for my emotional reaction; I only knew it wasn't sadness that caused my tears. I felt fortunate and blessed to have met so many kind and interesting people on my journey, including Sue and her friends.

I left Madison very early on Sunday. Since I didn't want to ride my bike through the maze of city traffic, I called for an Uber van on my cell. Kate, my driver, was talkative and friendly. I learned that she was married and had two children. She practiced the Bahá'í faith, a religion focused on unity, community, and service. Kate began volunteering early in life, which led her to Iraq during the Iraqi war and friendship with an Iraqi woman who introduced Kate to her cousin. Kate and the cousin fell in love and wanted to marry. They spoke with their parents about their decision and received the blessing of both families.

After a wedding in Iraq, Kate's husband and in-laws went through many difficulties. First, her father-in-law was abducted and never seen again; then Kate's husband was taken by Shiites and, later, by Americans troops, thinking he was one of the terrorists. Both times, he was tortured before being released. Her husband's cousin was also abducted by local gangs, and a ransom was demanded in exchange for his return. Kate's husband, also of the Bahá'í faith and a gentle soul, witnessed the murder, suffering, and starvation of many of his people. Kate said that despite all he had experienced, he remained gentle, kind, fun, generous, and very loving—especially to their children.

Kate spoke of the importance of being responsible in life. She said that life's greatest gift is the opportunity to be of service to others. I felt as if I was listening to someone from my Gratitude Training course. Our conversation flew. She invited me to breakfast, where our conversation continued until she had to leave for an engagement.

During our short meeting, Kate brought out the best in me. Her insights delighted me and connected us. It was a pleasure meeting her and sharing a brief, special moment. I felt as if I had known her for a very long time rather than only a short time.

In Madison, I had made reservations to take the ferry to Michigan. I met a nice couple on the ferry. Gwen and Tom were originally from Toronto but had recently moved to Michigan after twenty years of living in Illinois. They had just lost their dog, Spike, a Havanese, after having him for twenty-six years, and they fell in love with Jackson. We compared notes about our dogs, and Tom showed me a picture of Spike. I almost fell over. Spike looked exactly like Jackson, only grayer. As I always did, I told them about my bike journey and the reason behind it, and before we parted, Gwen gave me her phone number and address and invited me to stay at their place when I made it to Grand Rapids.

I also met a group of German pilots who had just attended an airshow in Oshkosh, Wisconsin. One of the guys worked for the EU and was an immune disease researcher. Coincidentally, he was working with other scientists on a cure for AIDS and the Zika virus. We had a long conversation, and he promised to share my mission with his colleagues in Europe.

When I exited the ferry and rode through town, I didn't see any signs for motels or campgrounds. I stopped at a busy ice cream shop, bought a cone for myself and water for Jackson, and asked another customer for directions to a cheap motel. The woman drew me a map while I told her, her husband, and her two sons about my journey. When she finished the map, they all wished me well. I thanked them and left.

In the parking lot, I looked at the hand-drawn map and saw that the closest motel was about eight miles away. As I was taking off, I heard someone call out to me from behind. I stopped and looked back. The woman who'd drawn the map ran up to me. She said she and her family wanted to have me over to their house to stay the night. Surprised, I returned with her to the ice cream shop. She drew another map with directions to their house, and I saw that it was five miles farther away than the motel. I didn't mind.

A short time later, I reached the family's street. The two boys, ages six and nine, waited at the end of the block on their bicycles to escort me to their house. They and their father and mother, whose name was Sarah, sat with me in their backyard and asked me all about my experiences on the road.

I talked about all of the connections I had made with total strangers who went out of their way to help me. I shared how those connections had changed me; I had grown because of them. Sarah and her family were now added to my list.

Sarah and I were both moved to tears by my stories. She told me that she had never invited a total stranger into her house. At the ice cream shop, she had felt God's touch and a voice urging, "Invite her." Sarah and her husband trusted that instinct, and now Jackson and I sat in their yard. As I had been so many times on my road trip, I was amazed and humbled.

I found myself paying close attention to Sarah's interaction with her sons. Her tenderness and love for them was a beautiful thing to see. The boys obviously respected her in addition to loving her. I learned that Sarah was a teacher on disability due to a heart problem. Her husband, Jaron, worked as a youth correctional officer. I could tell that he was most likely the disciplinarian of the two when it came to the boys, although they required no discipline while I was with them.

The boys asked to see pictures of the bears, bison, moose, and other wildlife I had encountered on the road. One of the boys, Blake, said he wanted to be a photographer. His parents had bought him a camera. He went to get it, then shared his pictures with me as well.

Soon, one of their neighbors came by and invited us all over for birthday cake and root beer. The ninety-year-young birthday boy and his wife, Erika, were from Vienna, and I enjoyed talking to them in German.

Spending time with this family and their neighbors, being included in their birthday celebration as if I were an old friend rather than a stranger, moved me and filled my heart with joy and gratitude. The truth I'd come to learn while on my mission was reaffirmed: When I remained open, trusting, flexible, and loving—when I surrendered my expectations—miracles occurred.

The next morning, Sarah made an early breakfast; then she saw Jackson and I off as we left Muskegon.

We made it safely across to Grand Rapids by late afternoon, and I called Gwen and Tom, the couple I'd recently encountered on the ferry from Milwaukee to Michigan. Tom met me on the top of a hill that led to their house, relieved me of the weight of the saddle bags, which he put in his car, then guided me the rest of the way. I was exhausted and appreciated his help. Upon leaving Muskegon earlier, the temperature had soared, and by eleven o'clock, the heat and humidity were almost unbearable. I was relieved when I made it to Gwen and Tom's house.

I received a warm welcome from Gwen, and after a cold beer, a shower, and a change into fresh clothes, I felt like myself again. Gwen cooked a fabulous dinner. Their twenty-one-year-old daughter, Erika, joined us and told me she was studying to become a registered nurse. She volunteered in Haiti and Honduras and spoke fluent Spanish. She loved the work she and others did in those countries to help children.

The conversation flowed easily and continued until 11:30 pm. As we ended a lovely night, Gwen asked what time I planned to get back on the road the next morning. I explained that the next day was my birthday and was about to give her a time when she and Tom insisted that I stay with them to celebrate. Pleased by the offer, I agreed. They must've risen very early the next morning, because when I left my room and went to greet them, I found an adorable, tiny birthday cake awaiting

My Angels Gwen, Tom and their daughter Erica

My birthday cake for my 59th birthday

me on the kitchen table along with a birthday card and a streamer hung across the nook above.

After birthday hugs and well wishes all around, I took Jackson for a walk. When I returned, I found another birthday card in one of my saddlebags from Sarah and her family. When I opened it, I saw thirty dollars tucked away inside. I texted Sarah to thank them and told her I would send the money to amfAR—the beneficiary of my six-thousand-mile bicycle journey—in her family's name. She responded that the money was for me; she would donate to amfAR as well. Knowing that she was on disability and losing two thirds of her salary, I found her gesture to be more than generous.

At noon, Gwen drove me to town, where we had lunch. Later that evening, Tom and Gwen helped me celebrate even more by taking me out for dinner by the lake, where I learned even more about this loving couple and their children. Tom told me he was in the process of getting endorsements for a book he'd written that would soon be published. The book chronicled a two-year correspondence with his son after the young man left home to attend college in Chicago.

I could not have imagined a more beautiful birthday, surrounded by a kind, generous, and gracious family. That night, I slept like a baby—happy, safe, and content.

Chapter 16

Gifts, Mixed Emotions, & Giving Back

On August 2, I left Gwen and Tom's house and began another hot, humid ride from Grand Rapids toward Portland, Michigan, on Cascade Road. I had planned ahead to stay at a particular motel that night.

The trip took several hours, and six miles from my destination, a man named Dana stopped his vehicle and asked if I needed help. We soon had my bike, trailer, flag, and saddle bags on his truck.

Dana was retired, looked like John Wayne, and exuded the old-school paternalistic attitude of being in charge; he was a what-I-say-goes-don't-mess-with-me sort of guy. We took off and had only traveled a short distance when a police car pulled us over. Dana and I looked at each other wordlessly as the officer walked up to the driver-side door. Dana rolled down his window, and the officer requested to see his driver's license and insurance papers. He said that Dana had failed to stop at a stop sign earlier.

Dana couldn't find his license; he thought he'd left it in his other truck, so the officer asked to see mine. I fished it out of my back jersey pocket, all the while telling him about my six-thousand-mile ride.

The officer took my license back to his vehicle and was gone for quite some time. When he finally returned, he suggested that I drive the truck.

Dana said gruffly, "I'd rather she didn't drive my truck."

"I'm going to write you a ticket for running that stop sign," said the officer, reaching for his pen.

I couldn't fathom why running the sign deserved a ticket. We were far out in the country, without another vehicle in sight. In fact, I didn't see another living thing in any direction, not even a cow.

"It was partially my fault, sir," I told him. "I was distracting him by telling him all about my ride from Alaska to Key West, and he must've missed the sign."

The officer studied us a moment. "Why don't you want her to drive?" he asked Dana.

Dana explained that we'd just met minutes ago when he was acting as a good Samaritan and picked me up.

Looking unimpressed, the officer said, "I'll be going this direction when I leave…" He pointed. "If our paths should meet again, I don't want to see you driving this truck. Make sure you have your license on you next time you climb behind the wheel." He left without issuing a ticket.

Dana waited until the officer was out of sight before continuing on.

When we reached the motel, Dana helped carry my things inside. I could tell by his gruff attitude toward me that I had been quite an inconvenience for him. But by picking me up, he had saved himself from getting into a lot more trouble with the cop and saved me from six more miles of riding my bike in the heat.

After Jackson and I settled in, I found an email from Sue congratulating me on my birthday and checking in on my journey. I was so surprised to hear from her. All the feelings that I once felt about her came up to the forefront. I responded with a "thanks" and requested her phone number; when we had parted ways, I had deleted her contact information. She sent her number right away. I called, and she answered. I hadn't spoken with her since we broke up. Our conversation now focused mostly on my experiences on my bike trip, and she seemed amazed by my stories.

That night, I slept well, but I had a difficult time getting up the next morning. It was dark and foggy outside, and I worried about visibility. I finally managed to get everything ready, had breakfast, and Jackson and I left at 7:50 am.

We continued on Cascade Road for thirty miles to Lansing, Michigan. I couldn't find the motel I wanted due to being on a one-way road and had to re-think my route, adding at least five extra miles to the trip. After walking part of the way because of loose gravel on the road's shoulder, I took the first exit. It was intensely hot out, and the roadway system zig-zagged me around. Jackson panted in the trailer behind me, as he had for the past couple of days. Worried about him, I made frequent stops to let him out and give him water.

Even now, I'm not sure how I eventually made it to the Red Roof Inn. Once there, I was given a special rate after sharing the fact that I'd just had a birthday. The motel was located far away from restaurants, so Jackson and I walked along a six-lane highway to a gas station. I bought more drinking water, a sandwich for myself, and a cooked chicken breast for him. My nerves were frazzled by the time we made it back to the room. My appetite wasn't satisfied after eating the sandwich, but I wasn't about to make that trip to the gas station again; I preferred going to bed hungry.

Unlike me, Jackson's belly was full after eating the chicken breast in addition to his usual dry dog food. He was a happy little guy when he curled up for the night. Such a good boy.

The ride from Grand Rapids to Portland, Michigan over an uneven, pothole-riddled road the next day had me concerned for Jackson and the trailer. The weather forecasted more thunderstorms ahead. I didn't relish the idea of staying the night at another isolated motel, so when I met a nice man named Greg at the place I had planned to stay and he offered me a lift, I was ecstatic. We stopped for coffee at a Dunkin Donuts along the way, where Greg and I had a long talk.

When we arrived in Fremont, Ohio, rain was falling in sheets, lightning flashed, and thunder rumbled. I was glad to be safe, dry, and in good company. What would've been an all-day ride on my bike had been accomplished in an hour and a half, thanks to Greg. He dropped me off at a motel, and we parted ways—friends who had been strangers only two hours before.

I checked in, spent a little while settling into my room, then walked with Jackson into town. When I spotted a hair salon that took walk-ins, I went inside for a haircut. The owner, a woman named Debbi Wagner, told me that her best friend had died of AIDS. She asked about the AIDS Memorial quilt; she and her friends had made a quilt panel for him, and she'd never seen it displayed. I knew of the quilt and told her to contact the World AIDS Museum, as they have a digital display of all the panels. I also shared where it is stored as well as sharing that some of the quilt panels travel throughout the country for different events.

When my haircut was finished, Debbi contributed twenty dollars for my mission and told me my cut was on the house. I thanked her, tipped the hairdresser, and left the salon.

Jackson and I continued our exploration of Fremont, stopping at a small restaurant called Scarpetta's. I had my eyes on a portobello sandwich, and when the waitress said they were out of mushrooms, I asked for a sandwich that wasn't on the menu. She said she didn't know how to charge for what I wanted. I ordered a glass of wine and asked for some time to keep looking over the menu. The girl agreed, then came back and said they were out of wine.

My laughter over this news drew the attention of the restaurant owner. She came over to the table, and I told her about all the bad luck with my orders. Apologizing, she left the table for a moment and came back with a bottle of wine. She filled two glasses for me and insisted they were free. She explained that this was the restaurant's second day in business, and they were dealing with a few little glitches. She also told me that a fresh order of portobello mushrooms had just arrived, and the sandwich would also be free-of-charge, adding that she would see to it that I was brought a free dessert as well. My luck had changed!

While enjoying my free meal, I thought of my life from the beginning of the bicycle journey until that moment. Tears welled up in my eyes and rolled down my cheeks. I had seen such wild beauty and had met so many kind and generous angels along the way. And I had changed since the beginning. I had started off with enthusiasm, eagerness, love, and confidence. I was now exhausted, weary, and in pain. In the beginning, I had not imagined that the roads I traveled would be so congested—somewhat like someone tossed a pot of spaghetti against a wall and said, "Pick your route." I had become overwhelmingly emotional and might cry unexpectedly on a whim, as I was now.

I wiped my tears and watched the staff, all of them hard at work making prosciutto balls. I wanted to give something back, so I asked if I could help. I was told that I could. I jumped into the fray with great enthusiasm, happy to be useful. My upbeat attitude must've been contagious; the staff perked up, and I left Scarpetta's with a job offer that I felt was sincere. We had accomplished a lot in a short time after I stepped in to help. Best of all, everyone, including me, had an awesome time. I think the owners were impressed.

I slept in on Saturday, August 5. Both of my knees and my left hand hurt. I needed some rest. When I finally woke up, I took Jackson for a run and to a farmer's market, where I met two beautiful ladies who sold Mary Kay cosmetics. I liked them. We had a nice talk, and they gave me some lotion and their business cards.

I also visited with some guys from the fire department, and they let Jackson and me get into their truck, which was cool. The firefighters recommended that I visit former President Hayes' house and library. Hayes was 19th president of the United States from 1877 to 1881, after serving in the U.S. House of Representatives and as governor of Ohio. He also fought in the Civil War as a Union Army officer and was wounded in action before rising to the rank of Brevet

Me working in the kitchen of Scarpetta's in Fremont, Ohio

Major General. While still in the Army, he accepted the Cincinnati Republican nomination for the House of Representatives, but refused to campaign, explaining, "An officer fit for duty who at this crisis would abandon his post to electioneer … ought to be scalped." In 1853, he began defending runaway slaves who had fled across the Ohio River from Kentucky.

Jackson and I visited the museum, library, and house and found them fascinating. The Rutherford B. Hayes Presidential Center is comprised of the Rutherford B. Hayes Museum and Library, and Spiegel Grove, an estate encompassing the residence of several generations of the Hayes family. Opened in 1916, the Rutherford B. Hayes Center Library was one of the first presidential libraries in the country. Private foundations support the center—the Ohio Historical Society and Hayes Presidential Center, Inc.

The library has twelve thousand volumes from Rutherford B. Hayes' personal collection as well as materials relating to his military and political career, particularly his presidency. It also contains newspapers and journals from the time of the Civil War to the eve of World War I. The building was constructed by the State of Ohio in 1916 and expanded in 1922, then again in 1968.

Stephen A. Hayes, the great-great grandson of President Hayes, serves as president of the Board of Trustees for the Presidential Center. In 1998, the center became national news when the Associated Press reported about a real estate company in Florida sending a letter inviting the former president to buy a condominium. It read: "Rutherford, we're excited for you!" Of course, the center's director turned down the offer for the long-deceased President Hayes!

A volunteer from the museum drove me back into town. Exhausted and hungry, I stopped at the Golden Dragon for dinner. While there, Leah Ann, a prior girlfriend of Sue's, messaged me, and I responded. Her story with Sue mirrored mine.

After our messaging, a deep sadness engulfed me. I missed Alaska and Canada, and each time I thought about the beginning of my journey, I started crying. I told myself to sit with the emotions for a while and try to figure out what was going on with me. For certain, I knew that I missed the quiet, the beauty, and the simplicity of those places, as well as the beautiful people I had met while there.

Over the past weeks, the noise, traffic, impatient drivers, and confusing routes in the places I'd traveled overwhelmed me. I felt a longing for nature, stillness, and simplicity. Perhaps Sue's email had brought those feelings to the surface as well as feelings about our relationship and the resulting love and loneliness.

Friends have said I must've had a godly, angelic, or magical light surrounding me throughout the course of my journey; what else could explain the many times help arrived for me at a crucial point or all the other amazing, almost miraculous, events I experienced? I think that's far from true. I also encountered rude people and impatient drivers who seemed intent on pushing me off the road. The rooms I rented for a night were often filthy, and I'd had more than my share of bad service. But I chose to hold space for the magical to enter my life. By doing so, I received gifts and became a gift to others.

A message I received from Debbi, the owner of the hair salon where I received a free haircut, exemplified this idea. It read: *"Thank you for coming into the salon and sharing your travels for a very important cause. You are an amazing person, and we were all so glad you walked in and touched our lives. The ironic thing is, all week we've been hoping to get our own hair and nails done and also hoping to fill our books with appointments, and you walked in and shared with us your determination and unselfishness and gave us all a reality check on what the important needs in the world really are. Thank you for that. May your goal of a cure by 2020 become a reality...God Bless you."*

Chapter 17

Making Friends in Unfriendly Territory

After riding twenty-eight miles to Tiffin, Ohio, I stopped at the Tiffin Motel. I saw the owner, a man from India, praying in a corner behind the counter of the small lobby when I came inside to rent a room. Lifting his hands to his forehead, he closed his prayer.

"Namaste," I said in greeting. "I'd like to rent a room for one night."

He took a long look at me. "I've no rooms available," he said.

My heart sank. "Please. I'm on my bike, and I don't think I can ride another mile. Could I at least pitch my tent behind the motel?"

"No, I can't allow that. You'll have to leave."

A thunderstorm brewed outside. Desperate, I made my plea again. Again, he repeated that I would have to leave.

"A storm is coming," I told him. "I don't know where else to go."

He opened a drawer. Withdrawing a business card for another motel, he handed it to me.

"Would you mind calling for me and asking if they have a room?" I asked. "I don't want to ride all the way there in a thunderstorm and find out they're full. I would really appreciate it." He made the call, and after a brief conversation, informed me that the other motel was full as well.

Feeling defeated, I walked out of the office and over to my bike. A motel guest stood outside. As both of us watched the clouds roll in, we struck up a conversation. He asked about my flag and the sign that read: Alaska to Key West. As we visited, the motel owner stepped out and rudely asked when I would be leaving. I told him soon and returned my attention to the friendly guest with whom I'd been chatting, explaining that Jackson and I had traveled twenty-eight miles today on our journey.

"When I walked in here," I said, motioning to the office door where the motel owner still stood, "I found him praying to his God for kindness, but he treated me *unkindly*."

I glanced at the owner and saw the startled expression on his face; looking as if he'd been hit, he went back inside the office.

As I told the motel guest goodbye and prepared to climb back on my bike, the owner stepped out again. He walked over to me and handed me a key. "Room 22," he said.

I nodded, thanked him, and took the key.

He followed me a few steps to the room, and we went inside. It was simple and clean. "It's perfect," I told the owner, then went with him back to the office. I paid for a one-night stay.

After a "namaste" and a big "thank you" to the man, I settled into the room with Jackson. Tears filled my eyes. Again, we were safe from another storm.

The next morning was a Monday. After breakfast at a Denny's, Jackson and I traveled twenty-nine miles to Bucyrus. The ride was smooth, with little traffic, the route taking us through nothing but farmland. We made great time and arrived in Bucyrus early in the day— so early that I decided to press on to Galion, another sixteen miles away. I felt good and was confident I could do it.

When I had less than seven miles left to go, the wind picked up, and I had to get off and push my 250-pound rig through it. I made it to a motel in Galion and was greeted by another Indian owner who couldn't have been any nicer. After renting me a room, he helped me fix my trailer. It had taken a lot of abuse, carrying Jackson over gravel, rough roads, and potholes.

That day, I'd had a lot of time to think about the previous night's incident with the rude motel owner; it had impacted me. Since starting this journey, I had passed by many religious institutions—churches, bible centers, mosques, Sikhs, temples. I felt certain that each of them taught their followers about the love of God and the other elements of their faith. Why, then, did so many leave those houses of worship and immediately continue to judge and criticize others, to discriminate against people and practice intolerance? Why did they throw love and respect out the window when they stepped out of those buildings and into the world? I asked myself why we can't all hold our fellow human beings high, lift them up rather than put them down?

I've observed people of so many different faiths fighting over whose version of God is the right one—insisting that their religion teaches the one and only way to salvation. I imagined how different our world would be if people valued each other and accepted and embraced our differences. What if we valued other people more than the things they own—possessions, titles? What if we approached one another from a place of understanding and patience rather than judgement? Would we finally have peace on our planet if we loved each other and lifted each other up, even those whose bodies don't look the way society deems to be "ideal," or their clothes aren't trendy, or their lifestyle and beliefs don't mirror our own? Every human being wants to be accepted and loved, treated with kindness and respect. This journey had reminded me that I can have those things for myself—acceptance, love, kindness, respect—by giving them to others.

Earlier that day while on my ride, a big German shepherd appeared out of nowhere and started running next to me. He had a deep, frightening bark that took me back to an attack Jackson and I once experienced years ago in Hollywood, Florida. We were on a walk when a huge, muscular dog attacked Jackson. I tried to lift Jackson up by his leash but couldn't. On instinct, I threw my body over Jackson to protect him.

My fear had turned to aggression when the dog bit my arm. I grabbed him by his ear, smashed him to the ground, and began punching his face. I felt his teeth sink into my hand, and I totally lost it, screaming the F-word at the dog and at its owner. Everything seemed to shift into slow motion. People stood around me, but no one stepped in to help. Blood was everywhere.

I kept screaming until the dog's owner got hold of it and ended the nightmare. Once the dog was out of the way, the people who'd been watching ran over to help me. Someone wrapped a cloth around my arm and another around my hand. The police arrived, and I had to fill out a report. Afterward, I drove Jackson to his vet and left him, then took myself to an urgent care clinic.

All of that ran through my mind as the German shepherd growled and barked alongside my bike. I knew I couldn't outrun him, so I yelled, "Sit! Stay!" in the deepest, sternest voice I could muster. To my surprise, he obeyed my commands, and I continued my trek to Galion. I felt as if I could now add "dog whisperer" to my resume.

That resume already included "horse whisperer." When I rode in the AIDS ride from Montreal to Portland, Maine, in 2000, I made a pit stop in the country after about eighty-plus miles to watch riders chase two horses down the road. The horses had escaped a fence, and some observers had stopped the sparse traffic on the hilly road they ran down.

All at once, the horses changed direction and began running down the steep hill of the main road, coming at full speed toward me. I froze, praying silently as they approached at a gallop. When they were right in front of me, I threw my hands up. The horses bucked, and I managed to grab one of them by the mane and began running along next to it until it came to a stop. The second horse had followed us, and when it also stopped, I grabbed it too. I walked both horses to their barn.

That night, when I rode into camp for the second-to-last night of our four-day, 450-mile AIDS bicycle journey, big smiles and a cold beer greeted me. During the dinner announcement, I was presented with a little statue of a girl sitting on a white horse. On it were the words: "Our own horse whisperer." It was a proud moment.

In my motel room in Tiffin that night, Jackson stood up and started barking when someone knocked on the door. I climbed out of bed, looked out, and saw a motel guest I'd met earlier. We had chatted about my ride, AIDS, and Germany. Remembering that his name was Eric, I opened the door. He said I had inspired him, and he handed me forty dollars, a donation for the ride.

The support I had received for my mission, not only from my friends, but from the people I met on the road, overwhelmed me. It gave me hope for humanity, for our communities, and for our country. I began to believe again that anything was possible.

I headed to Mt. Vernon on August 8—a thirty-five-mile ride through beautiful country on a rough, torn-up road. On its last leg, the trailer rattled and shook, and Jackson panted inside. I wasn't sure how much more abuse the trailer could take.

The wind slowed me down; I got off and pushed the bike up several hills while admiring the stunning scenery around me. I began thinking about what slows me down in life, versus what I *allow* to slow me down. Where in my life do I have control, and where do I allow other people or situations to control me? It was something to ponder.

We took a pit stop at Candlewood Lake. Jackson played in a big grassy field, and I stretched my legs and my back. Down the road from the lake, I bought water at a store and met the owner, Dan, who asked about the AIDS flag on my bicycle. He shared that his brother-in-law had been living with HIV since the mid-nineties and struggled with side effects from his medicines. I told him that he could add a red ribbon to the AIDS Memorial Flag in honor of his brother-in-law, and he cut one and placed it on the flag. The moment was an emotional one for me. I cried as I explained to him that the flag represents all the loved ones we have lost to AIDS as well as those still alive with HIV/AIDS. I said that those of us on this mission for a cure would not give up our fight and would continue to try to inspire others to join us in it.

Eric hugged me, saying that it honored him that I would ride with his brother-in-law represented on the flag. I saw that he had tears in his eyes as he urged me to be careful and safe on the road, especially now that I had his brother-in law with me. I promised I would, hugging him again before Jackson and I left.

Back on the road, I saw an Amish buggy for the first time and felt a sudden yearning to belong to such a peaceful community. Then I considered the fact that belonging requires adherence to a set of rules too strict for my free spirit, and the yearning disappeared as quickly as it came.

Dan pinning red ribbon on my AIDS Memorial Flag in honor of his brother-in-law

We stopped at a campsite on a beautiful lake. I would've loved to stay and spend the night, but I had no food on my bike. I had only a small container of oatmeal from McDonald's to eat that day and needed more than a power bar to fill me up, so I took off again on a gorgeous, challenging ride, headed for the next motel.

At dinner that night, six senior citizens sat at a table behind me, and I couldn't help but overhear them gossiping about other people and talking about television shows and politics; they were Trump supporters. I became uncomfortable when I realized that I was one of the people they gossiped about. They maligned immigrants, the handicapped, Democrats, and gays. All me. I felt under attack. I tried not to listen, but they talked so loudly it was impossible to ignore them; I heard every slur.

"Immigrants just come to America to take jobs away from Americans and get free medical care; the women get pregnant in their home country than come to the United States so the baby is born here as a citizen, and they can stay. Gay people are perverts and sinners and should all go to hell."

The list of grievances against all that I am continued. I turned around and made eye contact with one of the gentlemen. He nodded, and I gave him a "thumbs-down" gesture. "I overheard your entire conversation," I said to the group. "I'm sorry you feel the way you do."

They stared at me, silent and wide-eyed, as if they couldn't believe I had dared to comment. I continued talking, telling them about my ride—that I had started in Alaska and would finish in Key West in a few months. I didn't share that a cure for AIDS was the reason behind my ride; I feared I would be verbally or physically attacked for being a dyke or a gay supporter. Instead, I told them about encounters with bears and cougar. I also told them that I am originally from Germany and am an immigrant, and that I haven't taken any welfare or other services from the American system, firmly stating that immigrants work hard.

They appeared to be flabbergasted and confused, I could only assume because I am white. They also seemed angry I had been so bold as to participate, uninvited, in their conversation. I didn't care.

I finished by adding, "There is a saying that you can either sit on the bleachers and talk about the game, or you can be on the field playing the game." I turned my back to them again and ate my dinner.

A few minutes later, on my way to the front of the restaurant to pay my bill, I stopped at their table and wished them all a good evening. One person nodded, while the rest remained silent. My knees shook as I walked out with my head held high.

On Wednesday, I had fifty-two miles awaiting me to make it to my destination of Zanesville, so Jackson and I got an early start. Rolling hills immediately challenged us. After getting off to push my bike over a few of the steep inclines, I became frustrated. I couldn't reach the speed I wanted and ride with ease. I felt like dropping the bike and trailer on the side of the road and walking back to Florida. But I pressed on, pushing the bike over another steep hill.

Then Kim showed up.

Kim saw me struggling with my bike and gear and pulled over to offer her help. A woman who normally had a full schedule, today she only had to meet her father for a family meeting, then go to a massage appointment later in the afternoon. To my surprise, she called her father and cancelled the family meeting on the spot so that she could take me, a stranger, the last two miles into town.

We shared so much about our lives during the drive—my mission regarding finding a cure for AIDS, her family situation. Once again, a stranger reached out to help me, and in only minutes, we became friends. Kim was an amazing person—a loving, powerful, graceful peacemaker. It was my pleasure and good fortune to meet her.

After finding a motel and checking in, I cleaned up and then explored the town. I met the owner of Gemini's Eclectic Emporium and had a good visit with him while walking around his store. I left the Emporium and had gone about a block when I heard my name called out and turned around to find the Emporium owner running after me. He said he wanted to give me a gift to take along on my trip and handed me a handmade "Little Travelers" doll pin from Africa. The dolls are used to raise funds for AIDS in that country, and every sale of one helps families living with the virus. A part of the profit goes toward feeding families, keeping their electricity on, sending children to school, and providing clean water. Perhaps most important, hope for many is restored.

As of this writing, more than seven hundred thousand Americans have died of HIV/AIDS and 49 million worldwide. Thirty-nine million are infected. That is why I ride.

I pinned the Little Traveler on my bike jersey, knowing the difference it would make for me on my ride. It would help to remind me to stay focused on the reason I made the journey and to keep in mind the people affected in Africa who are often forgotten. I took off again, thinking, *I ride for you! And for you! And for you!!*

Throughout the morning, I saw beautiful deer leaping from one side of the road to the other. Such a joyful sight! The hills I encountered reminded me of hills in Alaska and Alberta, Canada. Thinking of how far I'd traveled filled me with awe, emotion, and pride. Those feelings intensified when I received a message from Jeff, a man I'd met along the way. It read: *It was a great pleasure meeting you. Even though I talked to you only ten minutes, you affected my life. I thought a lot about your bike trip and what challenges you face. And when I find an obstacle in my way, I think about you on a six-thousand-mile bike ride and my minor issues seem to go away. Thank you for stopping to talk to us. It was the highlight of my weekend.*

I was ready to leave the motel early on the morning of Thursday,

Store owner who ran after me with the African doll

August 10, but I couldn't find the pin that secured the flag onto my bike. I searched the room, then went to the lobby and searched there too, without luck. The guy working the desk brought me a screw without a nut. I asked if he had electrical tape or fishing wire that I could use to secure the flag. He found some tape, and we managed to put the flag in the pole and tied it up.

The motel didn't serve breakfast. I rode for hours without stopping to eat since I didn't find anyplace open in town. I pushed myself to ride hard, expecting it to start raining at any minute; the sky was overcast with dark clouds. Still, it felt as if I barely made any progress. The wind slowed me down, and after a total of four hours on the road with a few breaks for Jackson, I was on my last reserve and stopped to eat a power bar. Jackson left the trailer while I ate to stretch and pee. Then we took off again.

Twenty minutes later, I spotted a man in a parking lot and stopped to ask him how far we were from McConnelsville. I thought I probably had another fourteen miles to go, and my spirits were low. When he said I was only two miles away, my heart soared. I literally jumped for joy and gave him a big hug. Reinvigorated, I pedaled those final two miles singing my heart out.

Fifty-five-thousand acres of public land surrounds the village of McConnelsville, providing outdoor enthusiasts an area for hunting, fishing, hiking, or just observing the abundant wildlife. I looked forward to exploring a bit after checking into a motel. I ended up staying at the Three Sisters Sunset Inn that night, a privately-owned hotel located in the historic area of McConnelsville. I loved the quiet setting and the fact that it only had twelve rooms. The price was affordable as well.

Located across from the Muskingum River, the inn is famous for its hand-operated lochs. I met Kelly in the office, and she welcomed me warmly. She helped me get my bike and all my gear into the basement since the weather forecast predicted rain and storms for the night.

After settling in and washing my bike outfit, I took Jackson for a walk and some play time. I thought he was going to drink half of the river while playing his favorite game in the water. When he finished playing, I rushed to a little deli store just before the storm hit and ordered some fried chicken, a salad, and a beer. I devoured it all while overlooking State Rd 60 and the Muskingum River.

Back in my room, I took a little nap, then prepared to treat myself to a hot bath. I couldn't find a stopper in the tub. I searched my supplies for something I could use to plug the drain and found an empty container. Placing it over the bathtub drain, I created a vacuum, and in no time, I had a hot bath drawn. Relaxing into the water, I closed my eyes and mentally mapped out tomorrow's route.

I had planned to leave the Three Sisters Sunset Inn by 7:30 am on Friday, but when loading up, I noticed the trailer was missing a screw and a nut and was very unstable. Kelly suggested that I stop at a gas station for a replacement and to have the trailer stabilized.

Jackson and me in front of the Three Sisters Sunset Inn in McConnelsville, Ohio

Jackson and I rode into town and found a station, where I met Chris. He said his mechanic would arrive by eight o'clock. While I waited, Chris and I visited. He found out about my ride, and I found out about his life. The mechanic didn't show up on time, and I wanted to leave to get on the road. Chris suggested that I walk my bike across the street to a car mechanic place. All the mechanics that worked there were veterans and couldn't have been any nicer to Jackson and me. A guy named Danny exchanged two of the screws on the trailer and tightened everything. When I tried to tip him, he refused to take my money, saying, "You might need it on the road." He made great suggestions regarding my route ahead and told me that as soon as I left town, I would encounter a long, steep hill.

I left the shop preparing myself mentally for that hill, which ended up taking me twenty-eight minutes to climb while pushing my bike. Upon reaching the top, I got back on the bike and rode for a few hours before a guy in a truck stopped me and said, "I can't believe you're already here." I'd never seen him before in my life, so I was puzzled. "I saw you two days ago in Zanesville climbing all those hills," he explained.

He was a motorcycle rider and said he had great respect for what I was doing. I ended up loading my gear in his truck and riding with him to get coffee in the next town. We had a wonderful conversation about the ride, Jackson, his love for the open country out West, and American history.

When we parted, I was a bit panicked about being behind; I'd had a late start due to the trailer issues, the steep hill, and now the coffee pit stop. I reminded myself to relax into the day and just experience whatever happened.

Continuing on, I stopped at a farmers' market and at a couple of open fields to let Jackson run and stretch. During one of those stops, I realized the bike pole, which was welded on my bike before I left on the trip so that I could travel securely with the AIDS Memorial Flag attached, had become wobbly and dangerous. I had played "MacGyver" throughout my journey to repair things and did so now, using bungee cords and robs to tighten the flag close to the bike carrier.

Ten miles later, I pulled in at the Red Roof Inn in Parkersburg, a thriving and growing river town steeped in history. I took Jackson to a veterinarian after settling in at the motel. He had been eating a lot of grass lately, and that worried me. While there, I had them check his nails, ears, and anal gland. The vet gave Jackson a clean bill of health. He thought Jackson might be eating grass due to boredom. After returning to the hotel, Jackson received my full attention; we played for the rest of the evening

I woke up with a headache, after a long night of thoughts spinning through my mind: *What difference am I making? Why hasn't my ride raised more money for AIDS research? Am I really bringing more awareness to the cause?*

I also thought about the seven thousand dollars Jody had promised that I realized now I would never see. His insistence that I send him daily updates had become so overwhelming and overbearing that I was unable to hide my frustration with him the last time we spoke. It hadn't helped that he had recruited another friend to agree with him and spread the word about how badly my social media posts were written. After two months on my journey without raising much money, I asked him if he could please make the donation of seven thousand dollars he had promised me, and after that, he stopped all communication with me. Although that money would have helped immensely in researching a cure for AIDS, I felt immense relief at no longer having to deal with Jody.

Still, relieved or not, I no longer had the same enthusiasm and excitement I had when starting out. I was tired. My body hurt. Traffic congestion and occasional rude people were taking a toll on my spirit.

I took a taxi from the Parkersburg motel into Vienna to buy dog food, then on to Elkins, West Virginia. The vehicle was dirty, and so was the driver. His name was Jon, a big, obviously unhappy sixty-six-year-old fellow. Jon, a heavy-set man, chewed tobacco and spit it into an empty coke bottle that sat between his legs. He spit in that bottle every few minutes, and I wanted to gag as I watched it fill up with his brown saliva. I looked out of the window to avoid seeing it and tried to engage him in conversation, thinking that if he talked, he wouldn't be able to spit as often.

Jon was slow to open up. When he finally did, he told me the sad story of his life, which included being the eldest of five children growing up with a single mother on welfare. He and his siblings eventually ended up in foster care. One of his sisters became an addict and died of hepatitis C and pneumonia. Jon suspected she had AIDS as well.

Jon was a defiant Trump supporter. He didn't say it, but spoke of many of Trump's policies, one being coal. I asked him about his thoughts regarding clean energy, and his response was that we've had coal in the ground forever, although we didn't mine it for the last hundred years or so. He thought it should be used. I thought that was a pretty good argument coming from him and left it with that.

I became curious about what would come out of his mouth next, and I didn't have to wait long to find out. He talked about Germany and asked if Germany is an ally of the USA. I told him that after WWII ended, Germany became one of America's closest allies. I told him that Germany and many other European Countries fought with the U.S. in Iraq and Afghanistan, and that President Trump had strained those relationships.

Jon didn't respond to that. He returned the topic to Germany, stating that German women are "so cute."

I turned, looked at him, and said, "So, you think I'm cute?"

He smiled a big smile, not a smile of confirmation, but more of a you-pass-as-cute sort of smile. Then he asked if we, meaning Germany, have gay marriage.

"Yes," I said, adding, "and gay Germans can also serve openly in the military."

Jon sat on that for a while, then looked at me and stated, "Marriage should be between one man and one woman."

"Why does it bother you what others do in their bedroom?" I asked bluntly.

"It's just not right. This country didn't fight wars for gay rights."

I tried to reason with him about equal rights, but it soon became apparent I wouldn't get anywhere with reason. I gave up and just listened.

"The best thing we could do in this country," he said, "is to get rid of gay men. That would end the problem. Then mothers need to start dressing little boys like boys again and little girls like girls. Treat them like what they were born so they don't become gay."

I opened my mouth to respond, but had no words, so I just encouraged him to go on.

"Do they have men's bathrooms and women's bathrooms in Germany, or does everyone just use whatever bathroom they want to?"

I told him that Germans don't care what bathroom anyone uses.

His eyes bugged out. "A man needs to go to the men's room and a woman the ladies' room. No way will a woman get away with coming into the men's restroom if I'm in there."

I shut my mouth and let him have his opinion. After a few minutes of silence, I told him about my bicycle journey, leaving AIDS out of the information, hoping to encourage a more neutral subject to talk about. For some reason, my mention of the ride set him off on the topic of the Iraq war and his opinion that the United States would *never* launch a pre-emptive strike, nor would the police ever shoot innocent people.

It was a long ride.

Five miles from my Parkersburg motel in downtown Vienna, I found a big mall with many fast-food joints and chain restaurants. I went to

Walmart and bought dog food. They didn't have Jackson's brand, so I opted for another rather than trying a different store. I hoped he'd eat it.

Leaving Walmart, we walked to a coffee shop. The manager stood behind the glass front door, watching us approach. When Jackson and I reached the door, the man opened it just wide enough to allow us to talk.

"What do you want?" he asked in a gruff voice.

I smiled. "A cup of coffee."

"This isn't just a coffee shop," he said. "It's a casino."

I shrugged. "Okay, that's fine. I just want a coffee, though."

He glanced at Jackson and his service dog vest and said, "Dogs aren't allowed inside."

"He's a service dog. I have to have him with me."

The man jerked the door open wide, a furious expression on his face. I had not experienced such rage from anyone on this trip, and it startled me.

Tears welled in my eyes as I looked into his and said, "It must be a sad state of affairs for you to respond this way. I choose not to have coffee at your place." I walked away with a terrible feeling of sadness, tears running down my cheeks.

During my journey, I had encountered so much kindness and support from individuals I met along the way. But now, in the southern part of the United States, I witnessed and experienced too much of the opposite behavior. The rudeness and hate I often observed stunned me.

I watched the demonstration in Charlottesville, Virginia, on television, and sadness and fear engulfed me at what was happening in the United States under Trump's leadership. Trump had divided the country in half with his hatred and bullying. The fact that he reminded me of Adolf Hitler chilled me. I didn't understand why half of the country didn't recognize that we had a dictator in the White House.

I was now an American portrayed as an enemy of my own country because I am gay, an immigrant, handicapped, and a Democrat. I found the atmosphere in the South to be thick with hate, and I cried many tears over it.

Chapter 18

Heartache & Fear— Riding Through the Southern U.S.

While I stopped at Panera Bread for coffee, I received a call from Rosita, a former co-worker of mine. We worked together at WLRN Public Radio and TV in Miami. When she retired, she moved to Saint Augustine, and we stayed in touch. It was wonderful to hear her voice, and I cried for that reason and many others. I cried about the events taking place in our country and the nature and divisiveness of our president. I cried because I was no longer certain my ride made a difference, and I found myself rushing along now, not really seeing the country I rode through. I couldn't believe I was in West Virginia. I cried because I was homesick and felt so alone. Finally, I cried because my ride would soon end.

Rosita was a wonderful listener, and I found it easy to share my feelings with her. Our conversation and her encouraging words made me feel a lot better. Perhaps I had just needed a good cry.

I called a taxi to take me back to the motel. Deb, the driver, was the same as the last driver, Jon: dirty taxi, dirty driver. The vehicle was banged up, and Deb was poorly groomed. A small suitcase sat between us, serving as an armrest. Deb exuded a toughness that I knew I wouldn't want to cross, and she wasn't much of a talker. I didn't try to encourage her.

While watching the news, I couldn't contain my fright, sadness, and anger. I felt as if I'd gone back in time to the Third Reich. Shocked, I watched the Unite the Right rally taking place in Charlottesville,

Virginia, right around the corner from my location. Members of the far-right, alt-right, neo-Confederates, neo-fascists, white nationalists, neo-Nazis, Klansmen, and various right-wing militias made up the body of protesters—the worst of the worst, all in one place at the same time.

The rally turned violent after protesters clashed with counter-protesters, resulting in more than thirty injured. On the news, I watched Virginia Governor Terry McAuliffe declare a state of emergency, stating that public safety in Charlottesville could not be assured without assistance. Within an hour afterward, the rally was declared to be an unlawful assembly.

Later that day, a self-identified white supremacist named James Alex Fields, Jr., deliberately rammed his car into a crowd of counter-protesters, killing Heather Heyer and injuring nineteen other people. President Trump responded to the Charlottesville killing by stating, "There are very fine people on both sides. "

As I made my way through West Virginia and the rest of the South, I was afraid for my life. I am an immigrant gay woman with no breasts. One look at me, and I feared I might be burned at the stake.

Knowing I had a long day ahead, I left early on Sunday morning, August 13. I had called Don and Carole to see if we could meet. They lived in Virginia, but thought I was too far away from them. They said if I was in Elkins, they would come and pick me up.

West Virginia's political climate after the Charlottesville demonstration polluted the atmosphere. The air was so thick with tension I felt I could cut it with a knife. I was sick to my stomach over what had happened there and grieved the loss of the young activist who had been there to fight right wing extremism and neo-Nazism.

As someone from Germany and its history of the Third Reich, I often wished many more Germans had had the guts to stand up against Hitler, as did siblings Hans and Sophie Scholl and their friends, all members of White Rose, a non-violent student resistance movement in Nazi Germany Munich. Members of White Rose had distributed fliers against the war and Hitler's dictatorship. Sadly, Nazis killed them all. Sophie and Hans were both beheaded by guillotine. In Germany, they are now celebrated and remembered with pride, and Germans try to gain strength and inspiration from them. Hans and Sophie Scholl are recognized as symbols of the Christian German resistance movement against the totalitarian Nazi regime.

I wished many more Americans were like the Scholls and would speak out against Trump and his alignment with Neo Nazis and supremacists. I wondered if Americans would always remember thirty-two-year-old Heather Heyer for her bravery and commitment to fighting for our democracy. I fervently hoped we would.

I tried several times during the week to contact Sean from *Isthmus*, a Madison newspaper, but got no response. I wanted to ask about the interview I had given him. The paper had requested an exclusive, and I had agreed not to talk to another media outlet in Madison. In return, Sean had promised that the interview would be published.

It never appeared in their paper or even on their website.

As I prepared to leave Virginia, I felt heavy. I wondered how much more I could handle, both emotionally and physically. Exhausted, sore, and mentally drained, I constantly fought back tears. I was tired of the noise, the congestion, the traffic, the conflicts, the hate, and impatient people.

I remembered a conversation at Gratitude Training about Circumstances versus Commitment. I was totally caught up in my circumstances, and I knew I needed to move myself back into commitment. I understood that life is filled with circumstances. The question for me was, how did I want to be, and how would I choose to be in the face of my circumstances? The question became about commitment. Was I committed to a cure being found for AIDS by 2020, or would I let circumstances rule me?

As I continued to think about my mission and if it really mattered, I asked myself what action I needed to take to try to make it a reality. I recommitted to service and to trying to help find a cure for AIDS by 2020. However, my recommitment didn't erase my mental and physical pain; it simply meant I chose to move forward and not let the pain stop me.

I headed out for Clarksburg, West Virginia, a ride of about eighty miles. Upon my arrival, I found a cheap motel, settled in, and stayed the night. That day, I rode through elevations of up to one thousand feet, and I was hurting.

I left early the next morning for Elkins—a sixty-mile ride at an elevation of almost two thousand feet. As I rode, I continued to think of Heather Heyer and her family. Who else missed her? Would our society remember and celebrate her? A deep sadness filled my heart, and I silently prayed.

When I arrived in Elkins late in the afternoon, I rented a room in a cheap motel, settled in, and called Don and Carole. Delighted and relieved to learn I was close enough for them to meet me, they made plans to pick me up the next day. It would take five hours for them to drive to Elkins, so they would leave early.

I awoke the next morning and packed, then waited for Don and Carole to arrive. I played with Jackson, meditated, and prayed. I looked forward to leaving behind the heaviness and sadness of West Virginia.

Don and Carole's familiar faces were a wonderful sight. They greeted me with welcoming smiles and open arms. We packed their vehicle with my gear and left for Williamsburg, Virginia.

The drive through the Monongahela National Forest was steep and without a shoulder on the road. I felt thankful to be in a car as we maneuvered through the Appalachian Mountains. I had developed a rash on my butt, and my neck and knees hurt like crazy. Emotionally, I still felt deep sadness about what had happened in Charlottesville.

We stopped for lunch in a small mountain village and took a stroll before heading out again.

Upon our safe arrival at Don and Carole's home, Don suggested that I sit in their outdoor hot tub to relax my sore muscles. I didn't argue, and after dinner and a short rest, I soaked my road-weary body while staring up at the night sky, filled with gratitude and awe. I could scarcely believe my ride would soon come to an end. I reflected on my journey. On the day I had set out from Alaska, I had been unprepared for what lay ahead of me, but I had managed every difficult situation that arose. I felt a sense of pride and accomplishment.

The next day, Don and I called local newspapers about my journey. Don set up an interview with a journalist who would come to the house. She wrote a nice article.

> In May, Uli Schackmann quit her job, sold her car, rented out her house and caught a plane from Florida to Alaska — only to bike all the way back with her service dog, Jackson, raising awareness and money for HIV and AIDS. Her goal is to help find a cure by 2020. "Right now, the disease has become a silent disease," Schackmann said. "Nobody is really talking about it. Everybody is on medication, so it's not discussed at all."
>
> Schackmann said she's been involved in advocating for people affected by this disease since 1996 and was inspired by an annual event called The Smart Ride, where bikers raise

$1,250 minimum for the cause and then bike 165 miles from Miami to Key West, Florida. That's where she met longtime Williamsburg residents Don and Carole LaRuffa, who she's staying with to rest from the most recent leg of her journey. Schackmann's route would be challenging even if she wasn't pulling her food, water, tent, and dog behind her bicycle.

"I did train a little bit to make sure he (Jackson) gets in and out of the trailer, and he follows the commands, because we're on the roads, there are cars," Schackmann said. "Didn't prepare me for it. I'm in Florida, it's flat. Didn't prepare me for Alaska, Denali, the Rocky Mountains. There's no way you can train for it. There was more pushing than bicycling — I have great upper body strength again."

From Anchorage, Alaska, Schackmann bought some bear spray and a long knife, then departed for her route, which took her through parts of Canada, Minnesota, Wisconson, Michigan, Ohio, West Virginia, and now Virginia. The LaRuffas answered her request for a pickup from Elkins, West Virginia, and she was resting with them on Thursday, after visiting Colonial Williamsburg. The LaRuffas participate in The Smart Ride to support a longtime friend who has HIV. "The amount of cheering and love, it's just unbelievable," Don LaRuffa said.

From Williamsburg, it's a straight shot down the coast to her final destination, and Schackmann's looking forward to the flat ride. So far, she's raised more than $8,000 and spent more than $7,000 out of pocket, experiencing the best and worst of circumstances along the way. "I know I will never, ever do this again," Schackmann said. "And knowing I have done this, it's amazing. There's a sense of accomplishment, making a difference, inspiring others, motivating others."

Her goal is to raise $50,000 for the organization amfAR, which shares her goal of finding a cure in the next three years. According to HIV.gov, more than 1.1 million people in the United States are affected by HIV.

Between layering up to sleep in a tent in Alaska in the spring, climbing mountains, and learning to face fears of wild animals, Schackmann said she's had people express overwhelming kindness towards her.

She's had a man who was giving her a ride turn around to find her dog's trailer when it fell off his truck, restaurants pick up tabs for her meals, and one man at a Denny's give her an iPhone 6 — all without so much as a request.

Schackmann didn't know she was talking to a manager at the time. "I said, 'Man I've had a really rough day. I'm riding this bicycle from Alaska to Key West, and on top of everything else, I lost my phone, and I can't communicate with anybody.' I said, 'Bring me a big wine. I think I need it now,'" Schackmann said. "He did. Then he came back and said, 'You know what, I have two phones. I will give you my phone.'"

She's also encountered black, brown and grizzly bears, and has learned to scream and make noise as she bikes in the wilderness to let them know someone is coming.

She aims to be back in Miami by November, so she can meet up with the beginning of The Smart Ride and complete her transnational journey with them.

By Savannah Williams, August 18
https://www.dailypress.com/news/94375289-132.html

⌒⌒

Don and Carole gave me a lift out of the congested area of Williamsburg. We stopped on Route 17, and after resting for two days, I was back on the road, headed to Edenton, North Carolina. My rash was healing, and I'd taken a couple of Aleve for pain.

I had come close to giving up on my journey. The news coverage of the riot in Charlottesville had left me sick to my stomach and depressed. It also reminded me of my own dark German history. I thought constantly about the young woman, Heather, who had died standing up to hatred. I reflected about what I stood for and what circumstances I allowed to divert me from my vision of finding a cure for AIDS by 2020. It was easy to make excuses and let fear run my life, to let it stop me from being a powerful leader or seeing my vision through. Would I stand by my word and my vision? I would. I had rededicated myself to my journey. So far, bears, mountains, breakdowns, fear, and hatred hadn't stopped me. I would push on.

Although quite hot, the ride went well. I stopped several times to buy water. After Jackson and I both drank our fill, I splashed us both down to cool off. We encountered a lot of annoying little black flies. They swarmed around my head, ears, neck, arms, and legs. I kept riding, hoping to leave them behind.

I met two couples at the Nothing Fancy Cafe. They lived in Virginia but vacationed in North Carolina for a few weeks each year. They were interested in hearing about my ride, especially my time in Alaska. One couple shared that they had traveled to Alaska with their church a few years back. They had built houses and rebuilt churches in Kodiak for the homeless, most of them Native American addicts.

I thought about the Natives I had met, my shaman pilgrimage, and how we, the white people, have treated our Native brothers and sisters. I found it ironic that a church had helped to rebuild churches and homes for addicted Natives. I wondered if they also apologized for bringing the addictions and diseases to the native Alaskan people, and for the destruction of their many nations.

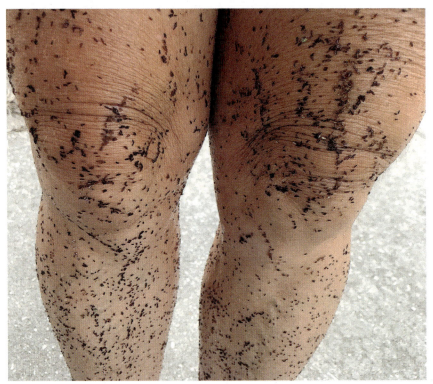

My legs covered with little flies

I found myself missing the stillness that I had experienced earlier in the ride. When I stayed in that stillness, I felt grounded, nurtured, peaceful, and connected to God and nature. I yearned for that connection that came so easily when I was alone on quiet wilderness roads.

I traveled through congested areas now. Cars zipped past me, and people surrounded me. While, before, retreating to that powerful place of connection had seemed almost automatic, it now took a lot of conscious effort.

I left the hotel at 5:30 am on Sunday and rode forty miles to Williamston. A mostly flat terrain with only one uphill bridge that required that I push the bike, made for an easy ride. My legs had become so much stronger than they'd been at the beginning of my journey, but I still appreciated level and downhill landscapes.

When Jackson and I arrived in Williamston, I saw a sign for the Village Inn. Excited to have found lodging with restaurants close by, I made my way there. At the motel entrance, I encountered a man and some women sitting outside listening to a religious radio station. I greeted them three times before getting a response. Although I found their reaction to me unsettling, I was determined to get a room, so I walked past them with Jackson.

I couldn't find the check-in desk. Looking around further, I came upon a big community room filled with senior citizens, all of them staring at me. Realizing that the Village Inn must be a senior citizen activity center rather than a motel, I smiled at my mistake and waved at everyone.

I headed out on Route 17 again. Fifteen minutes later, I found a motel. The place was cheap, and the room showed it. A piece of plexiglass covered a broken window, and bare bulbs served as lighting. The bathtub needed a deep cleaning, which I did before I took my shower. Nevertheless, I was thankful I could finally relax after an amazing day.

Jackson and I left the motel early the next morning and stopped at a nearby Burger King for coffee and oatmeal. In the middle of the night, I had awakened to something crawling on my leg. I quickly flattened it with my hand, unsure if it was a bed bug or a tick. After flushing it down the toilet, I had gone back to sleep.

After breakfast, I found a big field and let Jackson run around for a bit before we took off. It was so humid outside that I couldn't wear my glasses because they fogged up. Since I could only see about twenty feet ahead, I secured three extra red flasher lights to my flagpole to increase my visibility to the cars zipping by.

A foggy and lonely road

I was scheduled to meet my friend Flo at eleven o'clock that morning in Washington, North Carolina—a thirty-mile ride. Continuing to ride south on Route 17, I made it to Washington and took the first exit. After getting my bearings regarding my location, I contacted Flo.

I waited for her at O'Neal Drug Store, where Jackson and I enjoyed the cool air inside. I had left my SmartRide hat at the motel, just one of the many things I had forgotten, lost, or broken since starting my journey. I bought a baseball cap at the store, even though the people working there didn't treat me kindly. The proper lady at the counter kept looking me up and down with a suspicious expression on her face.

Little black flies covered my legs, attracted by my perspiration. To put the woman at ease, I explained that I was riding my bicycle from Alaska to Key West. She responded by saying, "That comes to seven dollars."

Surprised by her indifference, I replied, "I could have told you that a meteor is falling out of the sky."

She looked at me blankly and said, "Where are you riding from?"

"It's all good. Don't worry about it," I told her. I paid for my hat and left. When I come from judgment, I am not connected, and in that moment, I couldn't connect with her anymore. Love and compassion weren't present. She taught me a great lesson to be patient and non-judgmental of others.

Flo arrived, and it was awesome to see her smiling face and catch up. It had been years since I saw Flo. She drove us the few miles to her house, and we spent the rest of the afternoon there. The house is right on the Pamlico River, a tidal river that flows into the Pamlico Sound. Formed by the confluence of the Tar River and Tranters Creek, it's beautiful and still.

I listened to the waves and felt as if I was on a beach; I couldn't see the other side of the river, so it seemed much like the ocean. I was so relaxed that I fell asleep in Flo's hammock and was startled when I woke up, not knowing where I was. When I got up from the hammock, I couldn't move my head to the side, nor my left shoulder. The pain was intense, and we tried to ease it with medication, tequila, massage, and some muscle ointment. Nothing worked.

Concerned by my unrelenting pain, Flo called her chiropractor and got me an appointment right away. I went in and had a long conversation with the doctor about the ride. Afterward, he adjusted my neck and back, and I immediately felt better, although I still couldn't move my head and could barely move my shoulder. Worried about how I would manage to ride in that condition, I made another appointment for the next day.

Flo distracted me from my worries with a little side trip to Atlantic

Beach on a ferry. We met up with her daughter and her daughter's boyfriend, then I bought Flo lunch at a fabulous restaurant on the beach.

That evening, while sitting on Flo's deck watching her fly a kite, my heart ached. Had I reached the end of my journey? As I reflected on the trip and all the people I'd met, my eyes filled with tears. I felt blessed, fortunate, and amazed at how far I'd come and what I'd achieved. I wasn't ready to end the ride and go back to my ordinary life. I missed many of the friends I'd made along the way. I missed the stillness and connection to God that I had found on the journey, and it felt as though I was losing it. Now, everything around me was fast, loud, and impatient.

The next day, Flo took me back to the chiropractor for another treatment. First, he massaged my tense muscles, then did an adjustment. Finally, he applied heat. Afterward, Flo and I went to the farmers market for some produce so that I could make my fresh tomato salad.

Back at her house, we relaxed on the dock and shared a lot about our lives. Since I hadn't seen Flo in such a long time, I was as interested in her life as she was in mine. When Flo shared that her twenty-six-year-old grandson Zack was in prison, I fell silent; I saw the pain in her eyes. Zack had attacked and killed two men because one of them wore a ring that Zack thought he needed to save his family. Zack believed he was in a video game and that he and his family were under threat. He was convinced that the only safe way out for his family was to have that ring. When the men resisted, Zack stabbed and killed them both. Then the police arrived and shot Zack four times.

Flo's daughter, Zack's mom, got the call about her son. The entire family, in a state of shock, thought a mistake had been made; the Zack they knew would've never done such a thing. The injuries he sustained from the four bullets left his intestines damaged, and he had to wear a stoma bag and make frequent hospital visits.

Zack had been in prison for one year while awaiting his trial. He had yet to see a judge. His mom had hired an attorney for him, and they fought for him to get a life sentence rather than the death penalty. She and the rest of the family grieved over his situation.

Hearing about Zack made me realize that one moment can change a person's life in a lasting way. Flo and every member of her family changed the moment Zack killed two men. Their outlook on life changed. Their faith changed. Two people lost their lives, and three families were at a loss.

Flo's story about her grandson left me speechless. I could only listen and hold her in my arms. I was not prepared to see my friend in such a state of confusion and pain.

With lightning storms predicted for later in the day, I went to the chiropractor for a final adjustment. It was a Thursday, August 24. My mobility had improved, and I hoped I would get a good report so I could resume my ride.

The chiropractor was originally from Wisconsin and had been in South Carolina for twenty years. Married with two daughters, he talked a lot about parenting and claimed to be amazed by my sensibility and wisdom regarding the topic; he believed I would have made a great parent. While in my early teens, I thought I would love to have a whole bunch of sons, but that fantasy ended in my later teens, when I learned what was involved in getting a child.

The appointment was a success! The chiropractic treatments had worked. My mobility had returned. I could turn my head, which was important for changing lanes while riding my bike. I was grateful to be healed.

My thoughts turned to packing my bags and organizing gear. I planned to leave the next day.

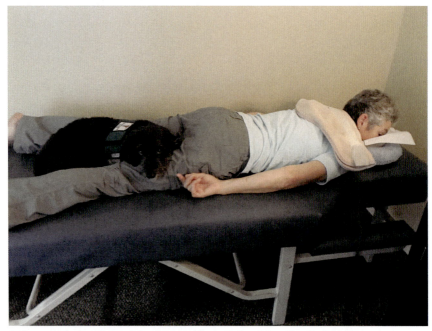
Chiropractic treatment for my neck and shoulder, North Carolina

Chapter 19

South Carolina—Campers, Connections, & Giving Back

On Friday, August 25, Flo and I left her house after a relaxing morning that included a hearty breakfast. Our plan was for her to drive me out of town and back onto Route 17. Along the way, we talked more about her grandson, Zack, and her faith in God, and both of us became so engrossed in the conversation that we missed the cutoff to Route 17. After about an hour, we realized our mistake. Flo looked at me and said, "Maybe I'm meant to go with you to get away for a while." She drove me all the way to Myrtle Beach.

The cheapest motel we found cost close to $300 for a double room, and neither of us could see spending that much money for one night. Flo suggested we camp at Myrtle Beach State Park. Since Flo had never camped before, I felt a bit nervous that she might become frustrated with insects, weather, and other things we could encounter while camping, like copperhead snakes; the State Park contained many warning signs about copperheads. The signs warned visitors to walk with caution, wear closed shoes, and carry a flashlight at night—all of which made me nervous. Despite the signs, Flo couldn't contain her excitement and enthusiasm when we reached the overflow area of the campsite.

After setting up our tent, we left for dinner in town at a restaurant on the beach. The place was a noisy, congested nightmare that served terrible food. However, we met a nice couple while waiting for an outside table, and I invited them to join us, explaining that we would leave soon after eating and they would have the table to themselves. We had a wonderful chat with them, then a nice stroll on the beach with Jackson before we headed back to our campsite.

Our tent sat between a family with five children on the right and a couple in their twenties on the left. Around one o'clock in the morning, a car stopped in front of the young couple's tent. While swearing loud enough for me to hear, the driver and his passenger exited the vehicle and proceeded to throw out all sorts of items—clothes, shoes, trash bags, and more. After emptying their car, they left.

About an hour later, our young man neighbor emerged from his tent and found a big mess in front of it. He also started to swear, favoring the F-word. At 2:39 am, the young couple, while still inside their tent, began talking so loudly they woke me up again for at least the third time that night. Tired and angry, I called out, "Hey! Shut up!"

"Go fuck yourself!" the young man yelled back, then continued to talk to his partner in a raised voice.

Flo and I rose early, both of us tired and cranky from being awakened so often during the night. After a quick breakfast, we left for the beach. The weather was beautiful. We found a quiet space underneath a long pier and settled down, protected from the sun. I listened to the surf crash onto the shore and drifted off to sleep.

Sometime later, I woke up with a start, unsure of where I was for a few moments. Red flags around the beach warned of a rough surf, yet some people ignored them and went into the turbulent water. Flo and I watched them for a few minutes, then went back to sleep. Due to all the noise from the previous night, even Jackson was exhausted.

When we woke up again, I took Jackson for a walk, enjoying the contrast between the rough water and the calmness within me.

Later, we went for dinner at Gordon Biersch, a restaurant recommended by a local. After an enjoyable dinner, we returned to our campsite to find that our neighbors to the right had departed. We felt such relief that they had gone.

Flo, Jackson, and I left the campsite just after 5:00 am Sunday morning. The town still slept, so we went to a gas station, where we bought coffee and banana bread. We returned to the campsite, ate, then packed. By 7:30 am, it was time to say goodbye to Flo. We both hit the road; Flo headed north, and I biked south to complete my journey. I had enjoyed spending time with Flo; she had made the trip more fun.

I almost flew down Route 17, a four-way highway without a shoulder. Vehicles came at me going fifty-plus miles per hour. A few impatient drivers pulled up next to me and honked, motioning for me to move over. Some of them honked from behind my bike, startling me every time.

After traveling close to forty miles, I made it to Georgetown and checked into a cheap motel. The next day, Clayton, from the Georgetown Times, interviewed me, and the article he wrote actually made it into the paper.

> Uli Schackmann is on a mission to put an end to HIV/AIDS, and she is on the final leg of a 5,000-mile bicycle journey from Alaska to Florida with her dog, Jackson.
>
> The dynamic duo stopped off in Georgetown Aug. 28 to share stories from their adventure and explain the "heartfelt" purpose behind their trek to Florida. Schackmann started her long trip from Anchorage, Alaska, on her way to Key West, Florida in May. Her purpose is to bring awareness and raise money for HIV/AIDS research and a cure.
>
> Schackmann, who is originally from Germany but lives in Fort Lauderdale, Florida, plans to arrive in Miami, Florida, just before Saturday, Nov. 17, when she will join bicyclists

there for the annual Smart Ride, which will be an additional 165 miles from Miami to Key West.

"Often in life, people have more regrets about things they didn't do than things they did," Schackmann said. "I wanted to see America and Canada and make a difference. Our goal is a cure for AIDS by 2020."

Schackmann quit her job, sold her car and rented her condominium before starting out in Anchorage with only her bicycle, complete with a dog compartment, camping equipment, clothing, food, bear spray, a bear drum (to store her food and other items that could attract bears) and a big knife. She also carries a flag displaying a large red ribbon made by a friend of hers who lost his fiance to AIDS.

"I brought some ribbons with me, so people can put a name on it and pin it to the flag," she said. "Then, I can take their loved one with me on this journey."

She traveled through the Yukon, British Columbia, Alberta, the Rocky Mountains, Calgary, Saskatchewan, Manitoba, Minnesota, Wisconsin, Ohio, West Virginia, Virginia and North Carolina before reaching South Carolina.

"In the Yukon, Jackson and I saw a grizzly bear with two pups," she said. "Luckily, the bear didn't smell us or see us."

Then, in Jasper, she saw two black bears and a cougar. Fortunately, she was not attacked because she took precautions like keeping food, deodorant and other scented items locked away, making a fire with lots of smoke and making noise to scare off wildlife.

"This has been an inspiring, powerful journey that has

helped me grow and learn about myself," she said. "I hope it has an impact on other people and that I raise enough money to make a difference."

Schackmann said she met a lot of helpful, caring people on her trip, including those who picked her up when her bike broke down, which was usually caused by either a popped chain or broken spokes.

"Strangers took me in and fed me," she said. "I experienced a lot of humanity, which has made me believe again in the kindness of the human spirit."

In Georgetown, Schackmann and Jackson stayed overnight at the Quality Inn on Church Street. She said people in this area have been very supportive of her cause.

"I am compelled to do this because I have witnessed the intimate nature of this disease and the human response to it," she wrote on her crowdwise.com page. "I don't need to explain that HIV knows no boundaries - globally impacting man, women and children, people of all racial, ethnic and socioeconomic backgrounds." HIV, which stands for Human Immunodeficiency Virus, lives in human blood, sexual fluids, and breast milk. It weakens the immune system, so the body has a hard time fighting off common germs, viruses, fungi and other invaders.

AIDS, which stands for Acquired Immune Deficiency Syndrome, is the condition that happens when the immune system stops working and a person gets sick because of HIV. According to the website hiv.gov, an estimated 35 million people have died from AIDS-related illnesses since the start of the epidemic.

According to webmd.com, the infection spreads from person to person when certain body fluids are shared, usually during unprotected sexual intercourse or when sharing drugs injected with needles.

It can also be passed from dirty needles from tattoos and body piercing and can be spread through oral sex, although it is unlikely. A mother can also pass HIV to her child during birth or through breast milk.

According to avert.org, an estimated 36.7 million people in 2016 were living with HIV, including 1.8 million children. Around 30 percent of them did not know that they had the virus.

"This journey is a life journey because you see what stops you in life, what fear holds you back, and what it must be like to live with HIV or any other serious illness," Schackmann said. "It really brings you closer to those living with the threat of diseases like HIV/AIDS and cancer."

People can donate to this cause by visiting <u>Crowdwise.com/Uli's Journey</u>. She has raised $6,000 so far, according to her Crowdrise page.

After the interview, I walked down Front Street and contemplated my journey. What difference had I made? Where and how had I grown? I felt the end approaching, and both sadness and pride filled me. Questions arose. What would come next in my life?

The ride had made me more patient with others. It had made me more aware of both my strengths and my weaknesses. I had learned to face my fears, and I had developed a better understanding of what stops me in life. I had come to realize the power of having a vision and of enrolling others into it. I had learned to trust, to surrender to strangers and situations. My connections to people had deepened, and I was more present to others. I had learned the importance of my support base—my real-life friends and Facebook friends—for getting me through days when I questioned myself. Perhaps most of all, I had come to understand that at our core, people are all the same, and that respect and love for one another will make the difference we so desperately seek.

When I started my journey, I brought to it enthusiasm, vulnerability, trust, connections, love, and surrender. As a result, I created miracles. I cried when I left Alaska and Canada; I felt as if I was leaving something special behind. But upon reentering the United States, I made incredible connections with Sara, Duran, Tom, Gwen, and so many others. It was as if the United States embraced me and welcomed me back. I reconnected to trust, love, and vulnerability.

Then I arrived in West Virginia, and something shifted. My experience became very different. I found myself more guarded and more in judgment of others. When I would tell someone about my ride for a cure for AIDS by 2020, I often got a distant reply along the lines of, "Oh, how nice." No curiosity. No encouragement. No enthusiasm. No respect.

While having dinner alone in Georgetown one evening, I noticed that my waitress was quite absentminded. I overheard the table of women next to me gossiping about her, and they had nothing good to say, even denigrating her body.

After a while of listening, I got up, introduced myself, and told the group about my journey. I also told them that I had felt included in their conversation about our waitress because I was able to hear them without eavesdropping, and since they had proclaimed to be good Southern Christians, I was surprised they would diminish her light rather than try to empower her to let her Christ light shine. I asked if they wouldn't rather share their dreams and visions with one another rather than talking about someone else's body.

They stared at me with confused expressions, so I closed the conversation by asking God to bless and empower them to uplift others. I asked God, too, to allow the food they were about to receive to nourish and heal them. Then I went back to my table. After I sat down, they began whispering, but I couldn't hear their words.

When the waitress came, I paid my bill and tipped her double, afraid the women might not leave a tip for her. Before leaving, I hugged the waitress and implored her to let her light shine, explaining that I believed that when her light shines, so does mine. I left with a sense of boldness and a big smile inside of me.

Georgetown is the third oldest city in the United States, and I enjoyed exploring it. Even though the population is only slightly more than nine thousand people, the city has many historical sites. Several historic plantation houses still stand, including Mansfield Plantation on the banks of the Black River and the Brookgreen Plantation at the center of Brookgreen Gardens Park.

Since the late 20th century, historic societies and independent plantations have worked to present a more authentic view of plantation life, including the experience of African-Americans that were enslaved at the sites. Following the American Revolution, rice surpassed indigo as the staple crop, and it was cultivated in the swampy lowlands along the rivers. Enslaved labor built large dams, gates, and canals to irrigate and drain the rice fields during cultivation. Large rice plantations were established along the five rivers around Georgetown, and planters often brought in slaves from rice-growing regions of West Africa. These slaves knew the technology for cultivation and processing.

The plantations and gardens are magnificent, and I enjoyed the beauty and stillness of the park. It amazed me to think about the enslaved people who created all of it; I wondered about how their lives must've been. They were stolen from their lands, separated from their families, and forced to do hard, brutal labor while suffering a multitude of threats and punishments. Their living conditions were usually horrific, yet they had created a beautiful, awe-inspiring place for which they received little to no credit. The plantations and gardens are presented today as a point of Southern pride rather than an accomplishment of the slaves who built and maintained them.

On Wednesday, August 12, we left Georgetown at 7:30 am with plans to camp thirty-one miles away at Bulls Bay. When weather reports predicted rain at midday and thunderstorms in the late afternoon and evening, I changed my mind and decided to ride fifty-seven miles to Mount Pleasant, hoping to find better shelter there.

The thunder and lightning storms, remnants of Hurricane Harvey, started around 4 pm and were predicted to continue until Sunday night. I resigned myself to not leaving Mount Pleasant until Monday.

I went to dinner at a Mexican food restaurant and met three people who worked there—Sophia, Jose, and Bella. They almost went through my entire photo album and acted so interested in my journey. Jose was engaged to be married in December, and I saw a longing for an adventure in his eyes; he seemed ready to hop on a bike and join me.

Sophia took some items off my bill. Divorced, and with her extended family all living in Mexico, she was raising three children on her own. Because she was a breast cancer survivor and I had a pre-cancer breast surgery we had much to talk about. I tipped her well, and by the time I left, I felt as if I was leaving a good friend behind.

After a good rest, Jackson and I made the most of a beautiful day by going to the Charleston Sea Aquarium. Inspired by a three-year-old girl who fearlessly fed the stingrays, I followed her lead and had the most amazing experience. When it came to stingrays, I had always been afraid of the unknown—the cold, slimy, poisonous ray on the back, the big mouth that could suck your hand in. But the little girl's boldness and joy helped me overcome my feelings of fear; she empowered me. We shared a big high five before parting ways. A person never knows who or what will inspire them. I was glad I had stayed open to the experience; she had given me a gift.

The sea otters couldn't get enough of Jackson. Behind the viewing window, they swam back and forth in front of him. Jackson smelled the glass and looked at them with big eyes, as if wondering what all the fuss was about.

Upstairs, we met a bald eagle named Liberty. After I talked to her, she posed for me. Afterwards, we went to the Fishery Landing, and I treated myself to a glass of wine and local food.

On September 1, Jackson and I spent all day at Patriot Point visiting the Yorktown aircraft carrier, the Laffy Destroyer, and a submarine. I had to carry Jackson up and down all the steep stairs. Few people were there, so I took my time and stayed very present during the amazing experience.

I felt my dad's essence nearby all day. He would have loved visiting Patriot Point, and I would have loved sharing the moment with him. Often, I closed my eyes and felt the energy of the sailors; it was as if I could hear the young men on the vessel. It felt impressive and powerful to stand on the deck of an aircraft carrier and beneath deck on the submarine.

Later in the day, Jackson and I stopped at the Fish House for something to eat. Our waitress, Angela, came from Durbin, South Africa, and we had a wonderful conversation about South Africa, Germany, our native foods, and our U.S. immigration experiences.

Three beautiful African American ladies sat at the table next to me. They were celebrating one woman's birthday, so I had the waitress add their drinks and food to my bill. I had received many gifts in my life and experienced so much goodness on my ride, and I wanted to share.

Jackson and I took an Uber to downtown Charleston the next day and walked around the old town. The cobblestone streets reminded me of my childhood in Germany, while the colorful houses reminded me of the Bahamas.

Filled with good memories and joy, I made my way down to the water and the Pineapple Fountain, where Jackson and I played. He thoroughly enjoyed himself, and so did I, until we got caught in the middle of a major downpour and had to rush back to the motel. My friend Judy Karkhoff had introduced me via phone and text to her best friend, Ardis, who lived in Mt. Pleasant. Ardis and I made dinner arrangements for 5:30 pm, and she picked me up at the motel. We went to a fabulous beachfront restaurant and had the chef's special, a four-course meal that Judy had paid for in advance over the phone. Ardis and I connected right away and shared a wonderful conversation.

That night, I went to bed thinking about how amazing the past couple of days had been.

Sunday, I took Jackson for a long walk by the visitor center and played with him. My heart filled with joy to see him carefree and happy, rolling in the grass and running off leash. Later, we went to the pier and spent some time there.

Back at the motel later, I did my laundry, gave Jackson a bath, packed my saddle bags, and prepared to get back on the road the next day.

At 6:30 that evening, Ardis met me again, and we went to Grace and Grit for another fabulous dinner. It was an enjoyable night.

We left the motel early the next morning. I took Jackson to the pier and visitor center to let him run on the huge, beautiful green lawn there before we took off.

We left for Route 17 at 7:30 am, and we almost made it to the top of the famous bridge—an eight-lane highway—when I heard sirens behind me. Since I didn't see a car in front of me, I knew the officer wanted me to stop. I pulled over and got off the bike.

After greeting him and wishing him a happy and safe Labor Day, I said, "I didn't go over the speed limit, did I?"

Laughing, he told me about a bike path I could use and said that he was worried about my safety. I assured him that I understood, but now that I had made it halfway over the bridge, I didn't have much more to climb before it would be downhill the rest of the way. I told him not to worry; I had been riding on major highways throughout my journey. There was no convincing him, however. He wanted me to turn around, go back to the visitor center, and find my way to the bike path—meaning I would have to climb the bridge again on the other side.

I personally thought it to be much more dangerous for him to drive backwards while escorting me off the bridge than it would be for me to ride the rest of the way across it. Still, I didn't argue, although I wasn't happy that I'd have to climb the bridge again. Fighting frustration, I rode next to him while he drove backward. Just when I thought I had dealt with my impatience, it showed up in my life again to test me.

A powerful wind made riding difficult and slow. My cellphone service flickered in and out, and I lost my navigational system. My

Police officer stopping me on top of a steep bridge. I had to go back.

frustration accelerated, and I reminded myself to let go and surrender to the way things were.

With thunder and lightning storms predicted over the next couple of days, I stopped at Lake Aire Campground and checked in for two nights. After putting up the tent, I covered the top, the floor, the bike, and the trailer with tarps that a camper had left behind. Certain that everything was rain safe, I took Jackson for a walk, and we met a nice group of year-round campers who invited me for a beer and dinner at 5:30.

Jackson and I arrived for dinner and joined the thirteen other campers who had come. I was surprised that everyone there had heard about our trip. Jackson kept our host John company while he grilled, and I shared travel stories.

The women opened up and told me about their lives. One of them, Tammy, was my age and in her third marriage to a man named David, who was also present. Tammy told me about her first marriage and her first child, who was born in 1984 and killed in 1988 when his father beat him to death. After finding him on the floor of her house, Tammy performed CPR on her son then rushed him to the hospital, where he was pronounced dead. Tammy donated his organs to science, and in his memory, she had his image tattooed on her back. She didn't mention what happened to his father, although I'm certain he must've gone to prison.

I also met a woman named Glenda and her husband, John. Glenda talked about her first husband, their abusive relationship, and the pain and suffering she had endured. For too long, she had stayed with the man, wanting the relationship to work, and because she had promised to be married to him "until death do us part." In the end, he became so abusive that she finally left. Glenda was thankful to be away from him. He had gone on to kill his next wife, and he had been on his way to find Glenda and kill her as well when the police arrested him. He went to prison on a life sentence.

Another woman at the dinner, who I'll call "Z" to protect her identity, told me she had been married for twenty-three years, and she and her husband had a fourteen-year-old son. When Z was twenty-two years old, her twenty-five-year-old sister was found dead in the trunk of her car, murdered by her husband. Z and her husband lived in Georgia at the time. The day before the murder, they had driven to South Carolina to surprise her sister with a visit. Z's sister was happy to see her, and the two young women spent the afternoon together. But when Z's sister suggested they have drinks at a bar that evening, Z said she was too tired from the long drive, and they made plans to get together the next morning.

Morning came, but Z did not hear from her sister and couldn't reach her by phone. Z and her husband picked up the sister's children

Campground in South Carolina with very friendly campers

and drove around, searching for the sister's car. They found it, and Z's husband opened the trunk and discovered his sister-in-law's body. The family suspected the sister's husband had killed her since he had a history of domestic violence. Due to a lack of evidence, however, he was not initially arrested or charged.

Time passed. Z's brother-in-law remarried three times, with each relationship showing signs of domestic violence. He received a five-year prison sentence for one incident but was released after three years on good behavior. In 2018, he overdosed on meth and died. In 2019, a home video surfaced of the party that Z's sister had attended on the night of her death, providing new witnesses to what took place. The case was reopened and was still being investigated at the time I met Z.

The dinner ended. After saying goodnight to everyone, Z asked me over to her camp for coffee, and we continued our conversation. We talked at length about her anger, fear, and violent feelings toward her former brother-in-law, even after his death. Z mentioned that she had sought therapy to work on those issues and to help her work through her grief over her sister's murder, her mother's recent death from cancer, another sister's death by heart attack, and her brother's suicide. Diagnosed with PTSD, she suffered from nightmares and feared going to sleep.

Z shared with me that when she was a teenager, her oldest sister's husband had molested and raped her, and it had taken a long time for her to find the courage to tell her mother and her sister. At that time, Z got involved with an older man, hoping that if she had a boyfriend, her brother-in-law would leave her alone. She got pregnant, and her older sister helped her to get an abortion, for which she still felt guilt and shame. I reminded her that she had been a child, and that a pedophile had manipulated and abused her.

When Z met Mike, her husband of twenty-three years and a calm, kind, generous, and loving soul, she knew that he was the one for her.

We finished our coffee. Z asked if I had any food with me at my camp, and I told her I didn't. She invited me for dinner the following night, and I accepted.

At 6:18 the next evening, Z called to make sure Jackson and I were coming, and we made our way over to her campsite and ate. Z said that the next day, she would be meeting with the prosecutor working on her murdered sister's case. She was nervous about seeing the video of the party her sister attended on the night of her death, and she didn't want to go through that alone. Her husband, Mike, had declined her request that he go with her; he had found her sister's body and didn't want to relive that horror. Z had asked a few friends to accompany her, but they had also declined. It seemed that no one wanted to dig up pain from the past.

"You are a wise woman," Z said to me. "I need someone like you to support me. Would you consider staying an extra day or two and go with me? By then, we'll also have a better idea about Hurricane Irma's route."

I sensed that she desperately wanted and needed me with her at the meeting with the prosecutor, and I didn't hesitate to agree to her request. We had only known each other a few hours, yet she had requested my support. How could I refuse? I considered the request a compliment and an honor. How many times had friends called on me for support in the past, but I was too busy or didn't want to get involved? How many times had friends refused to support me for the same reasons? One thing that I had learned on my cross-country journey was that nothing is more important than being present to help another human being in need. Many strangers had assisted me in my times of need on the trip. I now had an opportunity to do the same for a stranger. What a beautiful, powerful gift to be asked into someone's life in such an important way.

"You can count on me," I said. "I'll do my best to support you with grace, strength, and without judgement."

Z promised to remain open to counsel and said she would let go of the case if it became obvious that the evidence would not be enough for a conviction.

That night, I thought about all Z had told me about her life. Although she obviously had major grief and anger issues, she was a loving, intuitive, sensitive, and caring young woman. All the folks I had met at the campground were poor, yet most had been generous with me and authentic, like Z. They had shared not only their food, but the intimate details of their lives. Friends I had known for years had not shared as much about themselves.

For example, two brothers lived in a tent shelter behind my camp. One brother worked, while the other stayed at the campground all day due to a disability. They had lost everything—wives, family, houses, jobs—and were trying to rebuild their lives. The brother that worked took care of the disabled brother. I was astounded at their willingness to share their pain and suffering with me in such a profound way.

Ironically, all the people I met at the campground said that they voted for Trump. Z admitted that she regretted her vote for him; I wasn't sure about the others. Although they were kind and welcoming to me, some displayed an abundance of pent-up, misguided anger and rage. One woman talked in length about her frustration with Black people and their desire for "special rights." I listened, then tried to reason with her, explaining that my experience with Black friends and acquaintances was quite the opposite of what she described. I was relieved and pleased when several others in the group agreed with me.

Z had loaned me a big fan and extension cord for my hot, humid tent. It made sleeping much more comfortable for Jackson and me. Jackson had panted hard throughout the previous night, and I had slept topless, but sweat had drenched me, nonetheless.

Settled atop my sleeping bag with the fan blowing a nice breeze over us, I suddenly felt something curled up beneath me. Afraid it might be a snake, I pushed Jackson closer to the door. Before I could make my way to the door as well, I felt the "thing" move again beneath me. Definitely a snake.

My heart pounded as I put my flashlight in my mouth and grabbed my knife. Then I moved the sleeping bag zipper down slowly until I reached the snake. Pausing, I watched for movement. Nothing. I thought maybe the snake had died.

I proceeded with caution, anticipating the emergence of the snake at any moment, imagining it striking out at me. I wanted to scream, to run out of the tent, but I was afraid to startle it. Knife in hand, I pulled the last inch of the zipper down to where the snake lay curled.

The bag opened. I stared down at a twisted inner zipper—not a snake. Relieved, I laughed out loud. I thought of the many times my mind made up stories, and I went along, convinced the stories were true. Like the woman who had convinced herself that Black people posed a threat to her, my imagination often held me hostage, a prisoner to my fears.

Realizing we all have "snakes" in our minds, unfounded stories we've made up and persuaded ourselves to believe, I stretched out again, laughing and crying at once. My body relaxed as I released the adrenaline that had coursed through every fiber of my being. How many more snakes did I need to face and overcome? Far fewer than when I'd started my journey.

The next morning, I joined Z to visit the prosecutor and the detective working her sister's case. While she spoke with them, I stayed behind in the visiting room and concentrated on her, meditating and sending strength.

After a couple of hours, Z emerged and told me she had mixed feelings. She had watched the video from the party her sister attended on her last night alive; it was the first time Z had seen it. She had loved seeing her sister—her smile, her playfulness and joy. However, certain things Z witnessed in the video made her angry.

We talked for quite a while, and Z allowed me to support her. I took her to lunch, and she shared more about her experience watching the video and talking to the prosecutor and detective. Apparently, they still didn't have enough evidence to charge her sister's ex-husband for murder, and that disappointed Z.

After we returned to camp, Jackson and I spent a quiet afternoon and evening. I went to the gas station, bought food for us, and walked around. I would leave the campsite the next day.

Chapter 20

Hurricane Irma

I got up very early and packed the bicycle. When ready, I went over to see Z to say goodbye and have coffee. We had been tracking Irma, and it looked as if the hurricane had turned course and was now expected to impact South Carolina. I started to freak out when many campers approached to warn me to get out of South Carolina as fast as possible. I saw other campers packing up trailers and fifth wheels, bringing in flowerpots and grills, and making evacuation plans.

Z and I called a few car rental places, trying to find a vehicle for me; I would need one to drive away from the storm. We found the last small SUV available and immediately left for the Charleston airport to pick it up. Due to the unreliability of my cell phone navigation, I made sure the Nissan Pathfinder had a navigational system.

After Z drove me to the airport and I got the Pathfinder, I followed her back to camp. Once there, I packed the vehicle with Jackson's trailer, the carrier, four saddle bags, and the flag. Everything fit nicely inside.

Unsure of what direction I should head, I called friends in Atlanta, but they already had a full house of evacuees from Florida. After I hung up, my friend Cyndi called to check on me and find out my plans for outrunning the hurricane. She had already evacuated to Alabama and was staying with her second family, Greg and Edith. Greg and Edith invited me to come and stay with them as well.

I left the campground around 11:30 am and rode mostly on back roads with a speed limit of sixty miles per hour. I followed the navigational system and made frequent calls to Cyndi to check in. At 10:30 pm, I arrived in Alabama, exhausted and grateful to be in a safe, warm place and out of harm's way. People crowded the house. I met my generous host, Greg, and hostess, Edith, and everyone else who had come from Florida to escape Irma.

Greg and Edith told me they had a son who lived nearby, and he also hosted a family member from Florida at his house. The close connection between their family members impressed me, and I found their willingness to love, care, and share with friends and strangers amazing. I felt so thankful to them and to Cyndi for contacting me and inviting me into their home.

Outer bands of Hurricane Irma

Greg and Edith expected more friends and family from Florida to arrive during the night, so Cyndi and I made beds for the crowd, allowing for two to four people in each room. As I settled in with Cyndi in Greg's office—our makeshift bedroom—I thought about the friends I'd made at the campground: the two brothers who were camped behind me, Glenda, Tammy, and Z. I wondered if they had left yet and if they were safe. I hoped that someone had reached out to help them, too.

Nobody could sleep. We all gathered in front of the television to watch Irma approach the Caribbean and Florida and then head north along the East Coast. Watching the storm unfold was heart wrenching, and we didn't go to bed until early morning. Late arrivals trickled in during the night, all of them exhausted, relieved to be safe, and telling stories of evacuating Florida. They had had to deal with a gas shortage and horrific traffic jams.

Early the next morning, a couple named Angel and Anthony arrived with their two children, Stella and Charlotte. Although an outsider, I felt accepted by the large extended family gathered at the house. Everyone, including me, pitched in to show love and comfort to the children. We also came up with an activity and eating schedule that allowed for the large number of people and our varying diets.

In the end, fifteen humans, two dogs, and one cat found shelter with Greg and Edith, and another ten humans at their son's house. After four days, everyone left to make their way slowly back home, uncertain what awaited them in the aftermath of the hurricane.

I rented a small SUV to return to South Carolina and continue my journey from where I'd left off. Greg and Edith's son-in-law, Richard, needed a ride to Atlanta to catch a flight to Miami, so he came along with me.

After a seven-hour drive, with a quick stop at the Atlanta airport, I arrived in Savannah and got a motel room for the night. The next morning, I unloaded the car and drove it to the rental place at the Savannah airport to turn it in. Then I took an Uber back to the motel.

I decided to spend some time exploring the city. I needed to process everything that had happened over the past few weeks, as it all felt surreal. The people I had met at the campground with their amazing and vulnerable stories, the hurricane, the evacuation, and the new friends I had made in Alabama—so much had taken place in such a short time.

Jackson and I left Savannah early the next morning, and it was good to be on my bike again. Back on Route 17 and headed south, I became emotional; I felt a sense of freedom to be riding again, but the fact that I approached Florida and my journey's end weighed on my mind. I also felt enormous empathy for the people in the Keys and the Caribbean who had lost everything in the hurricane and would have to find a way to rebuild their lives. Irma took so much from so many.

Again, thoughts of my newfound friends from the Lake Aire Campground plagued me. I worried about them and hoped they were safe. I thought, too, about the new friends I had just left behind in Alabama, and tears streaked down my face, making it difficult for me to see clearly.

I wasn't sure what I was feeling, or why. So much had happened on my journey. I had made many friends and had shared deeply with many of them. Maybe my tears were because the ride would soon end, and I'd leave them all behind. Or maybe it was more than that—a combination of external and internal changes.

I had come to realize much about myself. For one thing, I didn't like who I became around certain people, especially strangers with an attitude. I thought back to some of them that I'd met on this trip: the casino/coffee shop owner who had not wanted me inside his establishment; the group of elderly seniors at breakfast one morning who badmouthed immigrants, gays, and liberals; the young camper who I'd yelled at when he and his partner talked loudly and cursed throughout the night. I reflected on those experiences and the people in them, and I regretted how some of those situations had played out. Whenever I encountered rude or impatient people, I often struggled to stand in patience, love, empathy, and power. And I often judged them harshly.

As I rode and reflected, I continued to cry. I wished for a shoulder to lean on. I wanted to rest in another person's arms and be reassured that everything would be okay. I thought I might be dying. My heart felt different lately; it worried me.

On television at a Waffle House, I watched news of a police officer being found guilty of shooting an unarmed Black man and planting a gun in the victim's car. Astounded, I understood the distrust Blacks felt toward white people.

I looked around the restaurant at the mostly Black faces and felt I was being evaluated, as if everyone wondered if I was a Trump supporter. I hoped they didn't think I was. I almost felt guilty making eye contact and smiling.

A nearby little girl, about two years old, initiated a conversation with me. When the girl's mother learned that my birthday was the same day as her husband's, she treated me like someone special. Relief flooded through me. I hoped she and her family knew that every white person is not a white supremacist. I hoped they could see that I'm not hateful.

What I saw on the news and in some people saddened me greatly. People claimed to want peace, love, and happiness, but many of those same people exhibited judgment, hatred, impatience, and rudeness. Our president made vulgar behavior acceptable to many.

I wished people could understand peace starts with each of us. What we put out into the Universe with our words, actions, and social media posts sets a tone for others. If I'm upset and use the "F-word," I'm not creating peace, love, connection, or happiness. I'm, instead, creating a disconnect. Change in the world starts when we change ourselves.

Jackson had diarrhea during the night. Thankful that Dr. Cords from Gentle Care Animal Hospital had made a first aid kit for Jackson to take on our trip, I cleaned up the bathroom floor and Jackson's behind, then gave him some medicine.

It was the morning of September 15, and we left the motel at 7:00 am, stopping at Starbucks for coffee and a scone. Twenty minutes later, we rode through town to Route 17. Along the way, I stopped at a produce stand and chatted with a nice farmer who gave us a cold bottle of water. I asked for directions to Midway, and he suddenly pulled a knife. Startled, I quickly put my hand on my own knife and stared at him with big eyes. Without a word, he bent down and started using the knife to draw a map in the sand. I released an inheld breath and relaxed.

The farmer reminded me of a wilderness scout. I bought a fresh tomato from him and ate it, enjoying the juice that ran down my fingers. We hugged, and I thanked him as he wished me well on my journey.

We arrived at the Midway Motel, and the owner, Rümmesh, greeted me. He explained that the credit card machine was broken and requested that I pay in cash, which I didn't have. I told him I could write a check. He insisted on cash, and I gave him a pleading look. I didn't want to get back on the road in the sweltering heat.

He studied me, then Jackson, and said, "You are a good person, and you are my guest." Rümmesh drove me into town to the nearest ATM. After I paid him in cash, we went back to the motel, and Jackson and I settled into our room.

A short while later, I became bored and went outside. Rümmesh and his wife were pulling tape off all the windows that had been used to put up protection during Hurricane Irma. I offered to help them, happy when they accepted my offer; I wanted to give them the gift of my assistance to thank them for their kindness.

After we finished, Jackson and I stayed in for the night.

I didn't have coffee or breakfast before setting out, and I rode thirty-seven miles before stopping at a gas station in Darien. A guy there named Loren was working on a white bicycle. We struck up a conversation, and I ended up fixing his tire. While I worked, we chatted. I told him about my ride from Alaska to Key West.

"I left Key West just before Hurricane Irma hit," he told me. "I've been on the road for the last three weeks."

"Where are you headed?" I asked.

"Savannah. I'm hoping to start over there," Loren said.

I noticed he wore a backpack. A duffle bag hung over his bicycle handlebars. "Where have you been staying at night?"

"Wherever I can. Last night, I slept for a few hours at a shopping center parking lot until the bugs got too much for me." He glanced at my bike, at Jackson. "So, what inspired you to ride from Alaska to Key West?"

"I'm riding to bring awareness to AIDS and to promote finding a cure by 2020," I explained.

Loren's eyes widened. "My partner died of AIDS. I not only lost him, I lost part of myself when he died."

He seemed astounded that I rode to bring awareness to the condition that had taken his partner and said that he counted himself lucky that I had stopped. Our meeting, he said, had briefly brought his partner back to him.

Loren proceeded to tell everyone pulling into the gas station about my mission. Some of them shook my hand and took photos. Before leaving, I took a picture of Loren and I together. He had reminded me why I was riding.

That evening, I checked into a cheap motel. After taking Jackson for a walk and tending to his needs, I discovered that the bathroom had a tub with jets. I filled it to the brim, turned on the jets, then soaked and relaxed for the longest time. What a treat! When I finally emerged from the tub, my skin looked shriveled up, like a sea monster.

After I dressed, Jackson and I made our way to the nearest restaurant, Ruby Tuesday, where I told the waitress about our travels. Soon, the manager and the rest of the staff came by to meet me, although they seemed more interested in Jackson. Everyone wanted to hear about our journey, and while I relayed my story of the struggles and successes of living out my dream, I saw in their eyes that they also had dreams and knew struggles and successes.

One woman, Sandy, joined me at the table while she took her break. It was nice to have company, and I listened as she told me about her life. She had started as a waitress at the restaurant and was now a manager. Years ago, she had chosen to have a mastectomy after being diagnosed pre-cancerous, like me. She had two sons, and before her divorce, they had lived with her in Tennessee, and she had worked long hours to help pay the rent and provide for their needs. But when she and her husband split up, he took the boys, left Tennessee, and moved to Georgia to raise them.

Sometime after the boys left, Sandy decided she was ready to start dating. Her first date was with a co-worker she had known for seven years. They ended up getting married and had been together for six happy years. She was content in her relationship, but life still wasn't always easy for Sandy.

"Two years ago," she explained, "I got a call that my son Karl was found unconscious in a motel room in New York. He had overdosed on heroine. A friend offered to pay for my plane ticket, and I flew out there.

When Sandy arrived at the hospital, she couldn't comprehend that her son was brain dead and on life support from a drug overdose. He had worked as a boat captain in Georgia, fishing for crab and grouper. She was forced to make the difficult decision to "pull the plug" on his life support. Afterward, Sandy learned that Karl was an organ donor. After his organs were harvested, she had her son cremated and the ashes sent to her.

At Karl's memorial service, his ex-girlfriend showed up and told Sandy that she was a grandmother. The girlfriend had never told Karl that he had a son. "Suddenly, I was mourning my son's death and celebrating my grandson's birth at the same time," said Sandy.

Sometime later, she received a couple of letters from people who had received Karl's organs. "It made me happy to know that his spirit lives on in other people," she said.

Sandy and her husband eventually bought a trailer and parked it near the place her two-year-old grandson lives and the marshes where Karl used to fish.

Sandy and I were both in tears by the time I finished my meal. She said she thinks we were meant to meet each other—that God sent me to her so that she could hear my story and learn about my journey; she needed to hear it, she said. We hugged before I left, and I went back to the motel feeling honored to have met such a determined, strong, loving woman.

I decided to stay another day in Darien. The motel's beautiful jet tub had helped me feel so much better the night before, and I looked forward to another soak.

It was Jackson's birthday. We went for a walk at a nearby mall parking lot where he was free to run and play. The mall had been beautifully designed. High-end retailers had once occupied the space, but only three stores remained open now. I spoke with the maintenance guy, who shared with me that the economy in town had not recovered since 2008.

While Jackson and I spent time there, a military convoy was using the empty parking lot as a refueling station, and a second convoy from Charleston, South Carolina, arrived. They were returning from their mission in Tampa, Florida, after Irma's landfall. I started a conversation with some of the soldiers, and they told me that over thirty thousand military personnel from South Carolina were in Florida. I saluted and thanked them for their service, then informed them it was Jackson's birthday and told them about our journey. Some of the guys wished Jackson a happy birthday and expressed their awe over what we were doing.

Later, back at the motel, I packed and prepared for the next day, then took another bubble bath, relaxing my sore body. When I finished,

Military convoy

I dressed, and we returned to Ruby Tuesday, where the girls on staff brought Jackson a grilled chicken breast for his birthday dinner. He was one happy camper, my Jackson.

We left early in the morning. I made good time and stopped after a while at an empty field to stretch and give Jackson some play time. After a few minutes, I was ready to take off again, but Jackson cried out, as if in pain. Upon closer inspection, I saw that little thorns were embedded in his coat. It hurt him terribly when I tried to pull them out, so I found his comb and used it to dislodge the thorns. It took more than thirty minutes to clean him up, and because of my poor posture while doing so, my back hurt afterward.

Once we got on the road, I realized we were barely moving and shifted gears. It didn't help. The wind blew against us from the south, making for tough riding. A horn blared behind me. A glance back alerted me to a pickup truck on my tail. Because the highway was only two lanes with little shoulder at the side and a lot of oncoming traffic, the truck couldn't pass me. The driver blasted his horn non-stop until he finally had an opportunity to pass.

As the driver came up alongside me, he yelled curse words out his window. Impatient and frustrated, I yelled back at him using similar language, despite my earlier commitment to handle such situations in a more mindful way. I felt a little better afterward but feared he might wait for me down the road and either hit me with his car or beat the shit out of me.

I brought my attention back to the road ahead. Roadkill littered Route 17. I saw a cute otter, lots of turtles, raccoons, parsons, birds, seagulls, and many armadillos lying dead along the way.

I had planned to ride thirty-seven miles to Woodbine and then another six miles outside of town to camping accommodations. But time passed quickly, and the heat was unbearable. I had traveled only about twenty miles, although it felt like fifty, when I came upon a motel. Weary, I stopped and checked in.

I didn't waste any time before heading for the hot tub and pool. Once in the hot tub, I discovered that the jets didn't work correctly. Water spewed out of the tub when I turned them on. The pool looked dirty, and the hot tub smelled strongly of chlorine. Disappointed, I returned to my room and took a hot bath, followed by a nap with Jackson.

A phone call from my tenant back in Florida woke me up. I had forgotten to send a check to Mike, my AC guy, for repairing the air-conditioner after Irma hit Florida, and my tenant told me the air-conditioner wasn't working. I ended the call and made my way to the motel's front desk to ask if I could buy an envelope and a stamp. The two ladies behind the desk smirked and told me no. I didn't respond to their rudeness. Instead, I found another employee who gave me directions to the nearest store, where I purchased what I needed.

Back in my room, I wrote Mike a check and put it in the envelope to mail; then Jackson and I went out for dinner at a little seafood shack where I drank two margaritas and pondered the difference in yesterday and today, the people with whom I'd interacted, and my motel facilities. Maybe it's true that you have to experience some "bad" to fully appreciate the "good."

That night, September 19, I went to sleep realizing that five and a half months before, I had started my six-thousand-mile adventure in Anchorage. I couldn't believe I was almost to Florida. What a journey it had been. I was in awe of how far I had come.

I had raised almost ten thousand dollars for AIDS research, met amazing people, and faced physical and emotional challenges. I had faced many of my fears, stood in trust, surrendered, and experienced miracles. I had become more flexible and softer with myself and others. I had learned to let go and live with minimal things, creating freedom and openness. I had faced loneliness and become more comfortable with myself. I had invited others into my circle, witnessed their light, and realized their contribution to my life. Physically, the journey had been very challenging, but I felt fortunate and blessed by every experience along the way.

Jackson and I continued our journey south. Roadkill still littered the road, but not as much as before. I didn't see any armadillos, but I did spot six rattlesnakes. I avoided the right shoulder of the road as much as possible and refrained from stopping, fearing a rattlesnake might be nearby.

Jackson needed to pee but had to hold it while I looked for a good place for him to go. Soon, I found the perfect spot at a fire station. We stopped, and he made use of the open space that was free of prickers and snakes.

While Jackson explored, a fireman named Bruce came over and

asked if we needed anything. He had been inventorying an ambulance when he noticed us. After I told him my story, he went inside the station to get some cold water for Jackson and me to drink.

Afternoons were unbearably hot on the road, and I knew the time had come to think about finding shelter for the night, but I wanted to take a picture with Bruce before we left. He agreed. He went back inside the station to get the rest of the crew to come out so they could all be in the photograph. I learned that some of the guys were with the National Guard, and they had recently returned from the Florida Keys where they had helped to clean up the devastation caused by Hurricane Irma. They were all friendly and interested in my mission, and we chatted for almost half an hour. Their wonderful, encouraging support made my day.

Jackson and I left, continuing our ride on Route 17. The brutal heat from the glaring sun soon weakened and nauseated me to the point that I found pushing forward difficult. Just when I thought I couldn't go on any longer, a little country bar appeared up ahead on my left. Relieved, I stopped and went inside to get water. When I opened the door, a cool breeze from the air-conditioner greeted me; it felt wonderful.

The few patrons inside turned to look at me as I entered and made my way to the bar. Since I felt guilty asking for free water, I ordered a cold beer and was glad I did after taking the first sip. It tasted delicious, and I felt my body relax as I began to cool down. I stayed inside the establishment for about an hour, chatting with the bartender and some of the guys sitting nearby while my temperature normalized.

When I told the bartender about my ride and mentioned the many rattlesnakes I had noticed earlier on the road, she told me that her kids had found a snake on their trampoline the day before. They scooped up their two puppies and ran inside the house. Later that night, her husband found a live alligator in the backyard. He killed it, and they now had gator meat in the freezer.

Eager to get back to my bike and back on the road, I asked about the distance to the nearest town and accommodations for the night and learned I had only a few miles to go. I said my goodbyes, but the heat hit me hard when I opened the door and walked outside. Jackson and I pushed on and soon found our next motel. We checked in and then went out for an early dinner. Later, I went to bed with the goal of reentering my home state of Florida the next day.

Chapter 20

Homecoming

Sadness about all the turmoil around the world overcame me as I watched the news the next morning. My heart broke for Mexico, Puerto Rico, and some of the other islands facing another category 4-5 hurricane. Texas and Florida were still in recovery and cleanup mode after experiencing Harvey and Irma. I said a silent prayer, sending strength, light, courage, empowerment, and love to all affected.

Leaving Kingsland, Georgia, soon after watching the news, I started off for Jacksonville. The many abandoned homes and farms along the way presented a sobering testament to the fact that the economy had not recovered in Georgia, along with other parts of the South. I wondered who had lived and worked in the now-deserted places I passed. Why had they failed? What had been missing? The many downed trees along the way, uprooted by Irma, added to my

"Welcome to Florida" sign

dismay. I rode hard, the wind at my back pushing me forward through my sadness and on into Florida.

At the outskirts of Jacksonville, I stopped at a gas station to get a cold drink. As I started for the door to go inside, a homeless man stopped me.

"This is a bad neighborhood, lady," he said. "You better get your ass out of here quick as you can."

I smiled at him. "Thanks for the warning."

He glanced at my bicycle, then gave me directions to I-95.

"I promise I'll leave just as a soon as I buy myself something to drink," I said, nodding at him, wondering if he really thought I'd be riding my bike on the interstate.

Later that day, I had no luck finding a cheap motel on Route 17. I rode on into Jacksonville, making my way through the grim, deteriorated neighborhoods. At a stop light, a man and a woman, both as downtrodden as the area, walked over to me and struck up a conversation. I raised my voice to be heard over the noise of the street.

After we chatted a while, they both gave me a thumbs-up, and the man asked, "Would you want to marry me?"

Laughing, I shook my head and gestured at the woman beside him, then at Jackson. "I think we're both already taken." They laughed with me as the light turned green, and I took off, waving at them.

The traffic was so dense it almost overwhelmed me, and I was nervous as I headed over the bridge leading into downtown. Relieved to see a Doubletree Hotel up ahead, I searched for access to the entrance and found it after a few minutes, only to be told when I went inside that they didn't have a room available. One of the clerks called a nearby Hampton Inn for me, and they said they had an available room. I thanked the Doubletree clerk, left, and rode over to the Hampton. The man behind the counter must've thought me a sad and pitiful sight; he took sixty dollars off my bill. I was so exhausted, overwhelmed, and teary-eyed, if he would've asked for three hundred dollars for the night,

I would've paid it without a second thought. I was beyond ready to be done for the day.

After getting settled in my room, I went outside and wiped down my bike with a damp cloth. Then I showered and taped my eyeglasses together. Earlier, I had broken them in half at the nose piece. It had been a very long ride and a very long day.

We left Jacksonville before seven the next morning. Before leaving, I had applied ointment all over my body to prepare my sore muscles for the forty-mile journey ahead of me.

As I rode, the flag on my bicycle gently caressed my cheeks. I felt embraced by the many souls for whom I rode. The wind picked up, and the gentle touch of the flag became a hard slap to my face and shoulders. I pushed on and arrived in St. Augustine, Florida, around one o'clock that afternoon in the middle of a rainstorm. The rain had soaked through my saddle bag protection and had managed to get

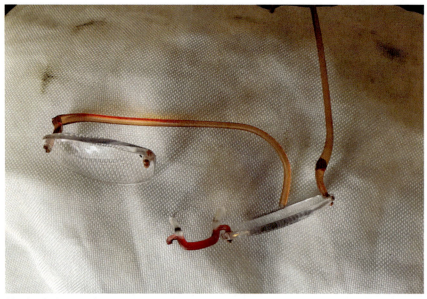

My broken eyeglasses

inside Jackson's trailer. We were both dripping wet by the time we made it to my friend Rosita's front door. I was happy to be home in Florida, yet a part of me longed to turn around and make the trip all over again. The journey had been amazing and powerful, and I reminded myself that it wasn't over yet; Jackson and I still had six hundred miles left to go.

After a warm welcome from Rosita, I took a quick, warm shower and emerged feeling like a different person.

Rosita's friend Cynthia had lived in the guest room with her cat since her house had flooded during Irma; it was the second time a hurricane had flooded her house—first Hurricane Matthew, and now Irma. Cynthia and her cat would be staying with Rosita until her home was made livable again. She spent her weekends and a few hours after work on weekdays getting her house ready, and she was still trying to get help from FEMA and her insurance company. Because Cynthia occupied the guest room, Jackson and I slept on the sofa bed.

I felt blessed by Rosita's friendship. She had been my rock since the day we met back in 2002 at WLRN, a public radio and TV station in Miami. I planned to stay with her in St. Augustine for at least a week. The bike needed a good tune up and some repair work. Jackson needed a good grooming. And I needed some rest and spoiling by my friend.

Despite my exhaustion, I slept very little my first night on Rosita's sofa bed. Jackson and Jack, Rosita's cat, took up much of the space, and I couldn't quiet my mind. I couldn't believe I was back in Florida. I missed the quiet peacefulness of the north; I had such a deep yearning within me for peace and quiet.

Lately, I had been dreaming about Alaska. Something elusive called out to me, attempting to draw me away from the busyness, the bars, the partying, and the congestion of the city. I longed for adventure, stillness, and isolation.

Earlier than expected, Cynthia moved back to her house, and Jackson and I moved into Rosita's guest room.

The days passed quietly. Rosita took me to a free live concert where we saw two different bands, and I met her friend Bernie. On Saturday, Rosita went to the Unitarian Universalist Fellowship of St. Augustine, a dynamic, loving community that nurtures spirit, mind, and ethical action. Guided by principles of liberal faith, Unitarians serve their congregation and the greater community. I'm also a Unitarian, and I would have loved to go with Rosita, but she had a long meeting afterward, so I decided to stay home.

I took Jackson for a long walk at the park. Out in nature, watching him play, I felt connected to God, a part of everything; I am always moved by nature. Afterward, I went to Publix and bought hummus, pomegranate seeds, and kefir. I was in heaven.

A couple of days later, I dropped my bicycle off at a bike store for repairs. It needed a new chain and a cassette that would have to be ordered. I bought new shirts and pants at a second-hand store and took Jackson to PetSmart to be groomed.

I was starting to feel weird and out of sorts, restless to get back on the road, but also happy to be going home. The energy around me seemed static, thick, and harsh. I picked up on it and became irritable. Aware of the negative changes taking place in me, I meditated and spoke to my angels, asking about the source of my foul mood. Answers came to me. All the people I had met on my journey were reflections of God. Through them, I had experienced his gifts of generosity, kindness, and love. However, now that my journey had stalled, I felt a disconnect, judgment, an absence of love. I received a message through my meditation: Bring the light. If I am light and love, it will reflect in others since we are all reflections of one another, even the parts we don't like

The next day, I took my blood pleasure. 139/87. My heart dropped. I needed to make some changes. My bike was back from the shop, and I would leave Rosita's the next day, October 2, to resume my ride.

Leaving just outside of Saint Augustine

News about the shootings that took place at a music festival in Las Vegas added to my sad and restless mood. I longed for uplifting words for myself and the world, but I couldn't find them. Once again, I vowed to show more compassion and patience toward others and to let everyone's light shine, including my own.

I resumed my journey with a heavy heart, questioning the significance of my ride. Did it really make any difference in the state of the world? Remembering the message received through my meditation, I tried not to despair and told myself that the world needs me and my light. I would stand in my power, stand in kindness, and let my light shine.

On October 4, I rode to Port Orange, just south of Daytona. After several stops at various motels that had no vacancy, I continued south until I finally found a room at the Scoot Inn, a biker motel. The owner's wife looked at Jackson and said, "I don't know about the dog. Wait for my husband."

When her husband, Mike, came out to talk to me, I told him about our journey.

"I'll give you and Jackson a room just because of what you've accomplished on your bike."

Mike rode his motorcycle long distances, yet he was totally impressed with my six-thousand-mile bicycle journey.

Happy to have a room, I showered and washed off my bike outfit. Then I walked to a fun little nearby restaurant for dinner. Two beautiful girls greeted us when Jackson and I walked in. I shared

Laundry day

stories about our travels, and the girls, Shyla and Ashlyne, treated Jackson and me like VIPs.

Mike, the guy from the biker motel, saw us off safely the next morning, and we rode forty-two miles through severe rainstorms and wind. We spent the night in a motel in Titusville. I made good use of their laundry facility.

I fell asleep thinking about the many fears I'd faced on my journey in order to grow. Bears, cougars, moose, calving elk, snakes, the Canadian Rockies, congested traffic, getting lost, bike breakdowns, extreme temperatures, storms, and high winds. All the while, I said, "Bring it on." Nothing stopped me. Playing small or thinking I'm not good enough would not get me through. The Universe put me in situations that forced me to show up, act powerful, and push through the fear.

I believed the Universe delighted in my strength, my power, and my shining bright light. I trusted and allowed it to guide me. I wished everyone knew of the beauty, strength, and power all humans hold within themselves.

Resuming my ride, I met Hassan, a handsome, peaceful man with blue eyes and black curly hair. He had been in the United States for fifteen years. A divorced father of one child, he claimed that he and his ex were good parents, despite their separation. They taught their child many good values, and both were proud of their son. Hassan owned a shoe repair shop, and he refereed high school and college soccer games in the evenings and on weekends. After his divorce, Hassan bought a nice sailboat and sailed around the world for two years. Upon his return, he created a partnership with his ex-wife, and they committed to raise their son to become the best he could be.

Hassan's story inspired me and made me realize that a person doesn't need to ride six thousand miles or climb Mount Everest to face their inner self. Being authentic with yourself and the people in your life can be an even more powerful journey.

Beautiful skies and a light breeze greeted us the next morning. We stopped at a little local diner, and I ordered one egg, grits, sausage, an English muffin, and a cup of hot coffee. The temperature climbed steadily when I resumed my trek, and I made several pit stops at gas stations. I also stopped at a church along the way so that Jackson and I could cool off.

We passed Rockledger later in the day. Excitement spiked my adrenaline as I realized how close to Melbourne we were. I had travelled forty-eight miles since breakfast.

While waiting on a red light, a driver in a vehicle on my right gave me a thumbs up, and an older couple in a big SUV smiled so wide at me that they made my heart sing. When the light changed, I continued riding on US-1. I passed another SUV parked in a lot on my right, and the driver waved me over. He and the woman with him appeared to be elderly, so I stopped and greeted them. They had heard about my ride and recognized me. Inspired by my effort, they made a U-turn when they spotted me so that they could meet me. The man gave me some money to buy lunch. Touched by the gift, I smiled and thanked them before taking off again.

Later that day, I had dinner at the Double Tapp Grill, a restaurant next door to my motel and another establishment called The Family Shooting Center. A cute woman carrying a huge gun walked by my table.

"Are you going to shoot us with your gun?" I asked in a teasing tone, glancing at Jackson, then back to her.

She smiled. "No. This is my boss's gun."

The woman continued walking out to her car, returning a minute later carrying a big bow. She explained that The Family Shooting Center had repaired both weapons, then told me she deer hunts and that she skins her kill and eats the meat.

While processing her statement, I heard the man at the table next to me talking aloud to himself. He appeared to be receiving a lot of text messages that irritated him. "I wish everyone would just leave me alone," he mumbled.

After overhearing a few of the man's loud outbursts, I caught his attention. "What's troubling you, sir?"

"People keep texting me. I just want peace and quiet right now."

I smiled gently. "You have choices, you know."

"If you mean I could say not to text me, I can't do that," he said gruffly. "Most of the texts are from a woman I've dated for two months."

"Oh, really?"

He nodded. "The first month we were together was awesome, but now everything about me is wrong, as far as she's concerned."

"That's too bad," I said, sincerely sad for him. "If you don't mind me asking, what do you want from this relationship?"

He shrugged. "I don't know. Just a partner, I guess. Doesn't pay to be picky. There aren't enough good women out there to go around, ya know."

"So, you're settling?" When he didn't respond, I asked, "What would you be committed to creating in this relationship? Would you commit to creating fun? Happiness? How about trust, ease, and vulnerability?"

He looked at me like I had two heads. "I want all that, but even if I committed to creating it, it wouldn't work. She finds fault with everything I do."

"Maybe she feels insecure and needs a little support," I said. "Could you give her that?"

He looked away for a minute. When he faced me again, he said, "I never thought of that. I just thought she didn't like me anymore." He smiled. "Yeah, you're right. I'll let her know I'm here for her and that I love her." With a laugh, he added, "Despite the texts."

At that moment, another text dinged on his phone. He looked at it and typed something back to the sender. After a minute, he told me it was the woman and that he'd responded exactly as he'd said he would. While we talked, another text came through. He paused to read it.

Looking up at me, he grinned. "She says she's relieved. And that she loves me too."

"I'm glad," I said. "Sometimes one word, one way of being, can shift a conversation or even a relationship. Don't ever forget that you have the power to do that."

"I won't." He pushed back his chair and stood. "Well, good to meet you. And thanks for the advice."

"Good to meet you as well. By the way, it's no coincidence that our paths crossed. We were both here at the same time for a reason."

He scowled. "How's that?"

"I believe that we meet people we need. Sort of like we're angels sent to guide one another."

"Angels, huh?" Smirking, he left a tip on the table. "Have a safe trip, ma'am."

"You, too." Watching him cross the restaurant, I felt good, even though it had seemed that he didn't believe a word I'd said.

After dinner, I walked Jackson for a while before returning to the motel. We passed a young couple, one of them wearing a bag that held a big weapon. *Holy shit.* I thought they must be on their way to The Family Shooting Center.

An hour into my ride the next morning, the wind picked up, blowing in from the southeast at eighteen miles per hour and slowing down my pace. By mid-morning, stifling heat and humidity had me stopping three times to cool down. I first stopped at a gas station, then at a Goodwill store. By the time I reached our third stop, a restaurant, I was nauseous. I ordered food to settle my stomach after I cooled down.

Despite all the fluids I had consumed, I didn't need to pee. In my mind, I heard Dr. Marah Lee from the SmartRide saying, "If you don't pee, we sag you." This meant she would pull any rider from the race who couldn't pee because that is a sign of dehydration.

Back on the road, I found I could go no further on my own. Even though it was still early in the day, I waved down a car and asked if the driver would drop us at the nearest motel. He did, and I got a room. I finally peed at three o'clock that afternoon.

On one of my many breaks to cool down the next day, I called my friend Nancy, who owns an antique store in Juniper. When she realized I wasn't doing well on this leg of the journey, she said I should stop for the night in Jupiter, and she'd come see me after work.

I jumped back on my bike and rode the last eight miles into Jupiter with a smile on my face, despite the wind and heat. I arrived just before two o'clock that afternoon and stopped at the Jupiter Waterfront Inn, a gorgeous place with hot tubs in the rooms. The waterfront (Intracoastal) was at the back of the building as well as an outdoor hot tub and a pool. One of the most expensive places I'd stayed, the hotel had the quiet, peaceful atmosphere I needed.

Nancy stopped by after work, and Jackson was all over her the minute she walked in the room. After all the years since he'd last seen her, he remembered her well. She took me to buy groceries, and I purchased a roasted chicken, treats for Jackson, a bottle of wine, and a bag of Epsom salts. We ate half of the roasted chicken with some tabouli and had a wonderful visit when we returned to my room.

After Nancy left, I filled up the jet tub and soaked my sore body in Epsom salts. While I relaxed, I reflected on how far I'd come and thought about what might be next for me. I went to bed feeling refreshed.

Unbeknownst to me, the previous guest had the radio alarm set for six in the morning. I had looked forward to sleeping in, but it was not to be. After taking Jackson outside to do his business, I returned to bed. When I got up an hour later, I greeted the beautiful day with gratitude.

Upon leaving my room, I met my next-door neighbor, a woman named Lisa, and her bearded dragon lizard. The lizard reminded me of when I came to the USA in 1986. The young couple I stayed with at the time had a boa constrictor and a huge, bearded dragon lizard, and both freaked me out.

Lisa told me she lived at the inn. I was so distracted by the lizard while she spoke that I could hardly pay attention. I did pick up on the fact that her house had flooded during Irma, and the resulting mildew made Lisa and her boyfriend sick. She was dealing with FEMA while drying out the different wet and mildewed areas in her home. I suggested she invest in a moisture measurement gun, and she told me that tip had made her day and probably saved her thousands of dollars.

"Pull over!"

Slightly alarmed, I glanced across at the guy yelling out of his car window at me.

"I have cold water for you to drink. I'll stop up ahead," he said.

Passing me, he stopped in a driveway a few yards ahead. I followed and parked next to him.

The guy smiled and handed me one of the coldest bottles of water I'd ever held. I immediately drank some of it while imagining pouring the icy water all over my body. It was the finest water I'd tasted in a long time, and it was served by a man with the biggest smile I might've ever seen. His name was Pete, and he was a homeless surfer. He had seen the sign on my bicycle that read: "Bicycling from Alaska to Key West."

Pete expressed his surprise that Jackson had been with me the entire trip. Reaching for his wallet, he gave me a folded stack of bills to support the cause. I found it incredible that a total stranger—a homeless man—would give me water and money and do so with a big smile and a thumbs up. He took a picture of us together before we parted ways.

I rode on and arrived in Lake Worth earlier than expected. I would be staying at my friend Jill's house in Lake Worth, even though she was in Portugal. She had arranged with her roommates, Casandra and

Brooke, to let me stay at their place for a night or two. They weren't home when I arrived, so I stopped at a local deli located only two minutes from their house.

My waitress, Sarah, claimed to get goosebumps when she heard my story. She took a long look at me, Jackson, and my bike, then offered me a ride to wherever I needed to go in town. Thanking her, I sat down to enjoy my sandwich.

As I ate, two old friends walked up to my table. Last year, I had attended Kim and Elle's wedding. They were now celebrating their one-year anniversary. I couldn't believe they had bumped into me while having lunch with their business partner, Tony. The three of them joined me at my table. They got some work done, and I shared a bit with them about my ride. I was surprised to learn that they had been following my journey on Facebook.

When I requested my bill, Sarah handed me a note that read: "Thank you for everything you do. You're an inspiration. Your bill has been taken care of. Sarah McChesney." Tears filled my eyes as I read the note. I left Sarah a nice tip.

I returned to Jill's house and found that her roommates were home. Casandra started to help me inside when Brooke called down from upstairs. She asked that we let the dogs meet outside before I came in. Their dog, Jack, and Jackson got along fine right away, so we were allowed to come in. Immediately, Casandra and Brook returned to their computers and continued to work. Uncomfortable sitting in the living room with them while they worked, I went upstairs and found my room.

Later in the day, Cassandra and Brooke left for a wine and food event. When they came home again, they had brought a woman named Nikki with them. I was happy to meet her and was eager to make a connection.

Early the next morning, I got up and readied myself for a short ride over to John and CindyLou's in Boynton Beach. I had met John in

Gratitude Training. CindyLou and I had worked together at the same company, Kids in Distress.

Brooke's dog had apparently heard Jackson and I stirring, so Brooke was awake and up with him when we went downstairs. When she returned from walking Jack, I gave her Jackson's leftover food with hamburger meat in it. She wished me a safe trip and returned to her bedroom with the dog.

My bike was in the garage, and I couldn't open the garage door. I had to ask Brooke to come down again, and she seemed annoyed as she helped me.

Thanking her and saying goodbye, I made my way slowly to Boynton Beach, stopping several times to play with Jackson and to eat breakfast. I had left Jill's house at 7:30 am, and I had told John and CindyLou that I wouldn't be at their place until ten or eleven.

After riding for a while, I had not found my friends' housing development and stopped at a restaurant for directions. I realized I had passed by their development about five miles back, and I was now in Delray. I turned around and headed back toward Boynton Beach. When I finally made it to the development, I found the key that John had left out for me.

I settled in, walked Jackson, and made some appointments. First, I called Steve from Bike America. Six of my gears weren't working correctly, and he told me where to go to have them fixed, adding that it would be a free service. Next, I contacted my eye doctor and made an appointment for the next day. I called to make an appointment for a haircut as well.

When John came home, he took me to drop my bike at Bike America before we headed to Luna Rosa in Delray for lunch. At his house earlier, he and I had had a long conversation. John had served twenty-five years in the military with four deployments to Iraq, Afghanistan, and other war zones. He said the deployments changed his kids, especially the youngest one, Franklin. Once, when John was about to be deployed,

Franklin asked, "Why are you leaving again? Why are the people over there more important than me? You should stay here. Our family needs you." That tore John up.

While on deployment, he worked out in the field and at secure areas. He once took out a convoy and lost nine men. Traumatized by the event, John began seeing a psychologist and was diagnosed with PTSD. Much better now, he practiced yoga and continued to see his therapist.

John remained involved with the military as a volunteer, talking to young recruits and working with veteran groups. Every Monday, he went to court to support veterans who'd been arrested for DUI, drug possession, and other crimes. He often volunteered at the Veterans Foundation, helping veterans apply for benefits. At the time of my ride, he also worked to support Puerto Rico after Hurricane Maria.

John amazed me. He had retired a year before my visit, but he was busier than he'd been while in the military. He was so proud of his family, especially his children. Grown now, they had a much better understanding of his time spent away from them during their childhoods. In fact, both children grew up and served in the military themselves. John also openly adored and loved his wife, CindyLou, calling her the rock of the family.

I slept well that night, and John drove me to Fort Lauderdale for my eye appointment the next day, then to my hair appointment. It took four hours to do my hair, and I left the salon exhausted. John picked me up, and despite enjoying my time with him and CindyLou, I felt depression setting in. I wanted to cry for the amazing people I had met, for the parts of myself I had left behind on my journey, for all the insights I had made and the growth I'd experienced, for the gifts God had bestowed upon me, and for the beauty in my life. I wanted to cry, too, because my journey was nearing its end.

As John drove us back to his house, we had a conversation about Trump. I was so centered and calm. John is a lovable, gentle and peaceful soul, and his support of Trump makes no sense other than that he trusts a man to lead the country more than a woman. John was fun and delightful, and he lifted my spirits.

I spent the next day connecting with CindyLou and John and doing my laundry. CindyLou and I went to dinner that evening and brought food home for John.

Early the following morning, on Saturday, October 14, Jackson and I left Boynton Beach and our beautiful, amazing friends. I was thankful for their hospitality, their love, their fun natures, and their stimulating discussions.

Chapter 21

Journey's End

I rode to Deerfield Beach, hoping I would bump into a rider or two while they were there training for the upcoming SmartRide in November. I did meet a few riders, but no SmartRiders. Many I met were with bike clubs and rode very fast, not single file, but with two to three riding next to one another. As they quickly passed by me, I thought about life—how fast we travel through it, allowing ourselves little time to smell the roses, as the saying goes.

I met James and Yamara at WLRN Public Radio and TV, where they volunteer. They had invited me to stay at their house should I pass through town, and when I arrived, they took Jackson and me to a restaurant on Deerfield Beach. I ordered a kale salad and a grilled cauliflower steak. We talked about Gratitude Training and the difference it had made in my life. We talked, too, about the importance of being responsible for and in charge of one's own life, about service and contribution, and about my experiences and the amazing people I had met on my trip.

The three of us spent the next day together, much of it watching the Dolphins football game on television and talking. I had known James and Yamara for twenty years and thought I knew everything about them. As it turned out, there was much about James that he'd never told me.

James is a painter, a designer, and a musician. All his friends were musicians when he was young. He wanted to follow their lead, but he didn't play an instrument. John invented his own instrument and was, for a time, the opening act for Bruce Springsteen. I discovered that he had also shared a stage with The Grateful Dead, Bonnie Raitt, and many other famous musicians.

When the opposing team had a 17/0 lead over the Dolphins,

Yamara and I left to take Jackson on a walk along Deerfield Beach. (We later found out that the Dolphins won 20–17 while we were away!) We also played in the ocean, and it was so refreshing and felt so amazingly good.

Yamara had met James on that very beach forty years earlier. She was new to the United States at the time, having moved from Brazil, and she didn't speak any English. She and James fell in love, married, and had children.

At the age of forty, Yamara went to college and earned a degree in education. She went on to teach children technology, problem solving, teamwork, creative thinking skills, and more. An amazing mother and wife, Yamara is a strong, independent woman.

Jeff Banning met me at the World AIDS Museum, where a group of people had gathered to welcome me back to Florida. Ian, from SFGN—South Florida Gay News—joined us for an interview. Everyone in attendance praised and congratulated me for what I'd achieved.

When the interview ended, I had lunch at Storks with Jeff and his friend Derick. I was glad to find Peter there and receive one of his hugs. He invited the three of us to join him.

I later rode to the home of a friend and former co-worker named Michael Baron. I played with his dog, Buddy, and showered. Then I took an Uber to the eyeglass place and picked up my new pair of glasses. I ended the day at George's Alibi, the place where I made my first journal entry for this book.

The next day, a Tuesday, I took an Uber to Dr. Fenton's office, and Rose, a longtime friend of mine, picked me up afterward and took me to life extension to get my prescription, then to buy dry food for Jackson. We had lunch at a place called Rosie's, where David Kitchen, a friend of mine from the yearly AIDS bicycle ride, greeted me with the biggest hug. John, the owner of Rosie's, and some of his staff came over

Kind homeless man giving me five dollars for the ride

to our table, and all their attention went to Jackson. Everyone seemed surprised to see me. We had a delicious lunch "on the house."

Rose became upset that John had picked up our check. She talked to the manager, but he would not take her money. Obviously embarrassed, she told me she was perfectly capable of paying her own way; she didn't need charity. Rose vowed to never go out to eat in a restaurant with me again. Before we left the restaurant, Rose left fifty dollars on the table.

Her intense reaction surprised me. I had been so happy to see John, David Kitchen, Angel, and the rest of the staff at Rosie's, and I had appreciated the free lunch.

At six o'clock that evening, Jackson and I walked with my former co-worker Michael to Mind Your Manors, where I met with Susan Kaulich, Greg Blue, Meghan Welsh, Maritza, and Maritza's friend Victoria. Maritza had been so supportive throughout my journey, and reconnecting with her and the rest of my friends thrilled me. I couldn't believe how close I was to my destination.

I stayed with Michael and his dog, Buddy, that night. I was sad to leave early the next morning, but I wanted to get started before the heat and humidity spiked.

I rode along US-1 and through the New River Tunnel amid heavy, dangerous traffic. Inpatient drivers tried to pass me, drawing frighteningly close. I emerged from the tunnel's opposite side an emotional wreck.

On this stretch of my ride to Miami, I met a man named Doug. He appeared to be extremely poor, possibly even homeless, yet my story inspired him so much that he gave me five dollars to buy food for Jackson.

I stayed with my friend Steffani that night, and we had dinner with another friend, her sister, Naomi, at the Quayside Restaurant. Later, Steffani left to attend the ballet, while Naomi and I stayed for happy hour at the restaurant. We had a wonderful conversation, and I felt more connected to Naomi than I ever had before.

As Jackson and I prepared to hit the road again on Saturday morning, I hugged Steffani and kissed her on the cheek. "Goodbye," I told her. "Thanks for everything."

"I have to say something," she said, meeting my gaze. "You are very disrespectful by stepping into my space and hugging me. You only do what you want to do. You ignore my wishes and everyone else's for that matter." I stepped back from her, stunned and a bit confused. "I'm sorry," I said. "I promise I'll pay attention to your needs next time."

I took off, but her cruel words stayed with me all morning. While I rode, I looked back at my life, searching for times when I'd been selfish at the expense of someone else, stung by Steffani's accusations.

⁓⌒⁓

I rode south on US-1 to Palmetto Bay, where I would be staying with my friend Adrienne and her husband, Bob. Adrienne is a former co-worker from WLRN Public Radio and TV and a powerful, strong, independent women. I always enjoyed her energy and working with her.

Adrienne moved a lot while growing up. Her father worked as a diplomat, and they had been stationed in Thailand, Malaysia, Australia, England, and many other Asian countries. When I worked with Adrienne, she told fabulous stories about her childhood living in different countries.

About the time I started working at WLRN, Adrienne received a breast cancer diagnosis. I watched her go through many surgeries, treatments, and hair loss. Through it all, she always showed up with amazing attitude, always making everyone laugh. She was my inspiration, my hero. I admired her courage and goodness.

Traffic grew dense as I drew nearer to Palmetto Bay and Adrienne's house. I exited US-1 and drove into the bus line express lane. I felt safer there, although I had to watch out for buses. Piles of debris littered the side of the road, left over from the hurricane. Work crews and big trucks worked to remove them.

I was grateful and relieved to reach my destination.

On Sunday, I went shopping for a new water bottle and flip flops. I had lost my old water bottle somewhere along the way, and I looked forward to wearing something other than the biking shoes I'd worn for the past six months.

We visited Adrienne's parents that night and had chicken curry together. I felt so spoiled. I enjoyed hearing more of their stories about life in Thailand and the many other countries where her dad had served as a United States ambassador. They had lived such a challenging and fascinating life, and their stories about experiencing the effects of changing politics often amused and even frightened me.

Adrienne woke me up early Monday morning. Bob had already gone for the day, and she had made coffee. We said our goodbyes, and she left for work. Soon after, her dad came over to help me close the house up before I took off. Spending time with Adrienne and her family had

Devastation from Hurrican Irma

been wonderful. I felt much gratitude for their uplifting, enthusiastic energy. I left, ready and eager to travel the last 160 miles of my journey.

I rode south on US-1 in the bike lane for as far as I could, avoiding the congested traffic as long as possible. After reaching Florida City, I traveled an eighteen-mile stretch on A1A with fencing on each side of the road and no turnaround. It felt as if I rode down a long prison hallway.

It was boiling hot out, and I kept myself and Jackson well-hydrated with the extra water I carried. Still, as before, I couldn't pee, and the smell from the hurricane debris made me gag. I told myself I couldn't throw up, or I'd be done for the day. I kept hearing Dr. Lee's voice in my head saying, "Drink and pee. If you are not peeing or if you throw up, you'll be sagged." I did my best.

I stopped at Gilbert's, depleted, exhausted, and nauseated by the stench on the road. I gulped down a cold beer to quench my thirst and tried to relax my muscles. While there, I met an awesome couple from outside of Chicago. The woman had been following the Florida Keys postings on Facebook and recognized me. She wanted a picture. As she snapped a shot of the two of us, another Facebook follower named Eli came by and gave me a hug. The Chicago couple gave me twenty dollars for the cause, and Eli gave me sixty dollars, moving me to tears.

Later, after ordering a meal, another man came over and asked if his wife could take a picture with me. Her uncle had died of AIDS, and she admired my efforts for the cause.

"How does she know about me?" I asked.

"Everyone here knows about what you're doing!" he exclaimed.

Surprised, I finished my sandwich, then walked with the man and his wife to the bicycle. I gave the woman a red ribbon. She signed it and pinned it to the red ribbon flag. We made a video and took pictures.

Back on my bike, I felt boosted by the food and drink, but mostly by the generosity and support of the people I had met. I headed for my next destination—the Florida Keys, home of my friends Paul and Jack, who I knew from our local AIDS bicycle SmartRide group.

Jack welcomed me into his house after we stored my bicycle and trailer in the garage. We chatted for a bit before I went to take a shower.

When I emerged, I found a formal table set for myself, Paul, Jack, and another friend from our local SmartRide group named Keith, and Keith's mom Ronnie. Ronnie is German, and we spoke to each other in our native language for a few minutes before sitting down to eat. Paul, Jack, Keith, and I had participated in SmartRide events for years and had built a wonderful, supportive, and loving community.

Sitting at a nicely set table for a change felt wonderful, graceful, and elegant, even while wearing my biking outfit. However, after enjoying a delicious meal and good conversation with wonderful friends, I was ready for bed.

Jack, Paul, and I had breakfast together the next morning. Wind and rain pummeled the landscape outside, and Paul suggested I stay until the rain subsided. I agreed and I left as soon as the rain stopped.

Wind still gusted from the northwest as I headed back out on the road again. It pushed me south and into the traffic lane. I forged on. Going over bridges proved difficult; I had to get off my bike and push it.

The wind blasted against me as cars rushed by. Remnants of debris from Irma lined the roadside in piles as tall as a three-story building; decayed animals, rotting filth, refrigerators, trailers, boats—all piled high. The disgusting stench of it blew around me; I spit and cleared my throat all day. My mouth and lips became so dry that I drank water as often as possible, all the while wondering what had happened to the people whose lives the castoff trash represented.

I had planned to cover forty-nine miles, and I still had twelve miles to travel before I would reach my destination. As I crossed one of the bridges, I saw a big pickup truck parked on the far side of the bridge. I asked the occupants if they were driving to Marathon. They explained that they had been on the way to Key West when they passed me on the bridge. They loved dogs, having four of their own, and when they saw Jackson in the trailer, they wanted to help. The driver said he was astounded that I had managed to cross the bridge in wind so strong the gusts had pushed his truck toward the left side of the road.

I accepted a ride into Marathon, where a Facebook friend named Susan had arranged for me to stay with a woman named Paige. Paige lived on a motorboat, and it took me a while to find the marina. Eventually, I found her boat amongst other ripped, stranded, overturned, and broken boats.

Paige's neighbors greeted and welcomed me. Aware of who I was, they let me onto Paige's boat, even though she wasn't there. I settled in, showered, and washed my biking clothes.

At six o'clock that evening, the neighbors knocked on the door to see if I wanted to go out for dinner. We drove to Burdine's on the water. On our way to the restaurant, I learned that both neighbors spoke perfect German, and we talked and sang together in that language. The evening and my hosts turned out to be delightful and fun. The man had studied Germanistik (the study of German) and was a professor in Dresden. The woman taught in the United States, but often visited her husband in Germany, spending summers and, sometimes, part of the winter there.

Burdine's, the restaurant, had only recently reopened after being hit by Hurricane Irma, and their food selection was smaller than usual. Two other couples sat nearby. Overhearing our joyous conversation and singing, they asked to join us. One, a young couple from Maine, lived on a houseboat in the Keys in the fall and winter, returning to Maine every May. The woman was a writer and had published two books. The other couple lived in Marathon. The woman was originally from Germany, and her husband was an American. They had lost their boat during Irma and had been driving along the shore looking for it. They had no insurance on it, and now their home was gone. They weren't alone. Many other people had become homeless when their boats or trailers were destroyed by the storm.

I thought of the tents I had seen in the mangroves while riding along US-1. People had lost their homes and jobs due to the hurricane's devastation. Recalling the refrigerators, boats, clothing, shoes, and personal items I'd passed on the roadside, I reminded myself that all of it had once belonged to people, had been a part of their lives—lives forever changed by the hurricane.

I had a great time at Burdine's. I loved experiencing togetherness and connection with total strangers. So many of the people I'd met along the Keys showed amazing spirit, attitude, and determination. They impressed me.

By the time we got back to the marina, my hostess Paige was at home after working a long shift at her hospital job. She explained that she was in her last year of nursing school. She had her two-year-old granddaughter with her, and I later learned that Paige was raising the girl. I found her dedication and affection for her grandchild beautiful. I spent some time getting to know them and even told the little girl a goodnight story from my travels before we all went to bed.

I had a short ride the following day. Arrangements had been made for me to stay in Big Pine Key with two lovely women—Bridget, a merchant marine captain for over twenty years and a dive master, and Rita, a professor who teaches nursing at a local college. They welcomed me and set me up in their guest cottage.

Even there, I saw devastation caused by Irma. My friend Susan Kaulich, who had made the arrangements for my stay with Bridget and Rita, had been in Big Pine Key helping to clean up after the hurricane when she met the two women. Their property was founded in 1970, and Rita and Bridget had been living and managing the place since 2005. The land was very green and lush, with many old-growth trees and Florida flora. I found it to be a peaceful place, and I loved that the owners had set it up as a safe, welcoming haven for lesbians, especially when traveling.

Bridget and Rita often hosted concerts for women as well as other activities. Many women from all over the United States had come there over the weeks since the storm to help rebuild and clean up the land.

Rita had free-range chickens but had lost a couple during the storm. She said that losing them had saddened her more than the building damage they had suffered. As soon as we got close to the chickens, she called them, and they all came running. The five that survived the storm ran right into Rita's open arms, and she introduced me to them.

The next day, I left Rita and Bridget's place rested and energized by our wonderful conversations. After coffee, toast, and long hugs, I got back on the road for the short jaunt into Key West. Riding was much easier than before. The wind had died down, and although the sun was out, it was less hot and humid. Piles of debris still littered the roadside for miles and miles, the smell even more intense and disgusting

This man lost everything during Hurricane Irma

than I remembered; it filled my nose and mouth, burning my throat. The sight of people's lives discarded—children's clothing, shoes, books, electronics, entire homes, boats, everything—made me cry again. The look of the Keys had changed, and it was sad to see. I passed empty lots with open wounds where homes had once stood. My heart ached.

After making it partway over the last of the bridges, I heard a funny noise coming from my back wheel. Thinking it was my spoke again, I got off to check, only to find a three-inch nail in my back tire. I had the first flat tire of my journey!

While still on the bridge I tried to remove the nail so I could push the bike into a safer area and change the tire. The nail wouldn't budge. While I worked on it, a gentleman driving a pickup truck stopped to warn me of the dangers of stopping on the bridge. Agreeing with him, I explained my situation, and he tried to remove the nail, without luck. I took apart my trailer, the saddle bags and flag, and loaded everything into the bed of his truck, and he drove me over the bridge to the nearest bike shop.

I had to wait a while to get the bike repaired. While waiting, I met a homeless man on his bike, and we chatted for a while about Hurricane Irma. He had lost everything; what I saw loaded on his bike was all he now owned. The man explained that he was on his way to Georgia to start a new job and a new life. He had been poor before the hurricane, but now he had nothing. I gave him twenty dollars and paid for repairs to his bicycle.

With my own bike fixed and ready to go, I hit the road again with a knot in my throat. I had only seven more miles to go to make it to the southernmost point of the state, where I would end my journey by taking a picture.

I arrived to find a big crowd of people standing in line for pictures of their own. I joined the line, and when my turn came, someone volunteered to take my picture and the crowd cheered as the shot was snapped.

Traveling alone on this journey had changed me. I returned home with a better idea of who I am and what I want from life. I returned a more confident and self-assured woman. I returned knowing I would travel alone again.

But at that moment, I had no time to think too much about the fact that my journey had ended. The entire town seemed excited for Fantasy Fest, and so was I. I was proud, too, of what I'd accomplished. It felt somewhat like a dream.

My friend Elaine had invited me to stay with her, so I rode over. We shared lunch and stories about the ride and talked about her possible move to Costa Rica. Afterward, we walked through town and saw a lot of people dressed up for Fantasy Fest. I felt overwhelmed and wonderful at the same time. I'd been thrown into all the action and wasn't completely

Arriving at Key West most southern point

comfortable with it. Too many people, too much noise. A part of me longed to be back in Alaska or on the quiet roads again, but there was no escape.

Key West AIDS Help, a beneficiary for the SmartRide for which I had been riding locally for twenty years, had invited me to participate in the Fantasy Fest parade. AIDS Help, a non-profit, community-based, full-service AIDS service organization, provides case-managed health care, affordable housing and housing assistance, food, counseling, referral, and support services for HIV-infected residents of the Florida Keys. I had accepted the invitation to be part of the AIDS Help team at Fantasy Fest.

Knowing I wouldn't get another invitation to walk in the Fantasy Fest parade anytime soon, I took Elaine's suggestion that I get my body painted for the event, as that's a "thing" at Fantasy Fest in Key West. I made an appointment to have a bike jersey and bike shorts painted on me. It was quite an experience, as I was painted in front of other people. Since my breasts have been removed, I wasn't too worried about my top being painted. However, when it came time to paint my bike shorts, I felt somewhat uncomfortable. My journey had taught me, however, to say "yes" in life whenever possible, and I said "yes" then.

AIDS Help is Florida's oldest continuously operating AIDS service organization (ASO) and remains the only agency in Monroe County that serves individuals living with HIV and AIDS across the demographic spectrum from Key Largo to Key West. AIDS Help provides case-managed health care, food, counseling, and referral and support services to assist in people living fuller, healthier lives. It also provides services not covered by other grants and resources, such as funding for non-covered prescription medications, alternative therapies, and a nutrition/fitness program. In addition, the Agency provides HIV education, outreach, intervention, testing, referral, and safe sex packet/condom distribution.

AIDS Help provided a total of ninety-six housing units for people

Body paint jersey

living with HIV/AIDS. It is the only ASO in the state to hold that distinction. I was honored to walk in the parade with AIDS Help.

The parade started late, and it was cold out. Lined up and ready to go, we waited for hours to start. I felt as if I were freezing by the time we got going, and I was grateful to be moving. I had to walk the bike, as the parade moved slowly, with a lot of stopping and starting.

Jackson walked next to me as the procession started off. At first, the atmosphere was almost as quiet as a funeral. Soon, however, we all started to scream, cheer, and whistle as we threw beaded necklaces into the crowds gathered at the roadside to watch. Everyone came alive!

After the parade, I couldn't shake the cold, and I had a sore throat. I slept most of the next day and woke up sick.

Walking during fantasy fest with Key West AIDS Help agency

Epilogue

I picked up an SUV from the Key West Airport at 1:30 pm and left Key West an hour later. I wasn't used to driving and felt almost as if I had to relearn. It would take time to adjust to life at home again. The traffic overwhelmed me, the aggressiveness, the noise. I felt nervous now, stressed out as I stayed in my lane and kept the speed limit, holding onto the steering wheel tightly.

Static, aggressive, impatient energy surrounded me. I felt in the wrong place and time. Aware of a post ride depression moving in on me, I longed to be on my journey again. My heart and mind remained on the road, and I thought often of the many people who had shown me support along the way.

My knees continued to ache after I arrived home, as did my elbows, my hands, my butt, and my neck. I continued to wonder if the trip had been worth it. Had talking to strangers about HIV/AIDS made any difference? Would my fundraising efforts to find a cure for AIDS help? Would I have the strength to continue the fight? Most of all, what should I do next?

The journey had become my life.

Shortly after coming home, I had three amazing dreams. In the first dream, I showed dogs how to fly. In the second dream, I was Martin Luther King. The third dream was about flying.

As Air Force pilots acknowledged my gift and contributions to flight, I stood amidst the chaos, raising my hand and turning my back to a shooter who pummeled me with paintballs. Blue and purple and hurting, I stood in peace, looking down at other women standing knee deep in water. I jumped in with them, then lifted them out of the water and flew.

With the financial help of many people, Jackson and I raised over ten thousand dollars for amfAR to continue their research for a cure for AIDS. I am so thankful for everyone's steadfast support during my amazing journey. Many kind and encouraging words kept me going, especially when things got tough. I knew I had wonderful people on my side—angels—rooting for me. I wish I could tell each one personally, from the bottom of my heart, "Thank you. I love you so much."

These days, when thinking back on my trip, I have no regrets. My time on the road and the angels I met continue to touch my day-to-day life. I still eat dinner alone sometimes. I get up early to watch the sun rise. I accept defeat when I must.

Perhaps most of all, I always take the scenic route. The world is full of wonders, and if you're lucky, you not only get to see them; you also get to experience them.

The End

Made in United States
Orlando, FL
16 July 2023